The

W9-BPM-113

California

Homeschool

Guide

Edited by Karen Taylor

California Homeschool Network

Strengthening the Voice of California Homeschoolers™

CHN is a non-profit 501(c)3 parent-service organization

Second Edition

National Library of Canada
Cataloguing in Publication Data

Main entry under title:
 The California homeschool guide
 Includes index.
 ISBN 1-55212-712-5
 1. Home schooling--California--Handbooks, manuals, etc.
 I. Taylor, Karen II. California Homeschool Network.
 LC40.C34 2002   371.04'2'09794   C2001-903959-X

TRAFFORD

This book was published *on-demand* **in cooperation with Trafford Publishing.**
On-demand publishing is a unique process and service of making a book available for retail sale to the public taking advantage of on-demand manufacturing and Internet marketing.
On-demand publishing includes promotions, retail sales, manufacturing, order fulfilment, accounting and collecting royalties on behalf of the author.

Suite 6E, 2333 Government St., Victoria, B.C. V8T 4P4, CANADA

Phone	250-383-6864	Toll-free	1-888-232-4444 (Canada & US)
Fax	250-383-6804	E-mail	sales@trafford.com
Web site	www.trafford.com	TRAFFORD PUBLISHING IS A DIVISION OF TRAFFORD HOLDINGS LTD.	
Trafford Catalogue #01-0111		www.trafford.com/robots/01-0111.html	

10   9   8   7   6   5

Acknowledgements

Some day this book may no longer be needed, and homeschooling will be as accepted as public school is today. That day is not yet here. Even though many families homeschool, there are still opponents. Knowing your rights and becoming involved will help ensure that the day will indeed arrive when homeschooling books, such as this one, will no longer need to offer legal information and details about how to do something as natural as educating our own children. This is why our CHN volunteers donate their time!

Many talented and experienced homeschoolers contributed thoughtfully and generously to this book. Some articles were previously published in other CHN publications, including our bimonthly newsletter, and others were written for this guide. Several parents contributed the photographs of children homeschooling in California, and others contributed the technical support that was needed to complete a project of this size. It was indeed a family project—a family of homeschoolers—and we all wish your family many special years of homeschooling.

Karen Taylor
Editor

California Homeschool Network
www.CaliforniaHomeschool.net
800/327-5339
CHNmail@CaliforniaHomeschool.net
PO Box 55485, Hayward, CA 94545

Table of Contents

Dear Reader,

You are holding in your hands a *wonder* of the modern homeschool world in California. That's not an exaggeration. Just a decade ago, homeschooling in California was a clandestine activity and finding information on how to homeschool was next to impossible. My own story offers proof...

In August of 1991, at 9 p.m., I stepped aboard a tiny sailboat moored in a harbor on the San Francisco Bay. I was directed below deck. There, in the dark galley three other women and I squeezed into seats around a scaled down table. In the faint light of a single lantern we watched as our hostess revealed a large, black binder with the words "Proprietary Information" stenciled across it in big, bold, type. She held the book up as if it was a sacred scripture and seemed to speak in tongues as she cited a string of education codes including 33190, 48224, and 51745. She mumbled strange acronyms like DOE, CTA, HSLDA, and CHSPE to name a few. The mantra concluded, she translated for us, "This book contains the information you need to homeschool in California!" She passed it around for each of us to examine—but warned us not to reveal the contents of the sparse pages to other people as it might get into the "wrong hands." She was referring to truant officers. She suggested that like some impatient vultures, they would swoop down on our school-ravaged carcasses and carry our children off to state-approved foster homes and government schools if they got wind of our homeschooling plans. We passed the book around and tried to imprint its contents to our brains—and proceeded to ask urgent questions in hushed tones. Two hours later we left, with her admonishment to keep our children inside the house until 2 p.m. each day in order to avoid nosy neighbors who might report our kids as truant.

I left there frightened, but determined not to succumb to my fear. Since I had exhausted all of my other education options (public and private schools) I didn't have a choice. I was going to homeschool my children. It didn't matter that information was scarce, that the few support groups that existed operated like secret societies, and that there were just a handful of ready-made resources through which to develop a curriculum. I was not going to pay tuition for another year of tears and frustration at school. The light was dim that night, but I held hope for a brighter future for my family through homeschooling.
Fast forward 10 years...

If you are reading this, then you are holding the future that I hoped for that night. A book, available to anyone, that sheds light on all of the accurate information, support, and resources available to families who make the choice to educate their children at home in California. A guide that not only explains how to homeschool, but one that inspires the reader with the wisdom of personal stories, along with suggestions for resources and activities. A manual that provides support and encouragement, and most of all—one that declares loudly and clearly that homeschooling is not only legal in California, but a viable educational alternative to proudly proclaim without fear of retribution. A handbook that declares homeschooling to be an activity to be conducted in broad daylight with the security of knowing it is safeguarded through the diligent efforts of tens of thousands of families throughout the state who believe in a parent's fundamental right to determine the educational course of their own children.

The California Homeschool Network knows that information is power—and with this guide they are empowering families and giving them the courage to homeschool their children independently, without fear of government interference or regulation. This guide is a compendium of the wisdom and experience of veteran homeschoolers. In your hands you hold:

- Reliable information about how to get started in homeschooling including the legal ways to homeschool, and how to develop a course of study based on *your* child's interests, abilities, learning styles, and needs.

- The latest research studies about homeschooling and homeschoolers.

- "Insight" to a typical day in homeschooling and how homeschoolers use the world as their classroom.

- Answers to questions about socialization including "The Prom."

- Kids' views of homeschooling told in their own words.

- A Who's Who of famous homeschoolers.

- Practical advice like: scheduling; record keeping; withdrawing children from school; choosing curriculum.

- Advice on how to diplomatically tell your relatives about your plans to homeschool.

- Examples of how everyday experiences like reading aloud, planting a garden, visiting a factory, taking a hike, cooking a meal, and playing games are the best curriculum.

- A discussion of the various approaches to home education from traditional academics, to unit studies, to interest-initiated learning and more.

- Real Samples of Curriculum—see for yourself the resourcefulness and creativity that homeschooling parents bring to the task of teaching their kids at home.

- Advice on how to homeschool high school students, including information on the California High School Proficiency Exam, the GED, Driver's Education, and Work Permits.

- Helpful hints on college admissions procedures and testing (includes SAT, ACT, and AP Exams).

- Guidance for homeschooling kids with special needs.

- Suggestions for incorporating computers into your homeschool along with ideas for educational software, Internet research, and online classes.

- Sensible ideas for dealing with parent burn out, working with kids of different age or grade ranges, overscheduling, and dealing with parental inferiority complexes.

- Pennywise tips for frugal homeschooling.

- Suggestions for finding and developing homeschool support groups.

- A comprehensive directory of homeschool resources including a list of educational product suppliers and textbook publishers for every subject including math, science, language arts, foreign languages, history, social studies, music, art, writing and computer sciences.

And, as if that weren't enough, a Companion Guide to this book is available—a CD ROM containing many of the forms used by homeschoolers that will make getting started a breeze.

In 1991, aboard that little boat, the prospect of homeschooling in California was a dim light flickering amidst fear, prejudice, and ignorance. Today, thanks in large part to the efforts of grassroots organizations like the California Homeschool Network—homeschooling is flourishing. Like the ancient world wonder, The Lighthouse of Alexandria, that guided mariners to safe harbor—this book, *The California Homeschool Guide*, is a wonder too. It is a wonder of the modern homeschool world. It is a beacon illuminating the way and openly guiding California families toward homeschool success.

The California Homeschool Guide will help you to enjoy the wonder of homeschooling with your children!

Diane Flynn Keith
Editor/Publisher of *Homefires*

BABY BLUES

Reprinted with special permission of King Features Syndicate

If you are new to homeschooling, you may be feeling somewhat overwhelmed at this juncture. There are so many considerations, so many opportunities, and so many worries tugging at your sleeve. We're here to tell you that what you are experiencing is normal. We know because we have been where you are now. We are parents who had no expertise when we fixed our sights on homeschooling our kids. You will come through fine, just as we did, and perhaps you will be a wee bit ahead for having at your fingertips the information and wisdom contained in this book.

If you are a veteran homeschooler, you know that as your children grow you must keep up, helping them find academic materials and helping them face the "rites of passage"—learning to drive, finding that first job, and perhaps, entering college. The need for homeschooling information is ongoing, and this book will serve you well, too.

Our parent-powered, all-volunteer crew is proud to offer you this publication, along with our bimonthly newsletter, a system of local county contacts, our free 800#, an informative website, statewide homeschooling seminars, a book for grandparents and many other California Homeschool Network (CHN) projects. If legal or legislative developments threaten your right to educate at home, you can count on CHN for accurate, timely information and analysis.

CHN empowers individuals by sharing information so that they may make independent decisions. Please note that none of the information in this book is to be considered legal advice. Education codes are provided, and even interpretations from various individuals, but this is for the reader's information only, to aid in making individual informed decisions.

We hope this will be the beginning of our usefulness to you, and that you will join us as we grow our families and grow an ever-stronger California Homeschool Network.

California Homeschool Network
Mission Statement

California Homeschool Network is an inclusive, statewide homeschooling organization serving families across a diverse spectrum of homeschooling styles and philosophies.

California Homeschool Network exists to protect the fundamental right of the family to educate its children in the manner it deems appropriate without regulation or interference by federal, state or local agencies.

California Homeschool Network monitors and responds to legislation which may pose a threat to homeschooling, and to this end, maintains a dialog with local, state, and national homeschooling organizations.

California Homeschool Network serves to inform and empower homeschooling families, educate the public, and foster community among home educators in the state of California.

Strengthening the Voice of California Homeschoolers™

©Bill Taylor

1

You're Doing What?

"Homeschool students enjoy the usual

friendships and activities for children and youth

that any good parent would want for them."

©Bill Taylor

Breaking the News to Friends and Family

By Karen Taylor

Most parents, even if they are quite committed to the idea of homeschooling, have a few insecurities as the moment arrives to make that final decision and begin homeschooling. The school has an enrollment deadline, and you let it pass. The school bus goes by that first day and your child is not on it. Yes, you have begun, for better or worse. It is a decision that seems so final, and although we know it is right, there is that lingering fear planted from years of having attended school. Will we fail, and will our child be harmed? Will our child's future be ruined? It's a little message that says that the only way to get an education is to go to school. . . only the teacher knows what is right. . .be good, and do what you are told to do. If your child was not on that bus, or you are considering withdrawing him or her from school, you are no longer obeying that message, and some discomfort often accompanies that.

It's tough enough to make the personal decision to home educate without having to also tell others about your decision. Some parents make the announcement when their child is still an infant, and let family and friends (and perhaps themselves) have years to get accustomed to the idea. Others wait until the child is of school age just to avoid prolonging any arguments that might occur.

Yes, friends and family will have strong opinions about your choice to educate. Some will fear that it is illegal, and that you will get in trouble. Others are going to be concerned about your child's future because you don't have a teaching credential, or they will recall you weren't that terrific a student. They will look at a little five year old, and question how you will teach that child high school chemistry. Or they will worry that the child won't be admitted to college with "only" a homeschool education. They wonder how he/she will learn to get along with others, if not at school.

And, you might even be accused of doing this for selfish reasons because some will think you aren't willing to let your child leave you and establish an independent life—at the age of five. We worry a lot about apron strings in our society! We receive societal pressure that tells us it is a good thing to see a three-year-old who is happy being with strangers all day. It means they have adjusted well. If you and your child enjoy each other's company, then you will likely receive the message in some way, at some time, that you have failed as a parent. You will be reminded that your job is to separate from your child, and the sooner the better because this kind of dependence on loved ones is viewed as a weakness.

The pressure will indeed be on for any family deciding to homeschool. It is one of the reasons we recommend that you find a support group (see Chapter 13). It is also why we are starting out with some facts. Facts that will help reassure you, and facts that will help you enlighten others about the benefits of homeschooling. So, in this chapter, we start with the good news that research has shown how beneficial homeschooling is. You will first hear from Dr. Peavey, a professional educator, rather than a homeschooling parent. There is very positive news to report about homeschooling. Read about some of the research, and share it with the doubters in your life, and then read on to consider the interesting list of famous homeschoolers. It appears that homeschooling might not doom your children after all!

Home Education FACTS Not Misconceptions
By Sam B. Peavey, Ed.D.

The remarkable revival of home education in recent years may someday be seen as one of the most significant educational developments of this century. Home education is an integral part of the current movement toward freedom of choice among educational alternatives. However, there is reason to regard the homeschool as having an identity and integrity of its own. It is well worthy of study and understanding as the most private form of private school.

The renaissance of family-centered schooling is the natural outcome of a number of forces converging on a fateful era. Not the least of all those forces is the well-documented fact that both the American home and the American school have reached the lowest level of mediocrity in our history. Both have betrayed the birthright of our children. The homeschool is a normal response of concerned parents to that mounting crisis. The homeschool is a pointed effort to salvage and safeguard values that once undergirded schools as well as homes. Home education is a rejection of the trend toward almost total institutionalization of child rearing. It is a reaction to a decline in scholarship and character in the classroom. It is a testimony of faith in the family— a faith that is almost lost.

My experience as Private Education Liaison on the faculty of the School of Education of the University of Louisville gave me an informed sensitivity to the concerns of families seeking religious and educational freedom in the private sector. Further, as my state's representative for the Council for American Private Education, I have come to know homeschoolers throughout a number of states. I have visited in their homes, addressed their gatherings, examined their instructional materials, interviewed parents and children, observed teaching, reviewed instructional plans, verified achievement and testified in their behalf before legislatures and courts. I have counseled homeschooling parents facing threats of lawsuits, arrest, fines, charges of child neglect, imprisonment and harassment from civil and educational authorities. My firm conclusion is that it is time for citizens in general and educators in particular to recognize and respect home-based, family-centered education for what it is and for what it is achieving.

Too often the most uncompromising critics of home education are persons who know little about it. The increasing institutionalization of children's upbringing is espoused as liberation from traditional family roles. It seems difficult for many to believe that modern parents have the competence necessary to rear their own children. They find it hard to conceive of family-centered schooling in their communities where broken homes, working mothers, unwed parents, absentee fathers and latchkey children have become the norm. The point should be made clear: a homeschool is first of all a home. The first requirement for a successful homeschool is a successful home.

I am not a promoter of homeschooling per se. I am a promoter of free choice among educational alternatives. It is my professional judgment that home-based education is one of the most significant and successful alternatives available to parents today. I have testified under oath to that fact on numerous occasions in recent years. In the course of my testimony, the same predictable questions repeatedly arise. Allow me to focus briefly on the major concerns many people have about homeschools.

How Well Do Children Learn in a Homeschool?

There is ample evidence that homeschool students as a whole achieve at a higher level than students in regular school on standardized measures of basic knowledge and skills. Reliable studies in a number of states provide that evidence. A statewide test of the basic skills of homeschoolers in Tennessee where over half of the students are taught by parents with only a high school education showed impressive achievement. Ninety-one percent of the students were achieving at or above their grade levels, while 75% were a full year or more above grade level in reading. Any school would have reason to be proud of such a showing.

A 1987 testing of 873 homeschool students in Washington State on the Stanford Achievement Test showed them clearly at or above average in 104 of the 120 test categories. In Alaska, a statewide appraisal of basic skills found homeschool students at all grade levels averaging in the top fourth of the nation.

In Oregon, a study of 1,100 homeschoolers found 76% scoring at or above average in achievement. The Hewitt Research Foundation in Washington made a study of several thousand homeschool students throughout the U.S. They were on the average in the 75th to the 95th percentile on the Stanford and Iowa Achievement Tests.

I am not aware of any reliable and comprehensive study that shows homeschool students doing less well than their peers in the regular school. We in professional education might well be intrigued by how this superior level of learning is attained in such modest circumstances by teachers with only a limited formal education.

Are Ordinary Parents Qualified to Teach?

That question is a legitimate one for a person who has been equating teacher qualifications with a college diploma and a teaching certificate. I hold two advanced degrees from two distinguished universities in teacher education, that is, teaching teachers how to teach. It has been my privilege to help prepare thousands of university students to meet the qualifications for a teaching certificate or permit to teach. They were as a whole fine young people and many have done well in the classroom. It has been most interesting to me to see homeschool parents with high school diplomas doing as well or better than my certified teachers as measured by their students' standardized test results. Those [homeschool] parents revealed some things to me about living, loving, and learning that I was never taught by my distinguished professors at Harvard and Columbia.

I have observed that most home study materials and activities are designed to allow the student to proceed on his own a large part of the time as an independent learner. That is teaching at its best. The situation is so different from the classroom where the teacher must face a room full of children and spend a major part of her time and energy maintaining order while wondering what is taking place in individual minds. The parent in a homeschool situation actually plays a more professional role as a monitor, tutor, counselor and resource person. One mother said her best advice on teaching came from her ten-year-old son who urged her to stop acting like a teacher!

It is gratifying that state authorities have recognized the injustice and futility of trying to force state teaching certificates on parents who choose to educate their own children in their own homes and for whom the state certificate was never designed. It is significant to note that the parent-teachers in home education are clearly demonstrating for us what a half century of educational research has revealed—a total lack of any significant relationship between the teacher's certificate and the pupil's achievement. Those research findings have been known and ignored for many years. Some examples of these studies follow.

Freeman observed that teacher certification requirements appear to have been conceived through intuition and then converted into certification regulations. Freeman found no significant relation between teacher certification and performance in the classroom. (Legal Issues in Teacher Preparation and Certification, ERIC Clearing House on Teacher Education, Washington, D.C. 1977).

Hawk, Coble and Swanson of East Carolina University in their study of all available research evidence concluded that there is little, if any, documentation to support the assertion that the effectiveness of teachers is a function of increased certification requirements. (Journal of Teacher Education, 1985).

In spite of all that evidence to the contrary, state school authorities continue to maintain that the certified teacher is the qualified teacher. It is particularly painful to see state authorities harassing and criminalizing educators who shun that invalid credential. The only valid measure of effective teaching that we have found is the degree in which pupils are learning. On that score, the teachers in homeschools as a whole are demonstrating their effectiveness.

What About Social Life?

The formation of one's social character and social values occurs in an interaction of positive socialization and negative socialization. The same is true of a home, a school, or a total society. Few persons would deny that the forces of negative socialization that dominate our society today have undermined the social values and social character of children's homes, children's schools and children's lives. Tots and teens wander in a value vacuum. The forces of positive socialization have lost much of their effectiveness in the schools the state compels its children to attend. The community school of today is not the sheltered, unspoiled place one associates with an earlier era in which the forces of positive socialization were predominant. Every problem, pressure and perplexity of our modern day interacts in the socialization of children in the classroom.

There is increasing recognition that the organization of the school is also a negative factor in children's socialization. Hurrying children from bell to bell and from cell to cell with arbitrary grouping of their peers was never designed for the normal socialization of children. Rather, it evolved as an expedient structure for compulsory mass institutionalization of children. Most children learn to tolerate and conform to the process their elders have developed as the best way of processing children en masse. However, students of child behavior are coming to realize that under the false facade of compliance with institutional demands, children experience a host of pressures, tensions, and stresses that few of them could identify or verbalize. The nature of life and learning in such an environment generates abnormal values, roles, relationships and behaviors. Children are turned inward upon themselves and their peers in an interaction rife with peer pressure, peer dominance, peer images, and peer values.

Out of that situation emerges the diverse problems of children which teachers face in today's classroom—social isolation, identity crises, poor self-image, emotional stress, competition, frustration, delinquency, hostility, moral confusion, boredom, rejection, burn-out, sexual promiscuity, violence, vandalism, teen pregnancy, alcohol, drugs and certainly the most tragic of all, suicide.

On that background, it should not be necessary to explain further the deep concern homeschool parents feel for the social character and social behavior of their children. That concern alone might well stimulate the growth of homeschooling beyond anything we have yet imagined. More importantly, it could draw homeschoolers closer together as functional family units where both the parents and the children might well rediscover themselves and each other in their joint venture in living and learning.

A related study by John Taylor of Andrews University compared 224 homeschoolers in grades 4-12 with regular school students using the

Piers-Harris Children's Self-Concept Scale. It is generally conceded that a favorable self-concept is indicative of an individual's socialization. Taylor's study concluded, "The self-concept of home-schooling children is significantly higher than that of children attending the conventional school. Regarding socialization, it appears that very few home-schooling children are socially deprived... Apparently, the research data indicate that it is the conventionally schooled child who is actually deprived."

Bronfenbrenner, among others, found that children at least through the sixth grade who spend more of their elective time with their peers than with their parents generally become dependent on those peers. He noted that this brought a pervasive pessimism about themselves, their future, their parents, and even their peers. This does not support the idea that a child's association with many children necessarily contributes to positive socialization as many parents and educators assume.

First hand observations of homeschooled children commonly impress observers with their qualities of maturity, stability, responsiveness and self-assurance. In fact parents often report that their decision to homeschool their children came from observing the impressive social qualities of other homeschool students. Certainly one should not underestimate the contribution to social values and social character that comes from a firm foundation in moral and spiritual values common to most homeschools.

Are Homeschool Students Prepared for College?

Homeschoolers have little difficulty in entering and succeeding in college if they plan wisely and make the most of their opportunities. High school and college counselors are available to advise on planning for entrance into specific colleges and vocations. Instruction in advanced and specialized college preparatory courses is available through extension courses from schools and colleges, educational TV, part-time enrollment in the local high school and tutors. Lack of some college preparatory courses can often be made up in college while enrolled in a conditional admission status. In most colleges, admission is dependent primarily on standard admissions tests. GED certificates often suffice in lieu of a high school diploma. College admissions offices understand that diplomas and grades per se from the regular high school offer little assurance of college preparation or potential since the standards from different schools vary greatly.

Most homeschool programs are uniquely designed and conducted with a stress on independent study, individual responsibility, self-evaluation and the use of diverse resources—all of which prepare one for success in college study. Studies of genius indicate that the independent, self-directive, open, undistracted environment of most homeschools provides the best setting for the development of gifted and creative minds.

What is Homeschooling Really Like?

As often stated, homeschooling is the most private form of private education. It is not designed for isolation but for privacy—privacy of living and learning in an intimate family environment. The family, of course, maintains all normal relations with the social, civic, cultural, recreational, religious and business activities and resources of the community. Homeschool students enjoy the usual friendships and activities for children and youth that any good parent would want for them. Many public and private schools offer extension study status and part-time enrollment for homeschoolers, thus providing access to elective courses, school facilities, counseling and participation in certain activities.

An impressive variety of professionally designed curricula for kindergarten through high school is being used successfully by parent-tutors with only limited formal education. The curriculum publisher/distributor ordinarily provides the homeschool parent a continuing consultative service on procedures, problems, testing and additional resources. Colleges, universities and correspondence schools provide a wide range of courses for independent study. Rich resources continue to become more available and attractive. Complete courses plus enrichment experiences are increasingly offered on educational TV.

The concept of home education raises the question in some minds as to whether home-based schooling prepares students for "real life." However, most observers would conclude that the best preparation for real life is to live it everyday as homeschoolers do. It is the institutionalized student in the regular school who is compelled to live in an unreal setting. The homeschool commonly provides a much broader daily relationship with the community than does the classroom of the traditional school. Experience indicates that three or four hours at the most, of formal instruction and study in basic subjects each school day in the home are sufficient to maintain a student at grade level. The remainder of the day is devoted to individual projects, field trips, art, music, libraries, museums, educational television, volunteer work in community agencies, sharing family responsibilities, hobbies, and the establishment of "cottage industries" as money-making enterprises in such things as gardening, art crafts, bake sales, woodworking, pet raising and lawn care.

Any image of the homeschool as a worn and weary mother huddled with her brood in the kitchen is far from the full scenario of home education today. National, state, and community support groups provide forums for fellowship and exchange of ideas and experiences on the enlarging frontier of home education. Such support groups collaborate in planning field experiences and group activities for students and for sharing common concerns. Periodic workshops bring parents together to examine and acquire materials for teaching and learning and to hear consultants on pertinent matters. A helping hand is extended to beginners in homeschooling.

Why is Home Education Necessary?

In a democracy with a tradition of free enterprise, educational choice is a vital response to the state's sheltered monopoly over the molding of children's minds and characters. Although motives for turning to home education vary, the common motive of course, is the conviction that the home and family setting can provide for children an education superior to that offered through other available and affordable alternatives. The majority are reacting to the fact that the government school no longer allows open recognition and reverence for God or for the divine nature and destiny of man. Others are concerned with the academic deterioration of public education and find that their children attain much better achievement in homeschooling. Many are concerned over the modern degeneracy of home and family life and seek to maintain a close and caring environment for their own children. Some hold distinct philosophical and world views in which they want their children nurtured. Others subscribe to educational outlooks on child development that they feel can best be fostered at home.

Conclusion

Home education is not a passing fancy. Those of us in professional education have long known that the strongest influence on a child's school achievement is parental involvement. That factor is indeed paramount in the homeschool. As our schools have become more massive, technological, impersonal, antisocial, amoral and institutionalized, perhaps educators need a more simple, natural and humane laboratory in which to explore the basic elements of living and learning. I would suggest those basic elements are all there and thriving in a unique manner in the privacy and normalcy and simplicity of the homeschool.

Let us close with the observation that homeschooling is not for all. Neither is compulsory state institutionalization.

CHN wishes to thank Dr. Sam B. Peavey for his kind permission to reprint this article in The California Homeschool Guide. This text was originally prepared as expert testimony and given before both the Iowa and New Hampshire State Boards of Education. The author holds graduate degrees in education from both Harvard and Columbia, and recently retired from the University of Louisville School of Education.

Research About Homeschooling
By Jackie Orsi

Many people are curious about homeschooling. Some insist that they want to hear from independent observers about whether or not the glowing reports of homeschooling parents can be believed. As it happens, homeschooling is one of the hottest topics for research by graduate students at university departments of education. Leaving aside for the moment the valid question of whether children's development can be truly and accurately measured, we offer some of the notable findings of researchers. Over the last decade or more, the tests and scales, however imperfect, that our society uses to measure learning achievement and social adjustment have been applied to samples of children from public schools, homeschools, and sometimes, private schools. In each and every comparison, homeschooled children excel. It's all good news. There has yet to be a single study that is at odds with the experiences of homeschool parents. Some characteristic findings:

Academic Achievement

The national average on standardized achievement tests is the 50th percentile. It may be said that this figure represents the public school average, since public school children represent the vast majority of the testing pool. By comparison:

- In a recent Florida study, homeschoolers scored in the 72nd percentile on the battery composite; a 1990 Montana study produced the same result.

- A sample of homeschool students in Maine exceeded national averages by 12 to 33 percentile points on various sub-scores.

- In Canada, Dr. Brian Ray found homeschoolers in the 80th percentile on reading, 76th percentile in language, and 79th percentile in math.

Several additional studies are cited in the previous article "Home Education: FACTS not Misconceptions" by Dr. Sam B. Peavey. In *Homeschooling: Political, Historical, and Pedagogical Perspectives* (Van Galen and Pitman, eds.), researchers Brian Ray and Jon Wartes surveyed the various achievement comparisons and summarized, "It is clear that the research findings to date cast a flattering light on the ability of parents to transmit curricula and assist their home-educated children in progressing through the major agendas of American schooling."

Social and Psychological Development

More good news from the researchers: every social and psychological profile of homeschooled kids consistently shows that they are well adjusted, indeed oftentimes better adjusted than institutionally schooled children.

Numerous studies of the quantity of social contacts provided to homeschooled children confirm that their parents are by no means isolating or depriving their children.

Taylor (1986) employed the Piers-Harris Self-Concept Scale, and found "that the self-concept of home-schooled students was significantly higher for the global scale score than that of public-schooled students. The scores of the homeschooled were also significantly higher than the public-schooled on all six subscales."

Shyers (1992) also found homeschoolers possessing positive self-concepts. Delahooke (1986) compared homeschoolers and private schoolers and found a lower susceptibility to peer influence among homeschoolers.

Shyers (1992) arranged for observers to rate children at play, not telling them in advance which ones were homeschooled and which were public-schooled. The observers tallied "significantly fewer problem behaviors" among the homeschooled youngsters.

A study by Knowles (1992) surveyed 53 American adults homeschooled as children. They ranged in age from 17 to 77. Knowles found them leading successful lives, with 96% replying in the affirmative that they would wish to be home-educated if they had their lives to live over again.

For additional information, contact The National Home Education Research Institute (NHERI); Dr. Brian Ray, President; PO Box 13939, Salem, Oregon 97309.

Famous Homeschoolers
By Karen Taylor

Homeschooling is not new, and the names of famous people who have been homeschooled can be found throughout history. While that does not mean that all homeschoolers grow up brilliant and famous, it does appear that homeschooling certainly doesn't hold people back. For some very creative famous homeschoolers, it probably made a difference in what they were able to accomplish, and the same is often true for today's homeschooled children.

Some well-known people were educated at home because they had learning problems when they were young. For those homeschoolers who are struggling with math or reading, it might be a comfort to see that some exceptionally capable people also struggled when they were young. Other famous people were discipline problems in school and couldn't adapt to the one-way-fits-all method of mass instruction, just as some children today can't. At home, they thrived.

Others appeared so gifted at an early age that they were not sent to school, so that they could learn at their own accelerated pace. Others, for a variety of reasons, were either self-taught or were given a great deal of freedom to learn what they wanted. We might consider them autodidacts or perhaps unschoolers today, and for those who are taking that direction in their homeschooling, it's interesting to see that some very accomplished people have thrived in an environment where they determined their own education.

Some famous homeschoolers were completely educated at home, and others also attended schools for part of their childhood, the same as today's homeschoolers. Some had tutors, just as some parents today find mentors to help their children in certain subjects. At times, the parents of these famous homeschoolers broke with custom and tradition to give their children the education they knew they needed. Parents who choose to homeschool are doing the very same thing today.

The following is a list of some well-known people who
received all or part of their education at home:

Abigail Adams
First Lady and also Mother of a Homeschooled President
She learned at home at a time when girls typically did not receive an education.
"I regret the trifling narrow contracted education of the females of my own country."

Ansel Adams
Photographer and Conservationist
He was home educated after age 12 because he couldn't sit still
in school and got in trouble there.

John Quincy Adams
6th President
He was educated at home by his mother.

Susan B. Anthony
Women's Rights Activist
She was taught by her father until she was sent away to school at age 16.

Clara Barton
Founder of Red Cross
She was educated at home until age 15.

Alexander Graham Bell
Inventor
He was taught at home until he was 10.

Pearl Buck
Author, Awarded Nobel Prize in 1938 (Literature)
The child of missionaries in China, she was primarily taught at home
by her mother and a Chinese tutor.

Agatha Christie
Author
She was educated at home.
"I . . .had a very happy childhood with practically no lessons and lots of time to roam about the garden and imagine things. It was my mother who told me to write. She was a woman of great charm and great character, and was always convinced that her children could do anything!"

Winston Churchill
British Leader, Awarded Nobel Prize in 1953 (Literature)
He began school at 12, did poorly, and continued learning after he left school.

Pierre Curie
Physicist, Awarded Nobel Prize in 1903 (Physics)
He was educated at home until he attended the Faculty of Sciences.

Thomas Edison
Inventor
He began school at 7, but his teacher thought he was dull and couldn't learn,
and complained that he asked too many questions.
He also didn't like math. His mother brought him home to learn.

Benjamin Franklin
Inventor and Statesman
His formal education ended early. He was primarily self-educated, and never stopped learning. He taught himself advanced math, navigation, history, science, grammar, and five other languages, and he read everything available to him.
"The doors to wisdom are never shut."

William Henry Harrison
9th President
His early education was at home. He attended college, but didn't graduate.

Patrick Henry
Lawyer, Patriot, and Orator
He was educated at home by his father, and self-taught in law.

James Joule
Physicist
He was educated by his parents until they sent him to Cambridge at age 16.

C.S. Lewis
Author
He was educated by his mother until she died, when he was 10.

Abraham Lincoln
16th President
Lincoln's schooling totaled less than a year, and he was primarily self-taught.

James Madison
4th President
His fundamental instruction was at home, followed by prep school, then college,
where he received a classical education.

Margaret Mead
Anthropologist
Although she did attend some schools, her family traveled so often that she was
sometimes homeschooled by her grandmother.
"My grandmother wanted me to have an education so she kept me out of school."

Felix Mendelssohn
Composer and Musician
His education was supervised by his parents,
with private teachers employed for science and arts.

Wolfgang Mozart
Composer and Musician
He was taught at home by his father,
and also performed and traveled, starting at a young age.

John Muir
Naturalist
He left school at age 11 to help his family, and continued learning by reading.

Florence Nightingale
Nursing Pioneer
She received a classical education from her father.

Albert Jay Nock
Philosopher
He was primarily self-educated, with instruction in Latin and Greek from his father,
then attended a prep school before college.

Blaise Pascal
Mathematician
He showed exceptional ability as a child, and his father directed his home education.

George S. Patton, Jr.
WWII General
Patton was a late reader. He was home educated, with his father reading to him
extensively, until he learned to read on his own at age 12.

Franklin D. Roosevelt
32nd President
He was educated at home until he left for a private school
to prepare him for public service.

Theodore Roosevelt
26th President, Awarded Nobel Prize in 1906 (Peace)
He was a sick child, and was tutored until college.

Erwin Schrödinger
Physicist, Awarded Nobel Prize in 1933 (Physics)
He was taught at home by his parents and tutors until he was 11.

Herbert Spencer
Philosopher
He was taught informally by his father, a teacher.

Fred Terman
President of Stanford, Engineer, Chemist, "Father of Silicon Valley"
His father taught him through grade school, where he learned at an accelerated pace.

Phyllis Wheatley
Poet
Kidnapped in Africa and sold into slavery at age 7, she was a quick learner,
and the family that bought her educated her with their children at home.

Woodrow Wilson
28th President, Awarded Nobel Prize in 1919 (Peace)
He was dyslexic, and did not learn to read until he was 10.
His father taught him at home until he was 13.

Frank Lloyd Wright
Architect
His academic instruction came from his aunts and his mother at home.

Orville and Wilbur Wright
Inventors of the First Successful Airplane
While both brothers attended school at times, formal schooling
was sometimes interrupted by their other interests. Orville spent what would have
been his last year of high school studying special subjects.
*"We were lucky enough to grow up in an environment where there was always much
encouragement to children to pursue intellectual interests; to investigate whatever aroused
curiosity."* — Orville Wright

Andrew Wyeth
Artist
He was home educated after 3rd grade.
"I cherished the time alone because it made me utilize every moment..."

The Founders of Our Country
One third of the men who signed
The Declaration of Independence,
The Articles of Confederation and
The Constitution of the United States
were homeschooled.

Who will be on tomorrow's list of famous homeschoolers? It will be interesting to learn their stories, and learn how homeschooling made a difference in their lives.

Starting from Home, There are Many Paths to Genius
By Jackie Orsi

Poking through cartons of books at our annual library book sale some years ago, I came across a discarded copy of a reference book, *Asimov's Biographical Encyclopedia of Science and Technology*, the 1972 edition. The subtitle says it all: "The Lives and Achievements of 1195 Great Scientists from Ancient Times to the Present Chronologically Arranged."

This wonderful tome fascinates me. Beginning with Imhoptep, an Egyptian scholar who "flourished 2980-2950 BC," the prolific author Isaac Asimov introduces the major scientists of history, their lives and their contributions. Very little is known about the early years of most of the ancients, but by the mid-1600s, some solid information regarding childhood begins to appear in the biographies. Asimov reports, for example, Pierre de Fermat, 1601-1665, a French mathematician who founded the modern theory of numbers, "was educated at home."

Following the Fermat biography, Asimov tells of dozens more down through the centuries who were "taught at home" by parents or tutor, or who are described as "self-educated" or simply, "had little formal schooling." Essentially, they meet the modern definition of homeschooled because they were not institutionally schooled. By the end of the 800-page volume, we have a lengthy and impressive list of homeschool alumni, and have uncovered some other interesting biographical data, as well.

Asimov shows us that the paths to genius are many, some are unexpected, and quite a few begin at home.

The Major Luminaries

The list of homeschoolers and their contributions is a dazzling one, sure to give homeschooling's critics twinges of doubt.

Blaise Pascal, French mathematician and physicist, educated by his father, made contributions to geometry and laid the foundation of probability theory.

Anton van Leeuwenhoek, Dutch biologist, "had little schooling," yet he managed to make significant advancements in microscopy, discovering protozoa and numerous other microorganisms.

Ben Franklin, American inventor, with "only two years of formal schooling," made significant contributions to electricity, meteorology, and study of ocean currents. He invented bifocals, the stove and many other practical devices.

Joseph Priestly of England, a clergyman who "never studied science formally," is credited with many advances relating to chemistry of gases, including the discovery of oxygen.

James Watt, Scottish engineer, was taught to read by his mother. He invented the steam engine.

John Dalton "left school at the age of eleven and a year later. . . returned to begin teaching at a Quaker school" in his native England. Entirely self-educated in science, he is credited with the formulation of atomic theory.

Johan Karl Friedrich Gauss was born to a poor family who soon recognized his precocity when he began "correcting his father's sums" at the age of three. Self-taught reading and writing, Gauss is considered one of the greatest all-time geniuses of pure mathematics.

Sir Humphrey Davy, English chemist, was born to poverty. He hated school and apprenticed to an apothecary where he began a course of self-education and experimentation. (Asimov notes that an apothecary apprenticeship of yore provided a fine education for many young men who later made significant contributions to chemistry. Indeed, I counted several in the book who followed that course, rather than college.) Davy was the discoverer of potassium, sodium, barium, strontium, calcium and magnesium, made many contributions to electrochemistry and other fields, and invented the coal miner's lamp.

Michael Faraday, English physicist and chemist, was born to a blacksmith of very meager means. Faraday was largely self-educated. It was his good fortune to be apprenticed as a boy to a bookbinder who let him read the books they bound. He became a scientist of vast contributions. He propelled the science of electrochemistry into the modern age, created classical field theory and the laws of electrolysis, among other achievements.

Charles Babbage of England "taught himself mathematics." He is credited with numerous inventions, and due to his theoretical work is thought of as the grandfather of the modern computer.

Joseph Henry, an American, was born to a day-laborer and apprenticed to a watchmaker at age thirteen. Without formal schooling, he nevertheless could read. "The story goes that at 16 while Henry was on vacation at a relative's farm he chased a rabbit under a church building. He crawled underneath, found some of the floorboards missing and promptly abandoned the rabbit to explore the church. There he found a shelf of books." One was a book called Lectures on Experimental Philosophy that fired him with ambition to seek some training in engineering. Ultimately, he is credited with the discovery of electrical induction and self induction, with contributions toward the development of the telegraph, and with the creation of the first electric motor.

Sir William Rowan Hamilton, an Irish mathematician, "attended no school and was largely self-taught." He contributed to optics, the wave theory of light, and invented "quaternion," an algebraic approach to three dimensional geometry.

George Boole, English mathematician, was mainly self-educated. He devised Boolean algebra, the algebra of logic.

James Prescott Joule had some sort of spinal injury as a child. He was largely self-educated, encouraged by his father who gave him a home laboratory. His work in heat energy was groundbreaking.

Herbert Spencer, English sociologist, "had little formal education" and "was tutored by his father and his uncle." He became a major influence in the social philosophy of his era.

Johannes van der Waals, a Dutch physicist, was largely self-taught prior to entering Leiden University. He was awarded the Nobel Prize for his work in gas equations.

Thomas Edison, the brilliant American inventor, was educated at home by his mother. He patented nearly 1,300 inventions, including the electric light, the mimeograph, the motion picture and the phonograph.

George Eastman, inventor of numerous photographic processes and the Kodak camera, "had little chance at schooling" and "was working and supporting himself at age fourteen."

Pierre Curie, the French chemist, "received his early schooling at home." With his wife, Marie, he received the 1903 Nobel Prize in physics for research in magnetism and radioactivity.

Lesser Luminaries

I spotted 24 additional homeschooled scientists in my survey of the book, individuals who made contributions of lesser magnitude. No doubt more than these were homeschooled, since universal schooling is generally a development of the last century and a half, but this is information that probably was not available to Asimov.

Fast Starts and Slow

For every young scientist who was a child prodigy, there seems to have been one who was significantly delayed in his development. Thomas Young, English physicist, could read at age two; among his many accomplishments is the development of the wave theory of light. On the other hand, Edison's schoolteacher told his mother he was "addled," so infuriating her that she removed him from school. Lord Kelvin attended his father's mathematical lectures at the age of eight, and entered the University of Glasgow at age eleven. Einstein "was so slow in learning to speak that there was some feeling he might prove retarded." The Swedish chemist Arrhenius taught himself to read at age three, and earned a Nobel Prize in chemistry. Fresnel, by contrast, was eight before he could read, yet went on to major discoveries in optics and light theory. Norbert Wiener, another who could read by age three, earned his doctorate from Harvard at 18 and did pioneering work in cybernetics. Volta, a major contributor to the understanding of electricity, didn't talk until age four, and was considered "retarded" by his family. Haller, the founder of modern neurology, began scholarly writings at age eight and created a Greek dictionary at age 10. Others thought to be slow or unpromising as youngsters include the taxonomer Carolus Linnaeus,

Nobel Prize winner Ramon Y Cajal, and Pierre Curie. (Suggested reading: *Late Talking Children* by Thomas Sowell.)

Away from the Noise and Commotion

Illness and physical limitations may have actually been a boon to many young scientists, allowing them the luxury of staying home to read, study and dream. Described as frail, sickly children were Pascal, Priestly, Joule, Watt, Haller and Spencer. The profound genius Rene Descartes attended boarding school as a child, but he suffered ill health. His schoolmasters permitted him to lie in bed as much as he pleased. Asimov tells us that Descartes "retained the habit of doing much of his work in bed for the rest of his life."

A surprising number suffered from hearing impairment. These included Goodricke, a deaf-mute from birth, who made astronomical observations and hypothesized correctly the existence of "invisible stars." Tsiolkovsky, deaf from the age of nine, was self-educated; he was a pioneer of rocketry and space flight. Edison, as is well known, was hearing impaired, as was the French physicist Guillaume Amontons; both expressed that deafness was a kind of a blessing because it allowed them to concentrate on their work.

Just a Hobby

Countless scientific strides were made by people never formally trained for the fields they pursued as amateur hobbyists. Astronomy owes much to the painstaking research of hobbyists. William Bond, a 19th century American watch-maker, discovered Saturn's third ring. William Beer, a German banker, spent eight years mapping the features of the moon; William Lassell owned a brewery by day and studied the heavens at night. He is credited with the discoveries of Triton (a moon of Neptune), Hyperion (the eighth moon of Saturn), and Ariel and Umbriel, (two moons of Uranus). Milton Humason began his career in astronomy working as a janitor at the Mount Wilson Observatory. Later his work measuring the speed of galaxies helped set the stage for the Big Bang theory.

Botany and genetics are built upon the findings of amateurs turned careerists. Gregor Mendel, born a peasant in Russia, "tended fruit trees for the lord of the manor." Later, he entered a monastery and continued his interest in growing things. Eventually his work in plant breeding led to the Mendelian laws of inheritance. Luther Burbank, California's own botanist, had "only the equivalent of a high school education" and was entirely self trained in experimental methods. He is credited with developing countless hybrids and other botanical firsts.

A Place for Learning at Home

Asimov's research turned up few homeschoolers in the 20th century, when forced mass school became the norm. Still, it is possible to see the importance of independent learning and supportive home life. Alfred Werner built a home chemistry laboratory in his parents' barn and by eighteen had done credible original work. He won the Nobel Prize for chemistry in 1913. Grote Reber's teenage explorations with ham radio laid the groundwork for his lifetime fascinations, especially in the field of radio astronomy. Thirteen-year-old Linus Pauling was pals with a fellow who had a home chemistry lab. That set captivated the young Pauling. He went on to win the Nobel Prize in chemistry for his work on the structure of proteins.

History's Lesson

Those who insist that children must not be left to learn at home, who say one must obtain credentials before one is allowed to enter a field of endeavor, and who say they can predict what a child will become are clearly proven wrong by these great men of science and invention. Human potential naturally strives for expression, but never in the same way twice. History here shows us the wisdom of letting people learn where they want to, when they want to, and how they want to. The mechanistic premises of modern institutional schooling with its methodologies and sequences and bell curves and certificates are all too limited and limiting. One cannot help but wonder how many excellent minds have been inhibited, perhaps thwarted altogether by the one-size-fits-all system. We need a lot less scientific management and a lot more belief in people. There is an old saying that goes, "Geniuses are born, not made." It seems a correction may be in order: Geniuses are not born, they are self-made.

Aren't Our Local Schools Good Enough?

"...no one will attend to their questions

as closely or care about them as deeply as I do."

©Don Perry

When You Must Explain Homeschooling

By Christine Tykeson

Homeschooling has become commonplace enough that I can take for granted not having to automatically explain my decision to homeschool to others. Where I used to encounter questions about legality or socialization, I now meet responses of, "Oh, I have a friend [or know someone] who homeschools" or "Good for you" or "It must be a lot of work. I wish I could do it." But every once in a while I encounter the types of questions that used to come up.

Late last spring I was hit with a triple whammy series of questions. A woman fired off to me, in quick succession, not only, "Why are you homeschooling?" a question that defies a quick response (how can you summarize in a few sentences all the reasons that have brought you to homeschooling), but also, "Are the schools not good in your area?" and "Do you have special training to do this?" I admit I was taken as much off guard by my belief that homeschooling had grown beyond the stage of being scrutinized, as by the style of her questioning and the not-so-hidden assumptions contained in her questions. I did a passable job, I suppose. After a brief period of stunned silence in which I gathered my thoughts, I told her that I believe individually-tailored education is a superior form of education and that I could best provide it through homeschooling, that I liked my kids and enjoyed being home with them and felt that they received a better socialization experience at home, influenced primarily by parents rather than peers.

Not a bad response, but I stumbled for it more than I would have liked. Since then, I've come up with more complete responses to each of these questions. I'd discovered from personal experience what I already knew intellectually; there still are and will be, for a long time to come, people who challenge and question homeschooling.

Why are You Homeschooling?

This is not a question that's easy to answer in one or two sentences. Many reasons have influenced this decision. At this point one can offer to give a pamphlet about homeschooling to the questioner. CHN has some free brochures that would work well. First of all, I believe homeschooling provides a better education. My children can progress as fast as they can or take as long as they need to master skills and learn them according to a style that befits their natures. Second, the social atmosphere provided by a loving, functioning family out-scores the environment provided on any school playground.

Are the Schools Not Good in Your Area?

If you're asking if the schools in my area are good compared to other public schools then the answer is "yes". If you're asking if they are as good as they should be or as good as the individualized instruction homeschooling parents can provide, I have to say "no".

Do You Have Special Training to Do This?

I don't have or need training comparable to that of a school teacher's because teaching my own children is a much different activity than managing a classroom of children. Success in homeschooling relies less on teaching credentials and more on family relationship skills; skills which are learned while on the job of parenting and by self-education, i.e. reading parenting books, and talking with other parents. I am not against well-trained instruction for my children and I do make use of professional and specially trained people to teach my children. My son is taking Latin and Greek classes from teachers who are "experts". My children have also received instruction from specialists in art, music, and martial arts. I also count as their teachers the learning materials I have purchased, borrowed or rented: books, videos, computer programs, and craft kits. Books provide access to the best minds and teachers that are to be found. I don't need to teach math when I have Saxon Math materials, with their clear instructions and incremental progression, to do the job for me. I don't teach my children so much as direct their education. And as their parent, I am the best qualified and most motivated person to do this job.

Not-so-coincidentally, these "training" types of questions often come from people in professional circles who revere, and expect others to revere, expert training. Defending the importance of training is a practice of professional courtesy for them. Within this group you find the most diehard opponents to homeschooling. No matter what you say you will not convince them of the merits of homeschooling. If you are talking to a relatively open minded person, you might point out that training and getting results do not always go together. You might say, "Children who have been homeschooled have performed well as evidenced by standardized test score comparisons and anecdotal evidence. Training is valuable when used for the purpose of enhancing performance, which it usually does, but is sometimes used for protecting privilege, as it is by the teachers' union which has pushed to require licensing for teachers in private and home schools as well. Credentialing requirements would, ironically, reduce the quality of education by reducing competition as it effectively wipes out home and many private schools. It's important not to underestimate the benefits of self-education in providing training. Self-education infuses any field with creativity that is otherwise missing from a professional class graduated from cookie-cutter institutions."

These are the replies I would give if I had time to give and formulate them. Then I consider, perhaps short replies are best. I'm reminded of the first homeschooler I ever met, who, when asked if he sent his son to school, answered, "Why would I do that to him? He's my buddy!" This response elicited laughter, always a good tactic for disarming an argument. Although I would carefully gauge where to use this remark, it sums up my feelings precisely.

Homeschooling Sound Bites

All of us find ourselves, at one time or another, being asked questions about homeschooling, and quite often we are caught off guard and unable to come up with succinct responses exactly at the moment when needed. We turned to some of our experienced CHN Local Contacts and asked for help in coming up with a few one liners that would help all of us enlighten those who inquire about homeschooling. We thought you might enjoy these short, to-the-point sample answers to typical questions about homeschooling (we didn't make these up!).

What about socialization?

- Socialization is one of the main reasons why we chose to homeschool.

- Socialization means providing a model of adult behavior for children to emulate. My children are with adults quite often during the course of a week, so socialization isn't a problem.

How will your children meet other children their age?

- I don't think it is important for children to be with other children who are exactly their own age. I think they need to be with people of all ages—and they are as we go about our daily lives, especially in our local homeschool support group and our extracurricular activities.

- We have plenty of children in our neighborhood.

But what about sports?

- We have easily found athletic activities outside of school.

- My child participates with others at our homeschool park days.

How can you stand to be **with** your children all day?

- How can you stand to be *away* from your children all day? (*at least this is what we sometimes think, even if we're too polite to say it out loud!*)

- It's a joy and privilege to share our days together.

I want my child to know what it's like to be bored.

- Well, my children are sometimes bored at home. It forces them to search within themselves and discover what matters to them.

- I think that by having an interesting childhood, my child may be less apt to be bored as an adult. I see no need to stifle him with 13 years of boredom in school just so he'll be used to it when he is an adult.

How can you teach subjects you don't know?

- I view my role as a facilitator. Sometimes that means I teach, sometimes I lead them to the right materials and they teach themselves, and sometimes I find someone else to teach.

How will you teach math?

- My children are very independent and study math on their own. My husband and I can answer any questions that come up.

- When my daughter progresses to where I can't help her anymore, I'll go over to Whatsamatta U. and hire a student to tutor math.

How will you teach advanced science?

- A homeschooling parent in our local support group offers science instruction. When my children advance past what she can offer, they will be able to take lab classes at Whatsamatta U.

What about the prom?

- My children may not be interested in the prom. I wasn't. But if they are, they may be invited to someone else's prom or our local support group can organize one of our own.

- My son went to his girlfriend's prom last year and said he had a great time. He also said that it wouldn't have been worth all the hassle of going to school just to go to the prom. He liked his method better.

- We offered our daughter a choice: the prom or a trip to France for eight weeks. Sadly the cost was about the same.

- The prom doesn't really have anything to do with education.

How will your children learn to stand in line?

- My child has been standing in lines for years, and is quite good at it. There are lines everywhere—the bank, the library, the grocery store.

- We're planning to take a trip to England where standing in straight lines is taken very seriously. (They can spot sloppy Americans at a glance.)

Aren't you being overprotective keeping your children home with you?

- It is my responsibility as a parent to care for my children. Caring for their safety and well-being isn't being overprotective.

- Homeschoolers aren't protected any more than anyone else from life's trials. Due to home environments marked by trust and love, they are actually better prepared to deal with difficult situations and people. I think that's why homeschoolers are usually more confident, compassionate and mature.

I went to school and I turned out okay.

- Yes, I did too, but I'm starting a new tradition for my family. I didn't know any homeschoolers when I was growing up. Isn't it great that we have the freedom to decide for ourselves what is best for our children?

Isn't homeschooling expensive?

- One year costs less than one month of private school tuition.

- We may spend as little or as much as we choose to spend. There are resources available to fit everyone's finances, so that a tight budget need not be a primary factor when deciding to homeschool.

- Not at all. We use the library for free, and also buy used curriculum.

I don't want to protect my child from the mean people because he'll have to live and work with them when he grows up.

- Actually, adults have much greater freedom of association than you are implying. We can walk away from social situations, switch jobs or move to improve our lives. Unfortunately, children aren't allowed to quit their school nor are they given much choice about who they spend time with in school. Part of why we homeschool is to allow our children freedom of association.

- Having protected my children while they are young will help them grow up to know they have the choice to avoid mean, nasty people. My hope is that they will also grow up to be nicer people.

How do homeschoolers graduate from high school?

- Some graduate from the private school they attend, some graduate from the local community college at the same time they receive their high school diploma.

How will your children get a job without a high school transcript?

- They will have a transcript from our homeschool. Beyond that, homeschoolers have found that employers are more interested in work experience and solid references.

A Child's-Eye View of Homeschooling

There's an old saying, "If you want to know about racing, go ask the horse." So, for the scoop on homeschooling, who better to go to than the children? A group of homeschooled children between the ages of six and fourteen were surveyed. Half had never attended a traditional school. The survey yielded interesting insights.

"I am in control of my day and my activities."

When students were asked to tell the best thing about homeschooling, the majority of respondents answered "freedom." They prized the "freedom to choose" when, where, and what to study, and how best to work in extracurricular activities such as play, volunteering, sports, and field trips.

"I can't say that I ever have a typical day."

Our "experts" were asked to describe a "typical" day in their lives and to tell how their day was apportioned between particular activities. Fully half declared that there is no such thing as a "typical" day. Each indicated some personal flexibility in scheduling and pacing their studies. Reading, both assigned and reading-for-pleasure, ranked highest on the favorites list. Household chores, part-time jobs, volunteering, sports, and group/club activities were listed as daily activities.

"Homeschooling is better because it allows you to go outside and look at butterflies and learn about them."

The students were asked, "Describe your experience in conventional school if, in fact, you ever attended one." It is enlightening to know that the one word most often used to describe the experience was "boring." Some reported that they liked the "hands-on" part of the schools' daily fare; this response was usually attributed to their experience in the early elementary years. Memories of time spent in the later grades told a different story, however. Students described the system as boring, slow, and intrusive into their personal and family lives.

"I think the perfect school would be like a huge back yard with lakes, mountains, and maybe a chemistry lab."

What would the children envision as the most fabulous school possible? Not one student proposed conventional schools with predetermined curricula, and certainly none supported the idea of any kind of enforced, stifling seatwork. Instead, their ideas centered around museums, computers, laboratories, the great outdoors and worldwide travel.

"I get to be with other kids pretty regularly."

The children were asked to rate the frequency they were around kids other than their siblings. The majority saw friends and peers every day and were satisfied with the quality and amount of their social interactions.

"You get to be with your family all day."

Improved family unity and cohesiveness was another factor on the positive side of the ledger. These children really enjoy being with their parents and siblings.

"…when I grow up I want to work for Lego."

The future looked rosy to all respondents. Most imagined themselves involved in various exciting activities while continuing to homeschool or, especially for the older students, continuing to self-educate well into their adult years. Traveling, college, apprenticing in a trade, sports, sciences, or fine arts were high on the list of the children's future plans.

"I would homeschool my own kids because I think they learn more and I want a close family."

When asked if they would homeschool their own children someday, most of our respondents were overwhelmingly positive about continuing the family tradition of homeschooling. Many expressed that homeschooling would provide their offspring the best education possible. Some respondents stressed that they would allow their children a choice in how they would be educated.

Why I Choose to Homeschool

By Beth Haynes

To Protect and Nurture the Natural Love of Learning

Children are natural learning machines. From before birth, children accumulate and assimilate thousands of data points in order to understand the world around them. No one has to give formal lessons to teach them to walk or talk, or more importantly to want to walk and talk. The questions of toddlers and preschoolers are numerous, even unending. Kids want to know about the world. They want to gain competency at tasks important to living their lives and achieving their goals. If taken seriously and assisted when asked, children will learn most of the skills and gather much of the information needed to live their lives successfully.

We easily remember things when our learning suits our personal needs or passions. Learning in order to pass tests or please others is quickly forgotten because ultimately it remains irrelevant to us as individuals. Learning by someone else's plan or schedule is inefficient and soon turns to drudgery. Allowing and encouraging a personal path of discovery seems the best way to learn and do so joyfully.

To Protect and Nurture Their Maturing Self-Esteem

Self-esteem does not develop by having people tell you how wonderful you are, or by the handing out of praise and rewards. True self-esteem comes from gaining confidence through true competence. That means doing a good job on tasks that are meaningful and relevant to your life. It means the freedom to go at your own pace and make mistakes over and over again if necessary. It means having help and guidance readily available if and when you need it, and just enough to get you past a stuck point. Self-esteem requires the development of one's own standards of excellence, not blind acceptance of the standards of others.

My children already possess the most crucial elements for educating themselves: a boundless curiosity and a budding sense of self-confidence. I wish to nurture the unique individuals they are becoming and assist them in clarifying their own interests and goals. I watch in fascination the path they are mapping.

To Adapt Their Education to My Understanding of Childhood Development

My philosophy of education differs greatly from that of most institutions. Based on my understanding of Piaget and Montessori, early childhood needs to be filled with hands-on life experiences. This time is too precious and too short to be spent on "busy work" of any type. Objects need to be handled and manipulated directly (sensorimotor stage) then experimented with over and over so that a child can experience similarities and differences, cause and effect (concrete operational stage.) Emphasis on book learning is not appropriate until a child enters into the stage of abstract reasoning. This move to higher levels of thinking and learning is highly individualized, but tends not to be in synch with a typical school curriculum. Too much too soon can be as harmful to lifelong learning as too little too late. For learning to remain an exciting adventure, and not be boring or overwhelming, the pace and rhythm of each child must be carefully monitored and attended. No one will guard this balance for my children as carefully as I will.

To Provide the Experience and Responsibility of Setting One's Own Agenda

Most schools, private or government, are locked into a set curriculum. Goals and expectations are externally imposed. This is the nature of the beast. A classroom without lesson plans would be directionless and chaotic. A diploma that is not backed by some set of requirements and standards is meaningless. The teaching of subjects begins and ends by the clock and calendar rather than by level of interest or excitement. How could anyone ever have a chance to "milk a passion" when learning on someone else's timeline?

One of the things that has impressed me in reading about older homeschoolers is their own concern that their education be "well rounded." These children are used to being responsible for discovering and pursuing their own needs and interests. They take seriously the task of entering the adult world and want to be equipped to deal with the challenges. Careful and detailed thinking is necessary to outline the information and skills needed to make a success of your own unique life. That is a crucial task that schools will never allow you to do for yourself. That task begins as a habit of paying attention to what you enjoy and find interesting as well as figuring out for yourself what it will take to get you from Point A to Point B.

I realize that not all of the important stuff will be inherently obvious to my children. My job as their parent and mentor is to provide them with an adult perspective and a set of guidelines within which we work together to design their course of study. Some areas take more effort on my part to convince them of a subject's relevance and importance. As in all facets of parenting and family life, there will be constant give and take on both sides. Homeschooling allows us an incredible amount of flexibility in the paths we take to achieve the goal of raising mature, independent and happy individuals. Is that not the true purpose of an education?

To Keep the Focus of Their Learning on the Mastery of a Skill or Subject

School can all too easily become a game of doing just enough to get a good grade. When topics are not self-selected, motivation to achieve true mastery is difficult if not impossible. The standard to be met is no longer understanding a body of knowledge or perfecting a skill but the approval of the teacher. The flip side of this is that mistakes and lack of knowledge are viewed as failures rather than opportunities to discover what still needs to be learned. In our lives, we learn in order to "do it right" (e.g. baking bread, balancing a checkbook) not just to achieve 90% of someone else's standard. Education should be the same way. You should learn to spell in order to know how to spell, not to get an A on the test.

To Tailor Teaching to Individual Learning Styles

Each child has a unique way of gathering and assimilating information. For a child to flourish, he must be free to go at material in that unique way. There are several ways of learning including kinesthetically, visually, musically, inter- and intra-personally (see pages 111-112). Schools are aimed primarily at those who learn with a logical/linguistic style. This means that a child who learns best when moving or talking is often labeled ADD or learning disabled.

To Encourage Lots of Questions, Including a Healthy Dose of Questioning Authority

Doing what you are told to do is a virtue only if the request makes sense to you. If not, the virtuous act is to question the authority. This behavior is clearly not acceptable in the vast majority of schools. Even in preschool, the projects are to be done in a specific way with the blatant goal of preparing children to "follow instructions." But to what end? The end of keeping order and getting through the lesson plan. What is left in a sacrificial pile is the child's creativity, along with self-directed trial and error aimed at discovering the way that makes the most sense to him. If the main goal is to cultivate law-abiding citizens, schools may be on the right path. My goal is to help my children develop their powers of reasoning and their own criteria for right/wrong and good/bad using reality as the standard. Of course, there are times when following instructions is a crucial skill, but it is one which can be learned in the process of pursuing a specific goal, and should not be an end in itself.

Benjamin asks a hundred questions a day, every time he hears a word he doesn't understand, or whenever a subject pops into his head. That is the time to learn vocabulary or dive into a subject. That is the time it's going to stick because it has direct personal meaning for him. In a classroom, he would either have to quit asking so many questions or have the strength to be a pest.

To Provide Proper "Socialization"

I don't understand why people think that the way to learn to get along with other people is to be thrown into a mob. There simply is not enough supervision of children's interactions at school. There are too many children and not enough adults. Premature exposure to peer pressure and immature styles of conflict resolution are not the way to build character. I am homeschooling with Benjamin and Eva because I do not think they will get proper "socialization" at school.

Knowing your own self-worth is the key to giving others an appropriate measure of respect or disdain. A solid self-esteem allows one to stand up to bullies or to extend one's self with compassion. When a person sufficiently values himself, he does not need to take bullies seriously. Conversely, there is nothing to be gained by ridiculing those who are different. I want my children to grow up surrounded by a group of truly decent human beings who will treat them with respect and demand the same behavior from them. The rest is a matter of custom and good manners that are learned by example and emanate from a general sense of goodwill toward others.

To Give My Values First Shot

All teaching contains the teaching of values. I have very definite ideas and values that I want to impart to my children. The values and curricular biases taught at public schools are politically set and falsely presented as objective and unbiased. When my children are older, it will be crucial for them to explore and understand various points of view and then come to their own conclusions. Until their tools of rational evaluation are more developed, I want to be present as a filter and interpreter of the ideas to which they are exposed. This is both my right and my responsibility as their parent.

To Maximize My Children's Free Time

It has been repeatedly shown that a child absent from his classroom can easily keep up by spending less than two hours a day on schoolwork. What else are they doing while sitting inside at their desks for much of the day? In spite of this inefficient use of time, most children come home from school too tired to pursue academic topics that truly interest them. One on one teaching is more efficient. We can finish the formal lessons in a few hours each day. The rest of the day is open to them to pursue their interests and passions, or simply play and enjoy their lives.

To Maximize My Time with My Children

I love being with my children. I love exploring and discovering this world with them. Together we learn and play and grow and change. I learn almost as much from them as they from me. As long as I am able to teach them myself, I prefer to be the one to accompany them on this glorious adventure of learning.

In Summary, I Can Do a Better Job

I love learning. I find this world fascinating and fun. There are some teachers with this attitude, but there is no guarantee Benjamin and Eva will consistently end up with them. Besides, no one will attend to their questions as closely or care about them as deeply as I do. Life is an adventure and education is an integral part of that adventure, not a separate activity done primarily in a special building during specific hours of the day. I expect to have a great time learning alongside my children as they explore new vistas. That perhaps is the most important "lesson" I hope to teach: The purpose of your life is the identification and pursuit of your values. Life is meant to be enjoyed, and you are responsible for your own life and your own happiness.

Benjamin and Eva might survive school, but I believe they will have a greater chance to flourish by learning at home.

Reinforcing a Positive Image
By Karen Rafferty

Public schools are under attack in the media while homeschooling is getting increasingly positive press. It is hard for homeschoolers not to take a perverse delight in seeing the tables turned. I'm glad we're getting positive PR, but I don't foresee a deluge of new homeschoolers. Homeschooling takes a commitment of time and resources. I do believe that this is the season to reinforce our new, positive image. How? By getting out and meeting people. Once they meet interested, intelligent, well spoken, properly socialized, homeschooled kids, not to mention their dedicated parents, it is difficult for people to disparage homeschooling. We've found community service a great way to meet and build bridges to a variety of individuals. Our most recent venture started with a deficit of positive regard toward homeschooling.

The Parent-Teacher Association in our city operates a food bank called PTA-Helps. Throughout the year the food bank is available to fill emergency orders for a week's worth of groceries. During the holiday season families can apply for a Thanksgiving and Christmas food order through their local schools or city hall. Several hundred families are served for each holiday. It's a worthy cause.

Six years ago I became aware of this program while volunteering as a den leader for Cub Scouts. Each November our den would participate in a canned food drive and donate the items collected to a food bank in the area. When I learned about PTA-Helps, we decided to donate our cans to our own community through them.

Mid-November 1993, my son and I presented the cans to the volunteer coordinator. At the center we noticed a "Help Needed" sign and learned that they had been unable to keep the food bank open more than one day a week due to a lack of volunteers. Since we'd been tossing around the idea of finding an ongoing way to serve our community, we started asking questions. What work would we be doing? How many hours would we be expected to commit? Could my son and I work together? The last question caused an uproar. He wasn't going to school in Downey? I home what? Homeschooled? No, they didn't need me.

In the intervening years we found other ways to serve our community: the homeless shelter, citywide cleanups, booth workers at Kids Day and more. We continued to drop cans off at the food bank after the Cub Scout drive each November, but, since the same volunteer coordinator was in place, we believed we would not be welcomed as workers.

This December, the Community Relations Coordinator for our church called in a tizzy. "PTA-Helps called me to see if I could find them some volunteers. They are really short-handed. Since Andrew is homeschooled, is he available to help? Do you know any other homeschoolers you could bring with you? They are desperate!"

On the premise that desperation can break down barriers, I collected my son and three other homeschooled teens from our area, and we drove down to the food bank. The senior citizens who were volunteering were delighted when our more physically active crew arrived to load, carry and unload boxes. Madam Coordinator was there and, true to form, turned to me, a challenge in her voice, and asked, "Why aren't they in school?" Trying to avoid a confrontation, I responded, "They attend a private school, and we really encourage service to the community as part of the curriculum." I thought I was going to get away with it until one of the seniors piped up, "Oh, do you homeschool?" Caught! A moment of awkward silence followed, and then the coordinator said, "Well, have them sign in here."

The boys worked steadily for four hours. They were cheerful and outgoing, carrying on conversations with the families picking up food orders and the other volunteers. The older volunteers had nothing but praise for them. At lunchtime the volunteer coordinator went out of her way to invite them down for the first shift. As much as I was tempted to follow them down in case they needed defending, I kept working. It's a bit hard to walk around and carry bags with all your toes and fingers crossed, but I managed. I kept telling myself, "These guys can handle themselves." No queries were forthcoming and nothing negative was said.

When we signed out, the coordinator mentioned to me that she was impressed with how hard and competently the kids had worked. I told her we'd enjoyed ourselves and politely avoided mentioning homeschooling. While she didn't exactly invite us back, I think we'll show up again next year. And I believe we will be welcomed.

Through the years we've made it a rule not to try to convert people to homeschooling, but to work on converting them to supporting our right to homeschool. The bridges homeschoolers build now will help preserve our right to homeschool when it is challenged. When you're in a minority, you can never have too many friends.

Isn't Homeschooling Against the Law?

"...you will be empowered

with the information you need to...

homeschool legally..."

©Cheryl Maxwell

There are four legal ways to homeschool in California, but there is something you need to know first—

You Can't Homeschool...And Other Stories

By Karen Taylor

Just when we think we have heard it all, some school employee comes up with another creative reason to tell parents why they can't homeschool. Sadly, a few parents (I call them victims) believe the stories every year. Perhaps you will laugh at some of the reasons, and shake your head in disbelief at others. They are shared here so that you will be empowered with the information you need to be assured that you can indeed homeschool legally—our goal is to have no more victims of tall tales!

"Ma'am, You Can't Teach Without a Credential!"

Probably the most frequently used tall tale is the old standby claim that, "You need a teaching credential." You will learn later in this chapter why that is not true. Some other parents have at one time or another been told that they need fingerprinting, fire marshal checks, a business license, health department inspection, and an inspection of their curriculum to "evaluate" it. Rest assured that those parents who agree to an "evaluation" request will undoubtedly be told that their request to homeschool has been denied.

But, wait! Our list goes on. We know of a mom who was told that she had to call Child Protective Services (CPS), and the school even gave her the phone number to call—was she to call and report herself for contributing to truancy, we wondered? Another mom of a boy was told that the only reason to homeschool was pregnancy. She ignored them and has successfully homeschooled him for many years. One new homeschooler said her child's teacher told her she couldn't homeschool her children because it was illegal to homeschool on a military base, and it was also unpatriotic!

Parents are often told that they can't homeschool because homeschooling is illegal...or that they don't qualify. . .or that there is no room in the school district program for them, so the child must stay in the classroom. . . or that only "very special cases" can homeschool. . . or that the only way you can homeschool is "through" the school. . . or the child must have a broken leg. Who knows what will be next?

A Misguided Trust in Authorities

Yes, some of these tall tales are farfetched, but since they come from *authorities*, parents tend to believe them. The reason for sharing these stories is that the more you know, the better your rights will be protected. While CHN does not give legal advice, we do share what fellow homeschoolers have learned, and we network and support each other—empowerment! Our goal is that no parent who wants to homeschool will believe one of the above stories or a different version, and reluctantly return their child to the classroom.

The Truth About Homeschooling and Your Four Choices

In this chapter, you will learn about the *four legal ways* to homeschool in California. Not only do you need this practical information for yourself, but we know you have concerned neighbors and relatives who will be relieved by reading this information as well. We will share with you what we have learned over the years. You will read about what you need to know to get started, and you will even gain knowledge about the education codes. You will soon know what records are needed, how to withdraw your child from school, and where to turn if you have more questions. Keep in mind that most parents have no homeschool legal problems. But, even one attempt to hinder a parent from homeschooling is too much. The ones who are most likely to become "victims" are the ones who have not learned about their rights ahead of time. So, consider this your legal fire drill. Learn what you need, but also be aware that you will likely never have to put that knowledge to the test. Happy *legal* homeschooling!

The Four Ways to Homeschool in California

What Legal Option Should You Choose?

There are four options available to parents who would like to homeschool in California. Learn about each one, so that your decision will be an informed one. Each option has pros and cons, and the decision is going to be a very individual one.

- Option 1: *The Private School Affidavit* (PSA/R-4)
- Option 2: *Private Independent Study Programs (ISP)*
- Option 3: *Public School ISP or Charter School*
- Option 4: *Credentialed Teacher/Tutor*

Option #1 The Private School Affidavit

Home educators may establish a private school based in their home by filing a private school affidavit (PSA/R-4) with the State Department of Education. The following Education Codes, which are printed on the back of the PSA form, are pertinent to this right: §33190, §48222, and §48415. For quick referral, these codes and others are listed in the appendix of this book. The entire California Education Code may be accessed from the California Homeschool Network website, *www.CaliforniaHomeschool.net/*. The annual deadline for filing an affidavit for an existing school is October 15th, however, a new private school can be established, and an affidavit filed, any time during the year.

In the fall of 2002, a new filing procedure was instituted by the state. Local county offices no longer distribute or process the PSA, and instead homeschooling families have a new option of filing online at the state website *www.cde.ca.gov/privateschools*, or they can contine as they have in the past, by requesting a paper copy from the state, or filing their own in lieu statement. The law did not change in 2002, but this new online process ensured that the affidavit would not be denied to anyone who requested it. Further changes are a possiblity. It would be advisable to check the CHN website to look for updates regularly.

The PSA: A Statistical Tool

The private school affidavit does not license, evaluate, recognize, approve of, or endorse a private school. The State of California accredits neither public nor private schools. The affidavit is a statistical tool, and necessary to effect the pupil's exemption from compulsory public school enrollment and attendance. By filing an affidavit you are showing intent to establish a private school. Parents have been legally using this provision for many years to conduct their own home-based private schools.

The State Department of Education, as well as any county or local public school district, lacks jurisdiction over the establishment or operation of private elementary and secondary schools. The school district is authorized to verify that a specific child who is not in a public school is being educated privately, and sometimes they do. Giving the name of the private school or showing the PSA (or copy of your in lieu statement) is adequate. They are not authorized to make a home visit for purposes such as evaluating your curriculum, however, some school individuals occasionally ask, so it is important for homeschoolers to be clear about their rights regarding this. There is no statutory basis for this request, and you may decline it.

Filling Out the PSA: Simple Hints for Success!

If you choose to homeschool independently by filing an affidavit or statement, you must re-file every year between October 1-15. There is no charge for the state form, and it must be offered to anyone who requests it.

Whether you file online, send in your own statement, or use the state paper form, it is important to keep a copy for your school records. No confirmation or approval will be sent to you.

You will be asked to sign "under penalty of perjury," so fill it out accurately. We offer a sample in the appendix so you can see what the PSA looks like and how some homeschoolers have completed this simple form. It's common to have a few minor changes from year to year, but basically it remains the same.

One frequent question is what grade to put down. Some parents have a child who is working above or below grade level, and they wonder just what they should tell the state. Although you will want to teach your child at the level that is appropriate for him, for the purposes of this statistical document, put down the grade he would be in if he attended school. You also do not have to "fail" him if, for example, he is not quite up to where the public school thinks he should be. Just write in the next grade and keep on homeschooling.

Single parents often ask whether they should mark themselves as teacher or administrator, or both. The directions clearly say to count each person once, so pick teacher or administrator. We have heard the argument made both ways. Some will say that a school must have a teacher, but doesn't need an administrator, and others say just the opposite. Pick the one that seems best to you, remembering that this is only statistical information.

The hardest part about filling out an affidavit/statement is coming up with a name for your school that the entire family will agree upon, and that will take some time. Sorry, we can't help you with that!

When Your County Asks for Too Much

Families who wish to determine the current legal climate in their county may contact their CHN Local Contact (your contact's name and phone number is at the CHN website or you can call 800/327-5339 and ask for it), or speak with a local support-group leader. We also strongly recommend that you visit our website regularly so that you are up to date on all legal and legislative matters of concern to homeschoolers.

In the past, some counties requested extra information that exceeded the Education Code requirement. Others tried to institute a processing fee despite the fact that the PSA could be obtained and filed directly with the state for free. As long as the new policy having everyone filing with the state remains, this should no longer be important. It will continue to be necessary to monitor state requests to ensure that they are not requesting more than allowed by law.

Occasionally, homeschoolers have been asked to submit fingerprints at their expense. Education Code §44237.4 states that the fingerprinting requirement does not apply to a "parent or legal guardian working exclusively with his or her children." They may also be asked to show a teaching credential, but a teaching credential is not required of private school teachers [§48222].

Extra forms, such as a Student Enrollment List, Request for Investigation Exemption From Public School Attendance, and other variations of information-seeking also show up from time to time. The extra county form might request that the private school list the names, birthdays, home phones, and the last school attended for all students. These forms are not required by law, and homeschoolers need not comply.

The state office may be contacted at the address or phone number below, and they will mail an affidavit. The affidavit can be accessed online, or a family may write their own statement (see CHN's website for a sample). We suggest keeping in touch with CHN for the most up to date information. It would be reasonable to assume that this information will change every year, and possibly even more often than that.

Online form: http://www.cde.ca.gov/privateschools/

Call: 916/657-2772

Write: California Department of Education
Policy & Program Coordination Office Attn: PSA
1430 N Street, Suite 4309
Sacramento, CA 95814

California Private School Requirements

Education Code §48222, §48415, §33190, §51210, and §51220 (see appendix) set the criteria for a private school. The following legal requirements apply to all private schools regardless of size (this means the huge private school in town with the high tuition, or your own private school with one child):

1. The administrator of every private school must file an affidavit or statement with the Superintendent of Public Instruction between October 1st and October 15th of each year. These forms are currently not available at your county office of education, but only through the state office.

2. Private school instructors must be "capable of teaching." There is, however, no requirement in the California Education Code that mandates that teachers in a private school setting hold a state teaching credential or have the equivalent training. Parents are ofen incorrectly told otherwise.

3. The names and addresses of the faculty, including city and street, must be kept on file, as must a record of the educational qualifications of each instructor.

4. Instruction must be in English.

5. Instruction must be offered "in the several branches of study required to be taught in the public schools." (See Education Codes §51210 and §51220, appendix.) The materials and methods you use to teach these areas are up to you. Subjects are:

    Grades 1-6:   English, mathematics, social sciences, science, fine arts, health, physical education

    Grades 7-12:   All that is included in grades 1-6, plus foreign language, applied arts, vocational education, driver education

6. The courses of study offered by the institution shall be kept on file.

7. Attendance records of each enrolled student must be kept in a register that indicates every absence of a half-day or more.

8. California state law requires that schools keep two health forms on file:
    *   Form PM 286, the *California School Immunization Record.* If you do not fully immunize, the back has a place to sign for exemption.
    *   Form PM 171A, the *Report of Health Examination for School Entry.* Form PM 171B is a waiver form.

    These health forms are available from the county health department.

For convenience, all the above forms and more can be found in a convenient printable format on *The California Homeschool Guide Companion CD,* available from CHN. Place these records in your child's cumulative file.

Preschool and Kindergarten

At the time of this writing, kindergarten attendance is not mandatory in California, although bills requiring kindergarten have been proposed by the legislature in the last few years. Currently, a child is subject to compulsory education and entry into the first grade in September if his sixth birthday falls on or before December 2 of the same year. It is suggested that you contact CHN when your child is five to verify that this information has not changed.

Even if kindergarten remains optional, you may, of course, teach your young children under six at home. You do not need to indicate enrollment of these children on your affidavit, and there are good reasons not to do so. Preschools are regulated by law and must be licensed, and indicating kindergarten may subject your private school to additional requirements.

Withdrawing Your Child From School

If your children have previously been in school, you must officially withdraw them. This is standard procedure whether you are moving across the country and enrolling them in a new public school, staying in town and enrolling them in a traditional private school, or homeschooling. File an affidavit first so that you have a legally established private school, and then withdraw your children. If you follow the proper procedures, this should not be a problem. Some homeschoolers suggest that you become aware of the legal defense organizations prior to taking this step, but it is not mandatory (see page 59).

The easiest times of the year in which to withdraw your child from school are during natural breaks such as during holidays or vacations. As a responsible parent, you may recognize that your child needs rescuing, and that it's imperative to act quickly. If this is your situation, your child may be immediately withdrawn from school at any time of the year. If you suspect yours might be a more complicated case, or there are hints of hostility from the school, contact CHN for specific suggestions regarding your situation.

You've filed the affidavit, and you're now ready to withdraw your child. This is a time that leaves most parents feeling nervous about what the reaction will be. Hopefully, you have read this entire chapter so that you can appear confident. This is a time for the strength that comes from knowledge, and not a time to meekly go in and ask for permission to homeschool your child. Be firm and courteous in your dealings with school officials. There is no need to volunteer that you will be homeschooling your child. This information may be accepted and supported by some officials, but others may respond negatively and make your withdrawal more difficult. While you have the legal right to do this, naturally you want it to be as easy a transition as possible. There are two ways to withdraw your child from school:

1. Contact by phone: You may phone the office and inform the secretary that you are transferring your child to a private school. Be prepared to give the name and address of your school. The secretary may offer to send your child's records to the private school. More commonly, however, your child's school will request that the private school formally send for your child's records.

2. Contact by letter: You may contact the school by letter, addressed to the principal. State that as of (date) your child will be withdrawing from attendance at (school's name) and enrolling in (homeschool's name). Advise them that they will be receiving a letter from (your homeschool's name) requesting (child's name) cumulative records.

Formally Requesting Your Child's Cumulative File

If your child has been in school, you may request his cumulative file by letter. With the assistance of a computer, it is easy to make nice letterhead for your school so your letter will look quite professional. Your letter should include the date of withdrawal and the name, grade level, and date of birth of each child. Request that the cumulative file be forwarded as soon as possible. Sign your name as the school representative, which you now are (see page 360 for a sample letter).

School officials who know that you have plans to educate your child at home may occasionally question your right to receive a copy of your child's cumulative file. Education Code §49069 states that parents have "an absolute right to access any and all pupil records related to their children . . .The editing or withholding of any such records . . .is prohibited."

It is not uncommon for schools to be extremely slow in responding to a cumulative file request, and rather than take it personally, it might instead be viewed as just one more inefficiency in the entire school system. The cumulative file is customary, but the law doesn't describe it, which means maintenance of this record will be at your discretion.

Record Keeping

It is important that you keep accurate records as a private school, for your own sake and for the sake of the homeschooling community. Should you ever be challenged by school authorities, your records serve as verification and validation of your private school status. Likewise, if your child should return to a traditional school, you will need to be able to forward your child's academic records.

You may keep your files in whatever form you wish. Some parents choose to purchase official cumulative file folders from an educational supplier. Others make their own, using a loose-leaf 3-ring binder.

School Records

Certain school records are required by §33190 and include:
1. A copy of your private school affidavit.
2. Attendance register for each child. There is no minimum number of days, although many homeschools use the 185-day school year as required for public schools. The number of hours per day is also not regulated.
3. Course of study for each child each school year.
4. A document listing your faculty and their qualifications to teach. Credentials and college degrees are not mandatory.
5. Health immunization records or waiver.
6. Report of Health Examination for School Entry or waiver of Health Examination for School Entry within 90 days of entering the first grade.

[Note: For your convenience, *The California Homeschool Guide Companion CD* has the forms that make record keeping easy. Select the ones you need, then print them.]

Teaching Records

Keeping teaching records is not mandatory, but many experienced homeschoolers recommend keeping records of some kind. These records are for your use as a teacher, to be kept as part of your student's portfolio. They are not transferred with cumulative file records if the student transfers into another school. These records will vary with each school, but may include such things as: a quarterly review of goals and objectives, a yearly outline of studies, daily or monthly lesson plans, unit study outlines, photos of projects, field trip lists, sports activities, samples of the student's work, extracurricular activities or classes, a list of books read during the year, standardized tests scores (if given), job training programs, apprenticeships, 4-H projects, etc.

Again, there are various ways in which a parent can record this information. Educational stores sell lesson plan books and forms, as do many curriculum publishers and catalog suppliers. Blank books, spiral notebooks, and three-ring binders with pockets can also be used. For others, the portfolio for each child might consist of the "best of the best" placed in a box for safekeeping.

Cumulative File Records

Student records in the cumulative file may include:

1. Legal name of student
2. Date of birth
3. Verification of birth date (copy of birth certificate)
4. Sex of pupil
5. Place of birth
6. Name and address of parent of minor pupil
7. Entering and leaving date of each school year
8. Subjects taken
9. Grades, if given. Credits toward high school graduation, if recorded
10. Verification of, or exemption from, required immunizations
11. Date of high school graduation, CHSPE, or GED.

Correspondence Schools

Many first-time home educators choose this method of homeschooling. Families can purchase prepackaged grade-level curricula, individual subjects, and/or choose to enroll in a correspondence school (see pages 343-345).

Correspondence school programs must be in compliance with the California Educational Code. Families enrolled in out-of-state programs are still required by law to be enrolled in a California private school. Some correspondence schools file a California PSA every year. If the school you select has not, you will need to file an affidavit or enroll in a private independent study program (ISP).

Option #2 Private Independent Study Programs

Homeschooling parents may enroll their children in the independent study program (ISP) of a private school that has filed a private school affidavit with the State of California. These programs are known as private ISPs and may be comprised entirely of home educators or may be an extension program of a campus-based private school. Private ISPs maintain student records in accordance with state law and offer a varying range of guidance and support.

Because a student's cumulative files are transferred with that student if he/she moves from public school to private school, a number of parents deciding to homeschool while in the midst of a school year will choose a private ISP as a means of attracting the least amount of attention from public school officials.

The number of private California ISPs is growing rapidly. If you are considering a private ISP, we suggest you contact some, and find out what their requirements and services are. Some might be better for a particular family, for example one specializing in special needs, or it might offer extra support. Some offer local park days and activities, but will accept students anywhere in California. Prices and services vary. Check with your CHN Local Contact or local support-group leader for private ISPs in your area, or start with the list on page 345.

Option #3 Public School Independent Study Programs

Parents may educate their children at home by enrolling them in a public school independent study program or charter school. Children enrolled in public school ISPs or charter schools are public school students, subject to the rules and regulations of both the school district and the state. The school receives full average daily attendance (ADA) money for these students. The state mandates that public ISP/charter students be treated as traditional public school students. While the degree of intrusiveness varies, expect curriculum guidelines, administrative supervision, and/or record keeping requirements to be imposed.

In the public school homeschooling program, the homeschooling parent is considered the teacher's aide, and all required school work is done under the direct supervision of the program's resource teacher, also known as the facilitator.

Your local school district office can provide you with a list of the public school homeschooling programs in your area. If your district does not offer it at the elementary level, you have the right to obtain an inter-district transfer into a district that does. Most districts offer traditional high school independent study programs.

Option #4 Credentialed Teacher/Tutor

A child may be taught at home by a parent or a tutor with a valid California teacher's credential for the grades and subjects taught under the private tutorial exemption. Instruction must be for at least three hours a day between the hours of 8:00 and 4:00 for 175 days a year (see Education Code §48224 in appendix).

Parents may be able to locate a credentialed tutor for their child by contacting the "Certified Personnel" department at their local school district office.

Other Legal Considerations

The language and intent of our laws are frequently open to interpretation. There is no law in California regarding homeschooling. The private school sections of the California Education Code, §33190 and §48222, are short, ostensibly simple laws, yet they contain terms that can be interpreted in several different ways. Homeschoolers and attorneys reviewing these laws consistently arrive at a liberal interpretation, finding no reason why a family cannot establish its own private school. Public school officials opposed to homeschooling read these same laws and arrive at a more restrictive interpretation, some even unequivocally rejecting the legality of family-based private schools.

Thousands of California families homeschool each year without any interference from public authorities. Unfortunately, however, an unnerving ritual is performed annually in a scattering of school districts around the state. Public school officials may single out a family or two, declare that private homeschooling is not a valid fulfillment of the law, threaten to bring truancy charges against the children, and threaten action against the parents. Regrettably, some families cease homeschooling in response to this pressure. More frequently, however, parents respond firmly with a factual accounting of their compliance with Education Code §33190 and §48222. If the family holds its ground in this manner, school officials usually grumble and go away, knowing an expensive, lengthy process awaits them if they press charges. Instead, they move on in search of less informed families who will be easier to intimidate.

CHN and other state homeschooling organizations maintain that a liberal interpretation of the Education Code allows for the individual and parental rights guaranteed by the U.S. Constitution, while simultaneously satisfying the state's compelling interest in education.

Inquiries regarding legal issues should not be made to the State Department of Education. Misleading statements from an old letter drafted years ago by an assistant general counsel to the Department of Education are still being sent to those inquiring, keeping some parents from homeschooling, we imagine. The assistant general counsel's opinion and the Department of Education's position is not legally binding on private K-12 schools or home educators. The Department of Education serves only in an advisory capacity in K-12 private school legal issues.

We hope to have anticipated your questions;
if you have others, please contact CHN at 800/327-5339.

Join a Statewide Homeschool Organization

You may be wondering if it is worthwhile for you to join a statewide homeschool organization. You may already be associated with a local support group, or you may prefer to go your own way in your homeschooling adventure. Nevertheless, there are many advantages in joining and supporting a statewide organization.

Probably the greatest advantage is access to information. All the state homeschooling groups in California monitor state legislation and the legal climate in the various counties. They publish newsletters to communicate with their membership. Advice and support can also be found through Local Contacts in your county, 800 telephone service, webpages, and internet discussion groups.

Another important advantage statewide organizations offer is public relations activities in support of homeschooling. Without general public support for parents who are dedicated to educating their own children, our educational freedom would be in grave danger. Public support is the crucial buffer between homeschooling and draconian state legislation.

Finally, we all benefit from the experience of the many veteran homeschool activists who offer their expertise in the statewide groups. Without their knowledge and wisdom gained through many years of working to maintain our educational freedom, our homeschooling lifestyle would not be as secure as it is. Your membership dues to the statewide group of your choice is an investment in your family's homeschooling future. It is a small price to pay for liberty.

Legal Defense Organizations

The most typical charge brought against homeschoolers is that of truancy; less common are charges of educational neglect, or child abuse and/or child endangerment. Keep in mind, these are potential threats and they are not common occurrences. Because each year a few homeschooling families across the U.S. do receive unfriendly legal contact from government officials, a number of homeschooling legal defense organizations have been established. Interested families should contact these organizations for a better understanding of their services.

California Homeschool Network Legal Defense Fund
PO Box 55485, Hayward, CA 94545
800/ 327-5339 *www.CaliforniaHomeschool.net*

The CHN Legal Defense Fund made news throughout the country when it was established in the summer of 2000. In a grassroots effort, donations were quickly raised from members and non-members alike to start the fund because of a specific need. With the fund now established, in the future it will be used for specific cases, controversies or legal issues to produce legal decisions and rulings that will guarantee the right of homeschooling parents in California to educate their children in the least restrictive environment. While CHN does not offer legal services or advice, it has often been able to provide the information and support that parents have needed to avert problems. With the establishment of the Legal Defense Fund, CHN is now better able to help in certain serious cases, by hiring attorneys. Anyone who believes their case may fall under the fund guidelines may apply for this assistance, regardless of membership in CHN. The idea behind this is homeschoolers joining hands to help each other.

Homeschool Legal Defense Association
PO Box 3000, Purcellville, VA 20134
540/ 338-5600 *www.hslda.org*

HSLDA is a national homeschool Christian defense organization. The fee is $100, and it takes 2-4 weeks for approval. They provide consultation to members, correspond with local officials, and will pay litigation costs for the homeschool cases that they undertake. They do not guarantee representation for child neglect/abuse or divorce/custody cases.

Pacific Justice Institute
PO Box 4366, Citrus Heights, CA 95611
916/ 857-6900 *www.pacificjustice.org/*

Pacific Justice Institute assists those in a battle for religious freedoms, sanctity of life, parental rights and other civil liberties. It maintains a network of attorneys who represent individuals and religious organizations without charge.

Pacific Legal Foundation
10360 Old Placerville Road, Suite 100, Sacramento, California
(916) 362-2833 *plf@pacificlegal.org*

A legal advocacy institution that fights government abuses.

The Rutherford Institute
PO Box 7482, Charlottesville, VA 22906-7482
Legal Line 804/ 978-3888 *www.rutherford.org*

The Rutherford Institute will help homeschoolers, regardless of religious belief, who are having problems with their state or local school boards. If the Rutherford Institute decides to take your case, the association will pay all costs. The Rutherford Institute is a non-profit legal education organization that receives most of its support from donations.

Tracking Legislation in California

CHN and the other state homeschooling organizations work diligently to keep their members informed of legislation that could pose a threat to homeschooling rights in California. Supporting the state homeschooling organization of your choice is crucial to the voice and political strength of homeschooling in the state. In addition, the following organizations also track legislation within California, although their scope is not limited to homeschooling:

California Network of Educational Charters (CANEC)
926 J Street, Suite 820
Sacramento, CA 95814
916/448-0995 *www.canec.org/articles.html*

A non-profit organization that provides information regarding current and pending legislative matters related to California charter schools.

Capitol Resource Institute
1414 K Street, Suite 200, Sacramento, CA 95814
916/ 498-1940 *www.capitolresource.org*

Capitol Resource Institute is a nonprofit, state-based organization providing a variety of services and products that educate the public on family issues before the California Legislature.

Family Protection Ministries
PO Box 730, Lincoln, CA 95648-0730
916/ 786-3523

This is a privately funded Christian ministry monitoring legislative issues affecting families and home educators in California.

Editor's Note: We end this legal chapter on a light note, with some amusing questions-and-answers that originally appeared in California Homeschool Network's newsletter, CHNews. It was written by Jackie Orsi, CHN's first Legal Chair, and with her characteristic humor combined with impressive legal knowledge, you may find that your final questions are clarified here. Thanks, Jackie! *(see page 47 for county/state processing changes)*

The 25 Most Frequently Asked Legal Questions
By Jackie Orsi

[In a surprisingly candid interview, investigative journalist, Jackie Orsi, aggressively pins down former CHN Legal Chair Jackie Orsi to get the ultimate skinny on all things legal about homeschooling in California.]

1. **Are you a lawyer?**

    No. I am most assuredly not a lawyer. Not even close. I am something far more amazing. I am a mother.

2. **Do you give legal advice?**

    No. I liberally hand out all kinds of advice, except the legal kind.

3. **Prove that you are not a lawyer. Do you know any good lawyer jokes?**
Okay. Why is it that New Jersey got all the toxic waste dumps and California got all the lawyers? Because New Jersey got first choice.

4. **I feel better now. How do you feel?**
That was good for me.

5. **Okay, here come the real questions. When can I obtain an R-4 affidavit to file for private school status?**
R-4 blank forms are usually sent down by the state to county offices of education around mid-August, but I think it's good to wait till September to request the form.

6. **When do I file?**
The law requires that private schools file "between the first and 15th day of October." (Education Code §33190) If you create a private school later during the school year, it is appropriate and wise to file an affidavit at that time.

7. **I am not sending my children back to public school in September, but the Ed Code says I am supposed to file my R-4 between Oct 1 and 15. Are my children officially truant during the month of September? How do I handle this "twilight zone"?**
While I am always preaching taking the law exactly as written, I do not hold strictly to the Oct 1 – Oct 15th parameters. In this case, following Education Code Section 33190 exactly hurts us by creating the very "twilight zone" you describe. In practice, parents don't need to wait till October 1 to file their R-4 affidavit. They can file at any time of the year to indicate their intent to operate a private school. If you file on September 1, the State Department of Education will recognize it as applicable to that current school year. This is common practice and it works in our favor. Similarly, a person beginning a private school on March 1st, as I did, can file at that time. In these situations, filing the affidavit to create protection against truancy charges is the most important thing.

8. **Do I have to do a criminal background check?**
Education Code §44237 requires that private schools take fingerprints and do Department of Justice checks on employees who are not credentialed teachers. Volunteers need not be checked. Homeschool parents are presumably volunteers. Also a code section exempts parents working with their children.

9. **Do I have to have a business license?**

   Every so often, some overbearing bureaucrat insists that homeschoolers have to go get a business license, but you don't need one unless you are actively conducting business with the public, i.e. advertising, charging tuition, etc.

10. **Do I have to get a fire marshal's inspection, etc.?**

    Can't say for certain that you are exempt from local fire, health and safety ordinances, since there are too many cities to possibly take into account. You have to research that yourself. Probably if you called your local fire marshal and explained that you want your school (which is also your home) inspected for the safety of your students (who are also your children), you'd get a loud snicker in response. I never heard of anyone having difficulties because of failure to heed local ordinances. As for state laws, fire alarm laws and earthquake safety laws apply only to private schools enrolling 50 or more students.

11. **Are there any other laws pertaining to private schools that I need to know about?**

    Well, you may be sorry you asked, the state education code does require the following of private schools regardless of size:

    Take an "industrial quality" first aid kit on field trips (EC §3240). If entering an area where poisonous snakes hang out, make sure you have the proper stuff in your first aid kit and that your staff accompanying the field trip has American Red Cross certification (EC §32043).

    Keep toxic art supplies out of your school. (EC §32060 et seq.) (Just say "no" to glue.) Provide "industrial quality eye protective devices" when students handle or observe substances that may be hazardous to their eyes (EC §32031 and EC §32032).

    Discrimination on the basis of sex is prohibited, and you're supposed to have a written policy about how you'll deal with sexual harassment. (EC §212.5 and §212.6) Said sexual harassment policy is to be on display in a prominent location; I suggest you put it on the refrigerator door, held up by those corny magnets we all have.

12. **I got my child's cumulative file from the school and all they sent were photocopies. Shouldn't they have sent the originals?**

    No. EC §49068 says that either "a pupil's permanent record or a copy thereof shall be transferred."

13. My county Office of Education jerks homeschoolers around and tries to intimidate us. Do I have to put up with this?

I used to live in one of the most annoying counties, and I personally prefer counter-intimidation tactics consisting of firmly going about my business and filing my R-4 in spite of their nastiness. I harbor satisfaction in the idea that my persistence in the face of harassment drives them crazy.

But I also realize that not everyone is as ornery as I am, so I also suggest a second strategy: go around them. County Offices of Education distribute, collect and process R-4s for the state as a courtesy. They receive no special reimbursement for the service. The state prefers the arrangement because it saves them a lot of work. If you personally don't prefer the arrangement, you don't have to deal with it. You can file your R-4 directly with the State Superintendent of Public Instruction, California Department of Education. [note: see page 50 for address.]

14. Can my county Office of Education charge me a filing fee for receiving my R-4?

They can try, and several have tried, but you are under no obligation to pay any fees. There is no legal authority for such fees. If your county refuses your R-4 because you fail to enclose a fee, then file directly with the State Superintendent of Public Instruction. If the state bounces your affidavit back because you didn't go through your county (they haven't done this yet), then put all the correspondence in your files as proof that you tried to file according to the law, but were obstructed by misinformed bureaucrats.

15. Do I need to use the R-4?

No. Nothing in the law requires the use of the R-4. Many affidavits in letter form arrive each year in the State Department of Education. It's perfectly legal. Make sure you provide every scrap of information requested in EC §33190, and then make your affirmation that all of it is true under penalty of perjury, sign it, and send it in. Voila!

16. Should I send my R-4 or letter affidavit by certified mail, return receipt requested?

If you live in a problematic county, this might be a good idea, just to give you extra proof of your filing. I've never known of an instance where it made any difference in protecting a family, but you never know. It can't hurt and could help.

17. How do I know if I live in a "problematic" county?

Sometimes we find out totally by surprise, but mostly we know where the trouble is likely to happen; San Mateo County and Alameda County are the worst offenders, near as I can tell. San Luis Obispo County has had their share of irritations. Watch out also in Los Angeles County and in other counties that try to collect R-4 filling fees (see #14 above). I can't possibly monitor the currents and undercurrents in all 58 counties, so you are wise to test the waters a bit yourself. Find out about your county and school district by consulting with your CHN Local Contact and other local homeschoolers. If you don't know anyone to ask, call your county authorities without giving your name and see how they treat you.

18. So I have to teach three hours a day between 8 a.m. and 4 p.m. 175 days a year, right?

No, only tutors operating under the tutorial exemption (EC §48224) are given such explicit time requirements. Private schools need to be "full-time day schools" (EC §48222), a term which is not further defined. A document prepared by the Legal Office of the California Department of Education says, "A private school is not required to be maintained for the minimum school day required of public schools nor is it required to be maintained for any minimum number of days in each school year as are public schools."

19. So I have to teach all the courses listed in EC §51210 and §51220, right?

Not exactly. The first statute you mentioned, §51210, for grades one through six specifies the "adopted course of study," while §51220, for grades seven through 12, indicates what a school "shall offer" which gives some wiggle room to allow for student preferences and goals.

20. If I file a private school affidavit, what are the odds that my family will experience a serious challenge?

Homeschoolers in some regions routinely get threatening letters from their counties and/or school districts. I have managed to handsomely wallpaper my outhouse with the notices, letters and threats that have arrived over the years from my county and school district.

We can all take comfort in the fact that few families are ever singled out. Statewide, administrative challenges happen to maybe 20 or so families annually, and serious legal challenges are truly scarce. I qualify "administrative challenges" as those instances when a bureaucrat spouts scary sounding "facts" and threats, 99% of which are made of thinnest hot air. So the threats mostly dissipate on their own, or are blown away by a little bit of true information supplied by homeschoolers themselves. A handful of cases go on to Student Attendance Review Boards. Only about one case per decade goes to court for trial.

21. If we enroll in a private independent study program (ISP), we'll be safe from legal troubles, won't we?

Sorry, but no guarantees here. One of the stronger administrative challenges of 1997 and that decade's major legal challenge in court involved families enrolled in private ISPs. However, the legal foundation of private ISPs is still fully intact.

22. If we join a legal defense plan, we'll be safe, right?

Safe from administrative and legal challenges? No. Safe from possible legal conviction? No. The best anyone can offer you is a guarantee of representation.

23. Any last non-legal advice?

*First, learn your legal rights and responsibilities. Heed the oldest and truest of adages: Knowledge is Power. Second, if you choose private schooling, **protect your privacy**. Give no more information to any authority than is required in your affidavit. **Demand to be treated as any other private school**.*

24. Any more lawyer jokes?

I really shouldn't.

25. Please, oh please, oh please?

Oh, well, if you insist. A man walks into a bar in Wyoming and orders a drink. In a sudden outburst, he proclaims, "All lawyers are horses' asses!" The guy next to him says, "Hey, careful what you say. This is horse country."

Thanks, Jackie.

You're very welcome, Jackie.

How Will They Learn to Stand in Line If They Don't Go to School?

"Isn't it obvious that homeschooled children

are at least as well socialized as

their school counterparts?"

©Bill Taylor

What About Socialization?
By Karen Rafferty

Several years ago I'd had it with the "S" question, "What about socialization?" Isn't it obvious that homeschooled children are at least as well socialized as their school counterparts? Why does that question keep popping up? I decided to do a little research. I started querying the questioners, "What do you mean by socialization?" Over the years I've narrowed the responses to four categories: Odd Duck and the Pack, the Institutional Persona, the Warden Mentality and Suffering Builds Character.

Odd Duck and the Pack

A cartoon of a dog and a duck appeared 30 years ago in *The New Yorker*. The dog, while demonstrating, was condescendingly informing his feathered friend, "This is how a duck walks."

I clipped that cartoon because, as a quiet studious teenager who desired only one or two intimate friends, I was an odd duck. Adults (raised in a pack culture) objected to my reserved personality. In essence they kept saying, "This is what a teenager should be like." They assumed that as social creatures, we need lots of interaction with our peers to be well adjusted. Studies have proven that the contrary is true. The more exposure to peers, the more dependent we are. We don't dare act out of concert with group-held beliefs, because we have to survive in the group. We adopt group views of drugs, gangs, sex and violence. Outsiders, adults in the youth culture, are perceived as the enemy, hence a generation gap is manufactured with teens who are uncomfortable fraternizing with the enemy, behaving obnoxiously around them. Self-esteem is missing, because self is missing.

Institutional Persona

Let's face it, obedient, self-effacing children are easier to handle in group settings. In her book, *Raising Your Spirited Children*, Mary Sheedy Kurchinka introduces a temperament spectrum. A few of her opposites include:

Accepts no for an answer.............Sticks to her guns
Stays on task...............................Easily distracted
Quiet...Always on the move
Jumps right in..............................Holds back and watches
Adapts quickly............................Upset by change

The personality characteristics that work best in an institutional setting are those on the left of the spectrum. Children on the right side of the spectrum are seen as stubborn, distractible, wild, picky and inflexible. In other words, difficult, intransigent, and bad. Kurchinka suggests a change of labels from *stubborn* to *holds high standards*, from *distractible* to *perceptive*, from *wild* to *energetic*, from *picky* to *selective*, and from *inflexible* to *traditional*. Her book is affirming to parents of "bad" kids, because it is apparent that their "badness" comes from the paradigm of the institution. I can't resist mentioning that many of those "difficult" kids become the movers and shakers when loosed from the confines of the institution.

Warden Mentality

How will they ever learn to raise their hands? How will they learn to stand in line? This last question is frequently asked by the person standing in front or behind us in a grocery store or bank line.

Students for Educational Alternatives and Reform do an excellent job of spoofing this false framework of socialization when they compare schools and prisons. Authoritarian structure, dress code restrictions, emphasis on silence and order, lack of individual autonomy, negative reinforcement and a pass needed for going from one part of the facility to another are a few of the similarities they emphasize.

When we look at the recidivism rates, largely caused by the inability of prisoners to function in a more free, independent environment, it makes no sense to raise children who are comfortable in an institutional setting.

Suffering Builds Character

I believe this is by far the saddest definition of socialization. It acknowledges that the socialization in schools is often mean spirited and, in fact, the whole school experience is a dismal one. "How can you learn to deal with un-kindness unless you experience it?" they argue, while accusing homeschoolers of being overprotective parents.

Psychological studies indicate that the individuals most capable of dealing with negativity, stress and disaster are those who were raised in a nurturing, affirming environment. This is because they have not been undermined by a barrage of negativity. Our children, like budding plants, need the temporary protection of a greenhouse environment so that they can develop the healthy root system which will make them survivors when exposed to harsher elements.

So, What About Socialization?

Rightfully, parents are concerned with more than just the academic growth of their children. Education in its best sense is education of the whole person. Years ago, Leslie R. Severinghaus of the Haverford School near Philadelphia wrote:

> "Ultimate performance in society— not just brains and grades—should be the admissions criterion of top colleges…. Who says that brains and motivated performance represent the dimensions of excellence? Is not social concern a facet of excellence? Is it not exciting to find a candidate who believes that 'no man liveth unto himself?' What about leadership? Integrity? The ability to communicate both ideas and friendship? May we discount spiritual eagerness? And why should we pass over cooperation with others in good causes, even at some sacrifice of one's own scholastic achievement? What about graciousness and decency?"

Like Severinghaus, I am concerned with character and courtesy and inter-personal skills. And that is one of the main reasons I homeschool.

Homeschooling develops whole, self-actualized, inner-directed, fully-function-ing, conscious, awakened, no-limit people in many ways. It strengthens the family bond where children learn how to have intimate, fulfilling relationships, resolve disagreements, work well in a group and communicate effectively. It provides time for introspection and more opportunities to investigate personal interests. Homeschooling empowers children by providing sufficient free time to become involved in solving community problems. I'm not referring to an artificially produced, adult-directed service project, but a heartfelt choice to become in-volved. This participation gives a child faith in the future and his/her ability to impact it. It also provides a myriad of experiences and exposure to a variety of individuals. Differences will come to light in a setting where uniqueness may be valued instead of automatically ridiculed. Largely responsible for their own educational success, homeschoolers work for internal satisfaction not external rewards. They develop discipline to produce quality work and the skills to judge the quality of their own work. Because they have more choice in how they devote their time and energies, they learn to evaluate whether or not an endeavor is worthy.

In 1993, J. Gary Knowles, assistant professor of education at the University of Michigan released the results of a detailed study of 53 adults who were taught at home. It examined the long-term effects of homeschooling. The following is a quote from an interview with professor Knowles:

> *"One of the major arguments against home schooling is that it deprives children of the peer contacts needed for normal social development. Public school educators and other critics also question whether home-educated children will be able to become productive, participating members of a diverse and democratic society. But I found no evidence that these adults were even moderately disadvantaged in either respect. Two thirds of them were married—the norm for adults their age—and none were unemployed or on any form of welfare assistance. More than three-quarters felt that being taught at home had actually helped them interact with people from different levels of society...*
>
> *"They had many warm memories about their home schooling [96 percent said yes when asked whether they would want to be educated at home if they had their lives to live over again]. Many mentioned the strong relationship it engendered with their parents while others talked about the self-directed curriculum and individualized pace that a flexible program of home schooling permitted...*
>
> *"...this survey and the life history accounts that arose out of it clearly show that, done in an enlightened, broad-minded way, with plenty of flexibility in curriculum and methods, home schooling can be a positive experience for children with benefits that last for many years."*

The modern homeschooling movement is coming of age. I anxiously await the results as more and more of our youth enter colleges, companies and adult society. I believe they will have a tremendous impact on society. Who knows...they might even shift the current socialization paradigm.

> *Editor's note: Here are two modern-day homeschooling fables, poking a little fun at typical public worries about homeschoolers.*

Mr. Pointy Nose
By Tammy Drennan

Once upon a time, there lived a happy family in a great wood: Mother and Father, Brother, Sister and Baby. Father went off to work each day, and Mother planted seeds and tended her garden and loved her children and taught them to read and write. At night, when Father came home, the family sang songs and laughed and played together.

One day while Father was away at work, a knock came at the door of the family's home. Mother opened the door and found a stern man with sharp teeth and a very pointy nose standing on the doorstep.

"May I help you?" Mother asked.

"I am here," snarled the man, "to inspect your home and your children."

Mother was surprised. "Whatever for?" she asked.

"It has been reported," snapped Mr. Pointy Nose, "that you do not institutionalize your children, as is the norm. It has been reported that you spend an abnormal amount of time with your children, and you have been seen laughing with them, and they with you. It has been reported that your teen child is not embarrassed to be seen with you and that she smiles while working in your garden and hanging laundry. I will have to inspect your house and ask you some questions."

Mother invited Mr. Pointy Nose in and offered him a cup of tea. Mr. Pointy Nose pulled a great pile of papers from his briefcase and began asking important questions: "How many television sets do you own, how often do you dine out, why do you have so many books, what do you have against institutions, why do you grow your own food, do your children know who Madonna is, how about Beavis and Butthead?"

Mother was very kind and reassuring: "We have one television set in the closet," she told Mr. Pointy Nose, "and we dine outside several times a week in nice weather. We have so many books because we love to read. We have no personal grudge against institutions—we simply choose not to institutionalize. We grow food to eat, and of course my children know who the Madonna is. I'm not sure what a beavis is, and while butthead is a rather crude term, I have known a few."

Mr. Pointy Nose seemed insulted by this last statement and jumped up in a huff. "I must speak with your children," he announced.

Mother called Brother and Sister. Baby was too young to speak. Brother was six years old and Sister was 13. Mr. Pointy Nose asked Brother, "Have you ever heard of Beavis and Butthead?"

"Yes," said Brother. "We have beavers in the creek, and Butthead is my uncle's boss."

Sister giggled, but Mr. Pointy Nose was not amused. He addressed Brother again. "Do your parents ever yell at you?"

"You better believe it!" said Brother. "One time I climbed clear to the top of a 30 foot tree, and Dad yelled and yelled at me to stay up there till he could climb up, too. He doesn't get much time to climb trees, and I think he yelled so much 'cause he was excited at the chance."

Mr. Pointy Nose turned in disgust and asked Sister, "Wouldn't you like to be institution-alized with other children your age?"

"Well, most of my friends are institutionalized," Sister told him. "And I haven't been too impressed with it. They can hardly read anything—they don't even like Charles Dickens. And they all hate history and math. I like playing jump rope with them in the evening, but they talk about the most boring things, like clothes and make-up and what's on TV, and…oh—I know who Beavis and Butthead are. Do you know who Mr. Pickwick is?"

"No," said Mr. Pointy Nose curtly. "What sort of music do you listen to?"

"Oh, Beethoven is my favorite. Did you know he went deaf and just kept on writing music?"

"No," said Mr. Pointy Nose impatiently. "Why don't you listen to popular teenage music?"

Sister was surprised that a grown-up would ask such a question, but she answered as politely as possible, "Because it sounds simply wretched."

"Wretched! Wretched!?" screeched Mr. Pointy Nose. "That is not a seventh grade word! Where did you learn it?"

Mother had been in the kitchen preparing a snack of homemade bread and strawberry preserves. When she heard Mr. Pointy Nose screech, she rushed to the living room. "What's wretched?" she asked, a little alarmed.

"This child," Mr. Pointy Nose said indignantly, "correctly used the word wretched."

"Oh, I'm sure she wasn't referring to you," Mother said gently. "Here, have some fresh bread and jam."

Mr. Pointy Nose looked at the tray in Mother's hands suspiciously, then cautiously took her offering. As he ate he began to relax a little. "You made this yourself?" he asked.

"Oh, yes," said Mother.

"And I helped," chimed in Sister. Then she added, "I'm sorry for upsetting you. I didn't know you had an aversion to that word, or I would never have said it."

"Aversion?" Mr. Pointy Nose sighed. He slumped in his chair and looked at Mother. "How do you ever expect your children to fit into the world if you don't institutionalize them, and you encourage them to develop advanced vocabularies and you teach them self-sufficiency. This does not coincide with the new way—they must follow the new standards."

Mother looked at Mr. Pointy Nose thoughtfully. "I appreciate your apparent concern, kind sir," she said, "but you see, I am not raising children to follow standards—I am raising them to set standards."

Mr. Pointy Nose looked around in a musing way and murmured, "Yes, yes. I can see that." He left with a bread recipe and an invitation to visit again some time.

Conversation From the Future

By Tammy Drennan

Two women meet at a playground, where their children are swinging and playing ball. The women are sitting on a bench watching. Eventually, they begin to talk.

W1: Hi. My name is Maggie. My kids are the three in red shirts—helps me keep track of them.

W2: (Smiles) I'm Terri. Mine are in the pink and yellow shirts. Do you come here a lot?

W1: Usually two or three times a week, after we go to the library.

W2: Wow. Where do you find the time?

W1: We home school, so we do it during the day most of the time.

W2: Some of my neighbors home school, but I send my kids to public school.

W1: How do you do it?

W2: It's not easy. I go to all the PTO meetings and work with the kids every day after school and stay real involved.

W1: But what about socialization? Aren't you worried about them being cooped up all day with kids their own ages, never getting the opportunity for natural relationships?

W2: Well, yes. But I work hard to balance that. They have some friends who're homeschooled, and we visit their grandparents almost every month.

W1: Sounds like you're a very dedicated mom. But don't you worry about all the opportunities they're missing out on? I mean they're so isolated from real life—how will they know what the world is like—what people do to make a living—how to get along with all different kinds of people?

W2: Oh, we discussed that at PTO, and we started a fund to bring real people into the classrooms. Last month, we had a policeman and a doctor come in to talk to every class. And next month, we're having a woman from Japan and a man from Kenya came to speak.

W1: Oh, we met a man from Japan in the grocery store the other week, and he got to talking about his childhood in Tokyo. My kids were absolutely fascinated. We invited him to dinner and got to meet his wife and their three children.

W2: That's nice. Hmm. Maybe we should plan some Japanese food for the lunchroom on Multicultural Day.

W1: Maybe your Japanese guest could eat with the children.

W2: Oh, no. She's on a very tight schedule. She has two other schools to visit that day. It's a system-wide thing we're doing.

W1: Oh, I'm sorry. Well, maybe you'll meet someone interesting in the grocery store sometime and you'll end up having them over for dinner.

W2: I don't think so. I never talk to people in the store—certainly not people who might not even speak my language. What if that Japanese man hadn't spoken English?

W1: To tell you the truth, I never had time to think about it. Before I even saw him, my six-year-old had asked him what he was going to do with all the oranges he was buying.

W2: Your child talks to strangers?

W1: I was right there with him. He knows that as long as he's with me, he can talk to anyone he wishes.

W2: But you're developing dangerous habits in him. My children never talk to strangers.

W1: Not even when they're with you?

W2: They're never with me, except at home after school. So you see why it's so important for them to understand that talking to strangers is a big no-no.

W1: Yes, I do. But if they were with you, they could get to meet interesting people and still be safe. They'd get a taste of the real world, in real settings. They'd also get a real feel for how to tell when a situation is dangerous or suspicious.

W2: They'll get that in the third and fifth grades in their health course.

W1: Well, I can tell you're a very caring mom. Let me give you my number—if you ever want to talk, give me call. It was good to meet you.

How to "Socialize" a Homeschooled Teen
By Jackie Orsi

It is said that, "Homeschooled kids stay young longer, then grow up all at once." I don't know who originated that gem of wisdom. I can't even recall who passed it along to me in conversation some six or seven years ago. I only know that I have never forgotten it, and all my observations have confirmed that it is true, completely true. I can say that now...

I recall times when I was so glad that my daughters and their homeschooling pals were taking the long route to maturity. At ages ten, eleven, and twelve, they were charmingly unsophisticated, natural, carefree little girls, at a time when many of their public school peers were applying make-up with a trowel and worrying about who was "going with" which boy.

I recall also some mighty discouraging times when I was ready for my daughters to show the world how homeschooling turns out superior teens. I began to look for them to be the confident, articulate young people of my expectations. I had seen such phenomenal teens, the children of other homeschooling families I knew, and I was ready for my payoff. Hey, where was the poise? Where was the maturity? Why were my kids still gawky and bashful? Why weren't they getting their acts together? Where had I gone wrong?

Now, isn't that just like a mother? One minute you're babying them, and the next minute you're saying, "Oh, grow up!" I wanted it both ways: I wished them to be childish when it suited my needs, and then, especially when they were in public view, I wanted them to flip a switch to activate instant maturity.

Well, now I know. "Homeschooled kids stay young longer and then grow up all at once." And when it says, "stay young longer," it really does mean

77

longer. I was jumping the gun. The only thing wrong with my daughters during their early teens were my expectations. They were getting their acts together, and now that they are eighteen and sixteen, I can tell you that they are totally together.

Now other parents are coming to me to ooh and ahh over the fine young women I have raised up. They ask me how I did such a great job. I preen myself and tell them, "No sweat. I knew what I was doing at all times. I had matters completely under control." What a liar I am. Actually, for a few years there, I kind of lost my way as a parent. Homeschooling with teens was still not widely done, and the road map for how to do it was hazy, still is hazy. Some things are clear to me now, and I hope I can help point the way for others.

Homeschooled kids stay young longer and then grow up all at once. Actually, homeschooled kids don't take longer to grow up; they only seem to take longer. All children need a good long time, but only homeschooled kids are being given that time. The rest are being rushed—rushed and harmed, I believe.

The pseudo-sophistication of the eleven-year-old girl whose mind is on dating and her figure and her clothes comes at a terrible price. Psychologist Mary Pipher has documented the damage in her powerful book, *Reviving Ophelia* (1994). Long before Pipher, Dr. David Elkind warned us that our society is neglecting children's emotional needs in his books, *The Hurried Child* (1981), *All Grown Up & No Place to Go* (1984), and *Ties That Stress* (1994). The role that institutional schooling plays in inflicting damage on kids is considerable, and both of these authors know it full well. I read their books and I want to shout to them, "Recommend homeschooling as an alternative to this disastrous scenario, you big turkeys!" But they don't. I guess homeschooling is still a little too far out for these mainstream thinkers. Too bad.

Good for us homeschoolers that we've figured out that kids need more time with parents and other adults, and less time in peer-segregated situations. Good for us that we give kids ample time and space for their personal development. We seem to have this entirely figured out in respect to our little ones, the six, seven, eight-year-old set. It's only when adolescence looms that we begin to doubt the wisdom of those strategies.

Somehow I got it in my head that when my kids hit their teens they needed more teen social activities, that they needed to be apart from the littler kids that run around at park days and field trips. I also thought they needed less time with their parents at that stage.

Today I don't agree with those ideas at all. I had borrowed those assumptions from the mainstream model of raising teenagers. Now I think that the homeschool model of socialization, putting kids in multi-age groupings with lots of adult supervision works best not only when they are prepubescent, but also when they are teens.

In fact, I think they probably need more adult contact, rather than less, when they are teens. Adolescence triggers the major stage of development of the "social self," so to speak. They become aware of the larger social world, and they begin to look to that world for their place in it. They want to learn behaviors that will let them fit in and gain approval. They attempt to fashion a new social self that is acceptable, likeable, worthy of love and esteem. ***THIS IS THE WORST POSSIBLE TIME TO ABANDON THEM.*** This is when they most need the example of adults.

To see what I mean, you have only to throw a bunch of thirteen-year-old homeschooled boys and girls together in a social gathering "just for teens." It's so painful to watch that you just want to die for them. They are acutely aware that there is a right way and a wrong way to act in the situation, but darned if they know what! They are clueless, and in the absence of clues, they do the only safe thing: nothing. They freeze stiff. The silence among them positively roars. I know all this because I peeked in on a couple of these misguided attempts by homeschooling parents to provide for their teenager's social life. (Okay, I'll confess. I staged one of them.)

Throwing clueless kids together without adequate adult influence and supervision is what schools do best and the results in that setting are generally far worse than the awkward home-schooling scene I just depicted. If you leave kids without a social script to follow they will eventually invent a script for themselves to fill the void. We are hearing more and more about the kids who have left the adult world and fallen completely into a peer-invented, peer-dominated society. Vancouver psychologist Gordon Neufeld, recently related to the Calgary Herald, "This is scary …because, as the kids age and the orientation to peers strengthen, mob rule, a Lord of the Flies syndrome sets in, and parents and teachers are left in the dust, incapable of reaching children, morally and intellectually."

The alternative is not to put the kids in these often ridiculous, and potentially dangerous, situations where they are banished to their own deserted social island. If you and/or your homeschooled teen get to thinking that he or she needs "teen social activities," I urge you to examine whether you and/or your child are feeling pressured to mimic the mainstream model. Are you really sure you want to do that? I think most teens deep down don't really want to be segregated into teen groups. My own kids, when I would offer them a chance to have teen parties or other teen-only events, were incredibly unenthusiastic. Child psychologist Urie Bronfenbrenner wrote: "(It) would seem that the peer-oriented child is more a product of parental disregard than of the attractiveness of the peer group—that he turns to his age-mates less by choice than by default. The vacuum left by the withdrawal of parents and adults from the lives of children is filled with an undesired—and possibly undesirable—substitute of an age-segregated peer group."

So what is the social prescription for teen homeschoolers? More of what has worked so well to that point: multi-age activities and multi-generational events. It certainly is desirable to seek activities that are intellectually appropriate for the older student, thus leaving the younger children behind on occasion, but I wouldn't work overtime to stage purely social events for teens.

I've noticed that the homeschooled teens who develop the most natural social relationships are those who have grown up together and were playmates before puberty hit. The really challenging problem comes when new teens arrive upon the scene. The activities which seem to work best to break the ice are those for which kids already have a script for how to behave: multi-age events like ice skating and bowling offer kids an activity to get involved in, and lets the teens get to know each other slowly, on their own terms, without pressure. Multigenerational occasions like parties, and perhaps even dances can give teens a chance to learn from adults how to interact in new adult situations.

How to raise up a homeschooled teenager? Now it seems so simple to me: Give them lots of time and keep them close; they'll do the rest.

But What About the Prom?

By Jackie Orsi

Sure, we're all sick to death of that "What about socialization?" question. But at least there's some substance to the query, a genuine concern behind it. I want to talk about that other question, one that came up several times in the years I fielded questions about homeschooling at information nights.

On more occasions than I care to think about, *adults* in the audiences asked outright, for all to hear, "But what about the prom?"

And here's an equally amazing thing: nobody ever guffawed, nobody snickered, nobody turned in disbelief to see if the questioner had a twinkle in her eye and a smirk on her face. Perhaps they were all just too polite to show their astonishment and disgust. Let's hope that's why.

The first time somebody asked about the prom, I was taken completely off guard. I reacted politely and stupidly. I mouthed something about how homeschoolers can organize a prom if that's what they want to do. I went away bemused. "Poor thing," I thought. "That woman's life peaked on a June night when she was 17, and it's been all downhill for her ever since."

The second time the question came up, I was again too shocked to come up with a clever answer because I was thinking to myself, "Again with the prom question? A second person thinks this is worth discussing? Do I see a pattern here?"

I started to obsess about the prom question after that. It became my hot button. My daughters, who are now adults, still get a kick out of Mom, sputtering and fuming about the prom. It's become a family joke. I apologize profusely to them for choosing homeschooling and denying them their night at the prom, and they do their best to pout and appear bereft.

The last time a hand went up in the audience to ask about the prom, I was ready. I replied, "Yeah, well, what about the kids who have a prom but don't get a date?" Then I just moved on to the next question. It wasn't the crushing answer I wanted, but it felt better than an answer that awarded the question validity.

You think I'm making too big a deal about the prom question? I don't think so. Let's set the record straight; this is not sour grapes on my part. Back in high school I went to two proms—and not with some loser who asked me at the last minute. My main squeeze was a guy who was president of the student government and captain of the football team. (Aren't you impressed with me now?) For my proms, I had to come up with a gown, which for economy's sake my sister sewed for me. My date had to come up with tickets, a rented tux, and a corsage. Our smorgasbord was a potluck with an overabundance of macaroni salad. I recall those two occasions as slightly silly, tolerably boring, a little too stiff for comfort, and kind of sweet. Significantly, my favorite memory of proms has to do with hours of work and fun beforehand turning the gymnasium into our version of the streets of Paris, complete with an Eiffel Tower made out of lumber, chicken wire, and tissue paper. So I don't have a problem with the prom, you understand, if it is kept in proportion and in perspective—but neither is true of The Prom.

Today's Proms have moved from the gymnasium to the hotel ballroom. There is a limousine or sports car rental, a five-course meal, and a gown that costs hundreds. An entire national industry now serves The Prom. It's safe to claim that between the two of them, a teenaged couple easily drops over $1,000 on The Prom. Think about that. (So many people wail about how much their kid has to spend at the college bookstore to get his or her textbooks for one semester, but it is a mere fraction of what that same kid shelled out for The Prom three months previously.)

Now I am going to tell you a sickening story about what is actually happening in a small city I know. My friend's son entered high school last August as a sophomore, so she showed up for the first meeting of the Parents' Council, a group that is meant to promote education and support the school. Like most public schools, this one needs everything: lab equipment, library resources, computers, you-name-it. Only three other parents showed up for the meeting. You see, support for the Parents' Council in that town has dwindled so drastically in recent years that it is virtually a nonfunctional organization with an empty treasury.

Across town, however, the Grad Night Committee draws about 40 parents per meeting. Grad Night is the night-long party that keeps the kids off the highways after they collect their diplomas. Not a bad idea. My parents let me throw a prom night party at my house. Six couples were invited and we had a lot of fun, talking, laughing, snacking, playing games until morning when my mom cooked a huge breakfast we were too tired to eat. Fast forward almost 30 years to this town where Grad Night features a catered meal, elaborate decorations (fountains and waterfalls), a band, a fortune teller, bungee jumping, Sumo wrestlers (?!?!), door-prizes valued at $50 for each and every kid, and much, much more. Last year the Grad Night Committee successfully raised about $35,000 and spent every single penny of it. Imagine blowing $35,000 on one party. Sumo wrestlers sure don't come cheap.

Grad Night consumes most of the attention, energy, and finances of that town's parents and the community at large. Meanwhile, the handful of parents who are struggling to revive the Parents' Council find it hard to get local businesses to contribute for library books because they've already been squeezed dry by the Grad Night Committee.

The Prom or Grad Night—take your pick. They have become orgies of mis-directed materialism, and verge upon being orgies in the more traditional sense of the word as well. I have a copy of a magazine called *Your Prom*, published by *Modern Bride* magazine. It is 216 pages long, 90% devoted to advertising prom dresses. Well, they're called dresses today—we would have called them lingerie when I was 16 years old. Lots and lots of skin, so naturally one of the ads is for silicone breast enhancers in two styles, "push-up" and "deep cleavage." (Would that be "push-together"?) Articles show beauty make-overs for girls as young as 14, yet the models in the ads all appear to be in their mid-twenties and older, and their poses are more than a little provocative. May I turn your attention to the woman in the leopard skin dress pulling on the ponytail of a man crouched before her on all fours; he isn't wearing a shirt but he does have on a bow tie—this is the prom, after all. That lovely young girl standing over him may not get to be queen of the prom, but she'll be a nifty dominatrix for some lucky young man. Ah, sweet sixteen and never been whipped.

The cover of *Your Prom* promises a "Sex Quiz—How clued in are you?" Let's see how clued in *you* are. Here's question #4: "Conveniently for your new beau, his parents have left town for prom weekend. Now it's past midnight. You are in his bed and he's saying, 'You would if you loved me.' Your reply?" Turn to the answer page now. For question # 4, we are advised, "*. . .don't make any sperm of the moment decisions.*" (No, I am not making this up.)

Don't blame the kids. I'm thinking that more than the "new beau's" parents have left town; for The Prom to have grown into this annual spree of unrestrained indulgence, dissipation, and *prom*-iscuity, a whole generation of American parents must have mentally "left town." As a rite of passage, The Prom is the quintessence, the culmination of how we raise our children today. This one night idealizes all that is shallow: looks, clothes, extravagance, sexuality, short attention spans, thrill-seeking, and adolescent concepts of "popularity."

Parents who don't care leave their kids home alone for the weekend; parents who do care spend the weekend staging elaborate diversions to keep their children from drunken driving. How sad it is that elaborate Prom Night and Grad Night diversions differ not at all from the practice of distracting two-year-olds from toddling toward traffic by giving them shiny toys. Fifteen years later, children have made no progress toward self-control and their parents haven't found a better way to guide them.

Finally, think of all of this in the context of public school. The Prom is a young person's reward for sticking out another lousy year in high school. It's a fairy tale evening set in sharp relief against a year of boredom, stupefaction, pettiness, crassness, manipulation, coercion, and fear. Grad Night culminates thirteen years of endurance.

For me, these annual events represent everything homeschooling stands against. I homeschooled with my daughters so that every day of their lives might have some magic in it, not just a single night once a year. I wanted the magic to come from the precious discoveries they would make about themselves and the world not from the momentary thrills provided by a night of Sumo wrestlers and bungee jumping. I homeschooled so that my daughters would estimate their personal value based on the depth of their thoughts, not the depth of their cleavage. I gave them reality, not surreality. I gave them meaning, not glitter. I gave them my time and my love, but not baubles. I taught them right from wrong, instead of bribing them. I gave them higher goals than having a date for the prom.

I'm ready for the next homeschool information night: "The lady in the blue shirt in the fifth row has had her hand up for a long time. Thank you for being so patient. Go ahead with your question."

"What about the prom?"

"Ma'am, these parents around you have come here tonight to find out a better way to raise their children by homeschooling with them. They have deep concerns about their children's educational achievement, about safety in the schools, about the moral fabric of American society, about spirituality and life and death and the future of all that matters in the universe. I think, perhaps, you came to the wrong place. On the other side of town, the Grad Night Committee is meeting. They're looking for someone to towel down the Sumo wrestlers when they get sweaty. You are the answer to their prayers. Bye-bye."

The Socialization Issue
By Tammy Drennan

Psychologist Paul E. White, Ph.D. says that research has identified three critical areas of socialization skills (and numerous minor areas). These three areas are: role-taking ability (empathy), impulse control (the ability to delay gratification), and conflict resolution.

Can anyone think of three areas in which institutional schools have demonstrated greater failure? The failure has little to do with uncaring teachers or administrators. The institutionalization of children assures general failure in these areas, and the larger the institution, the greater the likelihood of socialization failure.

The question is why? Let's start with role-taking ability, otherwise known as empathy. Empathy is the ability to understand the feelings of others, to put yourself in the place of others and feel what they would feel. A degree of selflessness is needed to do this. The insecure child is unlikely to develop much in this area, because his focus is so much on his own needs, his own survival. Institutional schooling, where children are under constant scrutiny—by teachers and by peers, fosters insecurity. Children worry constantly about acceptance by other children, about having their appearances and personalities found wanting, about grades, and peer pressure and myriad other things—they don't have time for empathy. They are too consumed with their own survival. Empathy is not impossible to achieve in institutional settings, but the odds are against it.

But in the secure setting of the home, where each child knows he is loved and accepted, empathy can flourish. Parents can teach and demonstrate the ability to relate to others, and the odds are on their side. They even have a double advantage—not only is the child sufficiently secure to look beyond himself, but there are far more real opportunities to act on his empathy, because his time is not regulated to the point of precluding chances to reach out to others. If his little sister falls and hurts herself, no bell will call him away from comforting her. If Grandma is feeling lonely, he is completely and naturally free to talk to her on the phone as long as he wishes, and as long as she needs. Empathy thrives in a natural setting. It fights for its life in an institutional setting.

Next there is impulse control. This is the ability to delay gratification, to say "No, I will not play a video game until I have done my math and my chores; I will not have a cookie until Mom bakes more, because there aren't enough for everyone." Again, the institutional setting is hostile to this important socialization skill. Institutions engage in crowd control—as a matter of fact, this is one of their major functions and is taught heavily in all teachers' colleges. Impulse control is self-control, which cannot (so it is believed) be neglected. Self-control takes practice, and if a child does not get to practice it, he does not learn it. He becomes a teenager with no self-control and finally an adult still in the same boat. At home, a child can be afforded endless opportunity for practicing self-control. He learns to schedule his time wisely and fulfill his duties without any bells telling him when to begin and when to stop and without someone standing at the head of the room, watching his every move. These small areas of self-control grow into larger areas, unlike the situation with the institutionalized child who, once outside the reach of the school, does not know how to exercise self-control, unless his parents have taught him this vital socialization skill at home.

Finally, we have conflict resolution. Once again, an institutional school setting stands firmly as a roadblock to another important skill. It would seem the perfect place to learn conflict resolution—there is certainly plenty of conflict to resolve. But in order to learn to resolve conflicts, children must see it being done—they must see Mom and Dad have a disagreement and come to a peaceful resolution over it. They must see how people compromise and apologize, and they must be afforded the opportunity to do it themselves. Too often, schoolyard conflicts end with children being separated from one another and sent back to their routine—no apologies, no compromise, and no restitution. Even more harmful is the popular "no-fault" approach to conflicts today, where equal fault is assigned to all parties involved and all are punished equally. Schools are reacting to the increase of conflicts within their halls by instituting conflict-resolution classes and committees, never examining why conflicts continue to increase.

Unnatural approaches to learning social skills are at best thin thread holding the fabric of civilized humanity together. The thread eventually breaks, and the problem is worse than ever, because the out-of-control, unempathetic, conflict-obsessed individuals are no longer two-year-olds throwing tantrums over not getting cookies—they are adults, with the power and the wherewithal to hurt and kill.

Parents who understand the importance of these three major areas of socialization—role-taking ability, impulse control, and conflict resolution—will teach them to their children themselves, no matter where their children go to school.

Who is Uncle CHiN?
Does He Know Dear Abby?

". . .your children will meet all kinds of children,

on field trips, in homeschool support groups,

and in support group arranged classes."

©Luana Holzer

Who Is Uncle CHiN?

Kindly, old Uncle CHiN, the "Dear Abby" of homeschooling circles, imparts his wise advice in every issue of *California Homeschool News*. Few people, if any for that matter, have actually ever seen Uncle CHiN; he's a figure cloaked in mystery. ("*MY* uncle? I thought he was *YOUR* uncle!") But we are all glad he's there to help us sort through the touchy issues that homeschooling sometimes presents to us. Below he tackles some frequently asked questions from homeschoolers.

What about socialization? Doesn't he need to be with kids his own age?

Well, the best way to begin to answer that question for yourself is to define "socialization." For instance, do you want your child to be comfortable with adults and older children as friends and role models? Would you like him to be a friend and nurturer of younger kids? When conflicts and misunderstandings arise, are you available, if needed, for guidance and support?

Socialization is so much more than being "with kids his own age." Homeschooling can widen a child's social possibilities. Uncle CHiN has observed many a schoolyard in his time, and is not impressed (but is often appalled) with the socialization taking place there. Homeschooling families can easily satisfy their needs to be with other people. There are support group meetings, Scouts, 4-H, church activities, play groups, visiting friends, sports teams and lessons, art and science classes, volunteer activities . . . the possibilities are abundant.

Aren't homeschooled kids too protected? Shouldn't they be out in the "real world" where they have to deal with bullies and people who are different from them?

First, it is natural and good to protect your child from harmful situations and people. Second, many school kids have daily lives far more homogeneous and "protected" than many homeschoolers. Third, there is nothing about schools that is more real than the varied environments in which most homeschoolers spend their time: homes and parks, libraries and field trip sites, wilderness and grocery stores. Fourth, studies have shown that, in general, the people who can best cope with stress are the ones who had happy childhoods with good experiences, not the ones who "got tough" by facing bad experiences.

I don't feel qualified to teach some subjects. How am I going to handle those?

It would be a rare parent (or teacher) who could teach every subject your child wants or needs to learn about. Think of yourself as a facilitator, helping your child to find the resources necessary for learning. Look for creative ways to meet your children's educational needs. Collaborate with other families. Look around your community for resources: people, programs, and places. Jump in alongside the children and learn with them. Remember, there is no need to test, grade, or fail any learner, young or old. Here are a few actual examples of how some California homeschoolers are approaching their studies in science:

- One family regularly takes classes from a nearby science center.
- A support group discovered a wonderful science teacher and arranged to have her teach a series of classes to the group.
- Science museums offer numerous classes open to all students, and by special arrangement with homeschooling groups.
- A teen arranged to do volunteer work for a scientist.
- Most support groups arrange science field trips.

What do I tell my (choose one) relatives/friends/neighbors to convince them that homeschooling is not going to "ruin" my kids?

Here are some things that have helped others:
- Invite the doubter to meet other homeschoolers, including homeschooled children. Some new homeschoolers have won over their spouses or parents by taking them to a homeschool support group meeting.
- Give the doubter some good reading materials. Enlist their support by including them in plans and projects. Does Grandpa have woodworking skills to share? Would Aunt Sarah make a good pen pal? Is the neighbor an experienced gardener? Put them on your team.
- Be patient. Some folks hang on to their skepticism for years, even though your bright, well-adjusted children are right before their eyes.

We just pulled our child out of school, and he is bored and uncooperative with our homeschooling efforts. What can I do? Is this normal?

Yes, it is normal. Many experienced homeschoolers remember a tough transition time when they first pulled their children out of school. They found that their children needed "down time"—usually several months—time to sort through negative school experiences, time to recover their sense of who they are and what their interests are.

Also, each family needs time to discover for themselves their most comfortable way to homeschool; many parents begin homeschooling by trying to replicate school in their own home, because they don't know any other way. Allow yourself to experiment as you evolve your family's unique homeschool style. My advice is to relax, be there with your child, and be ready to listen to feelings, answer questions, and get involved with new interests when they emerge.

How can I find time for myself? I think I'd go nuts if I were home with the kids.

Parent burnout in the first year is probably the major cause of homeschool failure. It's not that the job is so hard, it's that the parents often make it so hard. RELAX! Experienced homeschooling parents don't teach their kids all day long, and don't even try. That's a good thing, because one thing that kids really need, but modern day kids so often can't have, is unstructured time that they can fill. Big chunks of it. Hours and hours of it. Go ahead and take some time for yourself to read the morning newspaper, work in the garden, or take a bath. Your kids need to have time to get bored, discover what they truly want to do, explore and mess around, daydream and wonder, and learn about themselves.

Remember, too, that your kids learn from you even when you are not "teaching" them. They learn from your example, from discussions with you, from interacting and playing with you, and from helping you with everyday tasks.

Of course, you do need to plan some free time for yourself. Your spouse, parents, in-laws, other relatives, friends, baby-sitters, other homeschooling parents, and homeschoolers of baby-sitting age may be able to help. Consider how you can work with other adults and teens to get the quiet time or errand-running time you need.

What do you do Monday morning?

Listen to what one family told me when I asked about their typical day: "Every Monday is different. We might go somewhere special. Or we might do what we usually do when we are home: play computer games and card games; study spelling, Algebra, and French; take walks and talk about the weather; play a little basketball; and (since it's Monday) either have a big blow-out laundry day or go grocery shopping (depending on whether the lack of food or lack of clean clothes seems most imminent). Most days, Mondays included, end with about one hour of read-alouds (and sometimes discussions) before, after, and sometimes during showers and toothbrushing."

There is an infinite range of homeschooling styles and philosophies. Some homeschooling parents purchase curricula and use them to cover all the subjects usually covered in schools. Some of the homeschool parents who belong to a public ISP use the same textbooks and workbooks that are used in the schools, and along roughly the same schedule. Some homeschool parents choose (some with the help of their kids) topics for unit studies. They then immerse themselves in the chosen topic, with reading, writing, math, science, and art all part of one cohesive whole: dinosaur studies, perhaps, or outer space, or Latin America. Some homeschooling families do not set up any particular or planned curriculum at all. Instead, they follow the interests of each child. You will find each of these, and other, homeschool families doing very different things on Monday morning. And that's more than okay—that's terrific. Monday, Tuesday, Wednesday...they're all yours to make of as you wish.

Are there any bad sides to homeschooling?

Yup. Every day you homeschool, life gives you a report card. Sometimes you get A+ and sometimes you get F. Homeschooling parents generally say that they love their lives and love their time with their children, so their days are mostly good. There are bad days, however, and bad weeks, bad patches of all lengths. Why? Because it's real life, and real life is messy. The whole business of raising kids is messy, too. Kids change as they grow, and you need to be flexible and creative to keep up with their developing educational needs and their emerging personalities. Children can be real stinkers at certain stages, especially when they test their limits. Of course, the truth about children is that they need your love the most when they deserve it the least. It's all part of the roller coaster ride you bought a ticket for when you decided to have a family. Count on this: parents and psychologists know that homeschooled children present far fewer behavioral problems than their institutionally schooled peers. In the long run, you'll have fewer bad days if you homeschool.

I am committed to homeschooling, and am interested in developing a plan for my daughter... She has all but mastered "Reader and Math Rabbit" at 3 years and 5 months and has the requisite curiosity to do more. Any suggestions?

No, I don't know what comes after the "Rabbit". I do know that your instincts will serve you well, just as they have done up to this point. Continue to feed her natural curiosity and to support her explorations. "The canary in the mine shaft" is her attitude toward learning, and as long as she's learning with a happy heart, you are doing well by her. So, trust yourself and trust her. You are both doing great, and if you just explore and grow alongside each other, your days will be eventful and uneven, but fine overall.

Guard against developing overblown expectations, however. Kids are quirky little imps, and they have a way of confounding their parents' fondest predictions and highest hopes. Your daughter may seem to have conquered every developmental pre-reading task, and yet it may be many months, or even years, before she actually begins to read on her own. Likewise, each and every child has a personal set of stumbling blocks, tasks or areas of achievement that will pose challenges throughout his or her lifetime. If you and your youngster run up against one of her hard-to-surmount challenges and you place too much stress on achieving success, you may put her in a painful position of wanting to please you, but unable to do so. This is the sort of scenario that is called "failure" and can leave permanent scars on a child. So don't hustle too hard, Mom, especially now when she is so young and tender. Just enjoy your time together. It will be gone before you know it.

How do homeschooling parents work with children at different grade levels?

It can be tough, sometimes, to work with (help or teach) children of different ages and abilities. But it's not tough for homeschoolers alone; let's face it, teachers in schools have to deal with many more children who have (even if a narrow range of age) a wide range of interests, maturity levels, learning styles, and abilities. Also, parents can have difficulties dealing with the conflicting needs and interests of their children even if they do not homeschool.

Homeschoolers often have a great benefit over schoolteachers and students: cross-age tutoring is school lingo for a proven technique that is far easier in the home than in a school. Homeschooled children tend to be closer to their siblings and more apt to spend time in mixed-age groups. Younger children tend to learn from older ones naturally, through observation and emulation; older siblings often enjoy "teaching" what they know, and thereby learn it twice as well as before, while imparting new skills or knowledge to their younger brothers and sisters.

Here are a few specifics from veteran homeschool parents:

"I try to spend a little one-on-one time in the morning with each of my children, discussing the day's plans and what they want to do."

"Each of us takes turns having fun with the youngest while the others are doing quiet projects, reading, or using the computer. For example, my oldest child will read a book to the 5-year-old while the other teen and I work on algebra. Then I spend some time with the oldest on geometry while the other two play checkers. Finally, I have a great time playing with number scales and colored rods with my youngest while my two teens do art projects and free reading."

"My children are close together in age (two years apart) and have always been interested in the same topics. So far, all three of us have learned about space and dinosaurs and such together, each assimilating facts and developing concepts in our own way, at our own level. When I read aloud, I always read to both at the same time. Then we discuss what we read. It works for us. (So far.)"

"When I had a third baby, life went on fairly normally for the first six months. I was still able to do fun projects with my older two children as the baby slept in a sling. But with toddlerhood, everything changed. I suddenly had to supervise the baby almost all the time, so I just couldn't work with the older kids very often. However, that time was kind of wonderful; my kids grew in maturity and responsibility and became much more independent, not only in academics, but also in life skills such as cooking."

Can't we deduct the expenses of homeschooling from our income taxes?

At one time or another, every independent homeschooling family entertains the thought that since they are doing the work of the public schools (better and more efficiently, I might add) then shouldn't the government cut them a little slack? I'm afraid there's not much hope of it, and trying could be dangerous. Here's the way it works:

1. You could try to run your homeschool as a for-profit business and file a Schedule C annually, detailing your income and expenses. The IRS expects to see signs of profitability after a few years, or it begins to suspect that the business is just a tax dodge. Since you would be your only tuition-paying customer, it should be soon apparent to the IRS that your business is not a "for-profit" at all. Boys and girls, can you say "audit"? Now, if you accept other people's children and receive tuition payments from them, you have essentially reinvented the commercial private school, and yes, certainly you are entitled to deduct legitimate business expenses. But then you may need to obtain a business license, obtain suitable insurance, and so forth. Complicated, and probably not worth the effort. Homeschooling other people's kids isn't all that easy, to boot.

2. Or you could try to get your homeschool accepted by the IRS as a tax-exempt organization. The odds of this happening are microscopic since the IRS carefully guards against anyone using tax-exempt status for personal or family gain. Boys and girls, can you say "tax fraud"? (Gee, imagine being able to convert our families into our favorite charities: what cheerful givers we would all be.)

So there you have it. You could say that Uncle Sam and his state and local pals haven't developed a proper appreciation for homeschoolers yet. Maybe that's just as well, since anytime the government allows or gives something, it tells you what you have to do to keep the privilege. In this case the privilege would be keeping a little bit of our own money to raise our own children, but by some perversion, we have become the people of the government, by the government, for the government. My, my, I seem to have launched on a tirade here. Whatever has come over me? I guess I'm just a wrung-out taxpayer myself.

My 14-year-old doesn't want to try anything new. He's content to sit around reading sci-fi and playing the guitar. Should I insist that he "do something"?

Uncle CHiN suspects you may know from both your experiences as a parent and from your experiences growing up, people go through different phases of growth and assimilation, risk and retreat, energy and rest. Your son may be in a phase of rest and renewal before he leaps into a more energetic life phase; or he may be in a very active phase, trying to perfect his music skills while expanding his mind with science fiction. Either way, you might take comfort from the knowledge that musical intelligence is a valid (and, by the way, quite mathematical) form of intelligence; you might take comfort from the idea that reading anything will tend to develop reading and vocabulary skills and will give background necessary for good writing; reading fiction (and biographies) often gives food for thought about social relationships and tends to nurture empathy (reading fiction is good practice for "putting yourself in someone else's shoes"); and reading good science fiction can, believe it or not, teach a lot about science facts and help develop the wondering, speculating part of scientific thinking.

Finally, your own role could include not only listening to your son if he wants to discuss his interests, and supporting him if he asks for help, but also continuing to make available to him other opportunities and activities, and being a good model, one who has interests and actively follows those interests.

How do homeschoolers keep from screaming at their children?

We don't. In fact, Uncle CHiN recommends frequent, heavy duty screaming at children, whether they need it or not.

Nah. Just kidding. I couldn't help myself. Please do not think that homeschooling parents are a special mutant breed of parents who have infinite-patience genes. And do not delude yourself that we have children equipped with obey-parent genes, or never-sass genes, or never-tease-siblings genes...Sigh. Genetic engineering has a long way to go. We're all just regular humans who sometimes lose our tempers. I can suggest two remedies.

First, set up your homeschool in ways that minimize friction. Keep it simple. A couple hours of bookwork is usually plenty. Don't stress yourselves by dragging your child through six or eight hours of do-this, do-that, as schools do. Give each other space. Children do not need your complete attention all the time. Parents and children should spend time apart, going about their separate business.

When a child reaches overload, stop the lesson. A child who is struggling with a new math concept can reach the point of tears in as little as fifteen minutes. When emotions have kicked in, learning can't happen, so it's time to go on to something else. When everyone is crabby, slam those books shut. Declare a holiday. Head to the park, a matinee, take a hike, whatever.

Create plenty of opportunities for your family to present gripes, discuss issues, and work on finding solutions and compromises. The idea here is to talk things out, rather than shouting them out.

Second, learn how you and the kids can let off steam in ways that don't do enduring damage to psyches and relationships. Big hairy yelling matches do happen, in spite of all we do to avoid them. The important thing is how you clean up after them. Uncle CHiN recommends that parents offer the first apology. One of the most important lessons your homeschool can teach is how to say "I'm sorry." No matter how horribly the child has behaved, there is always something dishonorable in the exchange that a parent can claim as well. Saying, "I was wrong when I hollered at you. I'm sorry," shows your child how to apologize with grace.

Treat apologies as great gifts. When a child says I'm sorry, accept it immediately with a hug. Do not use the occasion to recount the gruesome incident, deliver a lecture on behavior, or catalog the child's other faults.

I keep hearing from many homeschooling parents about how much running around they do, to the point of craziness. Why do parents have to stress themselves and children by running around?

It is true that many homeschoolers joke about calling it "carschooling." This is partly due to "September Syndrome," that heady rush of freedom every fall when school starts. You, of course, have far better ways to spend your time than school. Lots and lots of them. So do your homeschooling friends. Next thing you know you're adrift in a sea of field trips, group activities, classes, sports, and you think back to your first contact with homeschoolers. You remember asking, "What about socialization?" And how the long-time homeschoolers pretended not to chuckle patronizingly. Now you know.

It happens every fall, as surely as the pumpkins ripen. And about the time the Jack-o'-lantern is collapsing on the porch, homeschoolers are paring down their schedules to the things they care about most. After a couple of years even the slow learners are more cautious about the time/money costs of activities.

Then there's that more prosaic aspect of overscheduling that is not really overscheduling at all, just Life With Kids. That is to say, if you have two kids, and each kid has an indispensable activity (different ones, of course, since they're of different ages and temperaments) and you want to go to Park Day every week, and the occasional really interesting field trip, and it would be nice to get to the museum once in a while. . .you get my drift?

When your children are young, and you initiate most of their outside activities, the schedules of homeschoolers with older kids can seem crazy. Yet most homeschooling parents believe their greatest role is to help their children discover and pursue their own interests. It is an amazing experience to see your child take over her own educational process. The demands this makes on the family can be stressful, particularly when the needs of two or more children conflict, but let's get some perspective.

Is this "running around" more stressful than having a child who is miserable or bored in school? More stressful than working another job to pay for private school (which has many of the same problems as public school)? More stressful than the third rainy day in the house with an eight- and twelve-year-old?

Sure, homeschooling parents complain about how busy they are, but if you pin them down they usually admit they wouldn't change much, that they and their kids are doing what they want to do. Homeschooling is joyful, stimulating, exciting, wonderful, AND good for you, but nobody said it was easy, any more than parenting is easy. It's important to have a support group where you can make friends to share your highs and lows.

And don't forget, your Uncle CHiN will always have a sympathetic ear.

I really want to homeschool my children, but I'm not a teacher. I only have a high school education. There are so many things I don't know. How can I do it?

As Sam Peavey, Ed.D., wrote, after carefully reviewing half a century of educational studies, there is a "total lack of any significant relationship between the teacher's certificate and the pupil's achievement." Sam Peavey ought to know a great deal about the validity of credentials. He holds graduate degrees in education from both Harvard and Columbia and taught for years at the School of Education of the University of Louisville. Credentials do not make a teacher.

So what is a teacher? In the traditional classroom the teacher is exalted to the mountaintop. There he or she spews forth truths that cascade down the mountainside in a wondrous waterfall. At the foot of the mountain sit the students like little sponges. As the resulting river flows over them they soak up some of what is taught, subsequently wring it out onto a test, and are left with an uncomfortably damp feeling of almost total ignorance.

Frankly, I believe your uncertainty is your best qualification. You won't be tempted to organize every subject and incrementally dispense truths. Instead you can learn along with your child. Your inquisitiveness and excitement over new knowledge will model the joy and the need for lifelong learning. You are everything but inadequate. Go for it.

I've heard a lot of talk about "unschooling." What is it and how is it different from regular schooling?

You could consider the continuum of homeschooling as ranging from the ideal of unschooling (a completely child-led learning environment) to the ideal of rigid school-at-home (a completely parent-controlled learning environment.) All homeschooling is somewhere between these two impossible extremes.

Some families find their comfortable niche on the continuum and stick there, others tend to cycle back and forth in a wider area. The most idealistic follower of child-led learning will assert parental privilege when it comes to, say, safety, while the most idealistic school-at-homer finds times when everyone really needs to put the books away and take a walk. Folks nearer the unschooling end probably use fewer traditional school materials than folks near the schoolish end, but long observation has shown Uncle CHiN that even this is not always the case. In short, big surprise, homeschoolers are difficult if not impossible to classify.

Uncle CHiN has also observed that both fervent unschooling homeschoolers and adamantly structured homeschoolers find more common ground as their children get older. The moral? Don't put yourself in a box. Feel free to find what works best for your family, and be ready to be flexible when change is needed.

There are many homeschoolers that aren't schooling at all in my city. I am afraid the local school system will get wind of these parents and make it difficult for families like us who are providing a better education. What do you think?

There are almost as many ways to homeschool successfully as there are homeschoolers. Sometimes the very best homeschooling doesn't look like school at all. It might even look like nothing is happening. I bet a little research will help to allay your fears and boost your confidence in your fellow homeschoolers.

To find out about all the different styles of homeschooling, and especially to understand homeschooling that doesn't look like school, I recommend you start by reading *Growing Without Schooling* and *Home Education Magazine*. You'll find parents describing their children's learning experiences in an unstructured homeschool setting. (Yes, kids can and do teach themselves to read with Garfield and Tintin books. And they learn math through catalog ordering, budgeting their allowances, and studying for HAM radio licenses, among other activities.)

Next, attend local support group events like park days and spend some time talking to kids as well as parents. I know at least one of the kids will be happy to share his or her latest passion and research with you. (You'll not only learn something about a new topic, but you'll discover just how very good kids can be at teaching themselves.) And when you talk to the parents, you'll find that they are far from neglectful. In fact, they are very aware of what their children want and need to learn and are actively facilitating that learning by providing their students with books, materials, trips to places of interest, and more.

If you're feeling unsure, talk to your local librarian. Chances are, homeschoolers are among her favorite patrons because they have such great questions and want to research topics that are off the beaten path she frequently must help traditionally taught kids to travel. And finally, you might want to attend a homeschool conference or information night. Statewide and local groups sponsor these affairs regularly throughout the year. For information on upcoming events in your area, check with your CHN Local Contact or call us toll free.

We have a 3-year-old and a 22-month-old, and we are planning to homeschool. I worry a lot about how to start with a very curious and independent 3-year-old. I don't want to push him, yet I don't want to miss any windows of opportunity. He asks questions unceasingly. I have been told not to push him, to let him play, but he constantly asks, "What does that say?" when looking at labels, signs or books. Is that not a sign of reading readiness? What should I do? Or not do?

Your child's questions about words in his environment are indeed a sign of reading readiness. Other signs include: writing strings of letters and asking to have them "read," memorizing stories and "reading" them aloud, and recognizing some written words (his name, for example).

These signs are touted by some early childhood educators as proof that very young children should be receiving direct instruction in phonics and other word attack skills. Indeed, some children who receive such instruction at an early age do become independent readers more quickly than their peers. Studies have shown, however, that these early readers tend to lose this advantage as elementary school wears on. Eventually, many early readers become disinterested in books and stop reading for pleasure by the time they enter junior high.

Others who teach young children suggest that the direct teaching of reading be delayed or even omitted. These educators believe that time spent drilling phonics with preschoolers might be used more wisely. Very young children should be surrounded by interesting objects and attentive adults. Enrichment in the form of field trips and social opportunities provides little ones with the experiences which are required to make reading meaningful. In the absence of these experiences, early readers may be decoding words, but they cannot attach meaning to those words in the same way that these "experienced" children can.

Among homeschoolers, I have observed an alarming amount of reading going on. These outbreaks of literacy occur at all hours of the day and night. What made these children independent readers? They have grown up in a literate environment, their questions have been answered, and they have had an attentive adult (or older sibling) who was willing to spend time listening to their reading. Some homeschoolers have chosen to include flashcards and word lists in their homeschooling, others relied simply on books and their own love of reading. If you want to encourage your child to develop into an independent reader,

- DON'T: teach a child who is squirming or inattentive
- DON'T: force lessons over your child's protest
- DO: visit the library regularly, but leave when your child is ready
- DO: talk about words you see in your environment
- DO: play word games with your child
- DO: read for pleasure yourself
- DO: read aloud to your child

Most importantly, RELAX! Reading is not that hard to learn. Most kids will learn reading almost as naturally as they learned to talk, and pushing reading at a very young age can result in later difficulties. Do cultivate a literate environment, but don't push. Your Uncle CHiN hopes you both have fun!

How can I possibly teach my children everything that a school would teach them? I don't know all that stuff!

You mean you don't remember everything you supposedly learned in school? For shame! Doesn't that tell you something about true learning? Children will learn what is necessary for them to know, just as we did. They will also forget whatever they deem irrelevant, just as we have done. So don't worry about keeping up with the schools and giving your children lots of information to forget. Let them learn what is important to them. And if you don't have all the answers to their questions, learn something new with them. Have fun.

I feel like we didn't get enough done during the "school year." Should we homeschool through the summer?

Homeschool through summer if you think it will work for you—but please, do it because you're looking forward to some exciting new projects and juicy new books to read, not just because you're playing catch-up. The game of catch-up can't be won. If you ever end a "school year" feeling you accomplished enough with your children, you will be the first homeschooling parent to ever do so. If that day should arrive, please contact me so we can schedule your coronation.

Of course you fell short of your lofty goals this year! Your September dreams—every book finished, every new concept mastered, and every project realized—they belonged to some other family. Specifically, that would be the family of Mr. and Mrs. Downright R. Perfect of Paragon, CA. The Perfect Family gets their entire curriculum perfectly done right on schedule. They never get colds, keep library books overdue, nor do their children squabble over who reads first.

But alas, the Perfects are also *perfect bores.* They never go out and look for a rainbow after a shower. They never decide to chuck the books and go see a museum exhibit. They never turn over a rock to see what creatures live underneath. They never find anything so interesting that it deserves a closer look. Be glad you're not Perfect, cause you would have missed all those perfect moments you had this year. You had a bunch of them, if you'll let yourself remember.

Get used to the idea that you will never really finish anything with your children. Their education is never going to be complete in your eyes. It's not just a matter of a few more chapters in their science book; it's a matter of trying to give them all the wisdom, knowledge, and strength you want to give them.

You'll never do it to your satisfaction, not if you kept them home till you are over 100. So, since completion will never happen, you might as well not let it bother you. Perhaps summer has its own special curriculum in store for you and your children. Go! Enjoy! Learn!

I'm concerned that my children won't be exposed to a wide enough variety of children from different backgrounds. What about the tough kids? Without being exposed to difficult people, how will they learn to cope when they get into the real world? Also, they will miss out on observing a teacher deal with difficult children.

Wow! It seems to me that you've asked a series of stealth "What about socialization?" questions, but Uncle CHiN has not been fooled. First, let me assure you that your children will meet all kinds of children, on field trips, in homeschool support groups, and in support group arranged classes. Lots of people of many religions, ethnicities and incomes homeschool.

Second, if your children play in public places, they will run into challenging people, young and old. They will be out in the public with you, observing you handle difficult people and situations. There will even be spats and issues to work out in the homeschool support group setting. They will have the gentle guidance of you and other adults to help them work things out. Also, homeschooled children typically possess a greater degree of self-confidence than their schooled peers and therefore are better able, overall, to deal with tough people and situations themselves. (Psst...homeschooled children are actually more in the "real world" than schooled children...But that's another column.) In closing, why would you want your child to be in a classroom, watching a teacher deal with difficult children instead of having that teacher focus exclusively on children's learning? At home, you can give loving, one-on-one attention, without wasting anyone's precious time or energy on disruptive classmates.

Are homeschooled children subject to statewide, standardized tests typically given in public school? Should I give my homeschooled children these tests?

Homeschooled children are not required to take standardized tests such as those given in public schools. However, some homeschooling parents do have their children tested. To test or not to test is left to the family to decide. Some homeschoolers test yearly, others only occasionally and some not at all. If you would like to test your child there are companies that sell the tests to homeschoolers and you can administer the test in your own home (see page 346). There are also private independent study programs that offer testing as a service to homeschoolers. And some support groups get together every year and conduct tests that are administered by a credentialed teacher who is usually also a homeschooling parent.

Testing can be a useful tool if not overused and taking practice tests can alleviate anxiety in a child who is taking an entrance exam for high school or junior college. Some high schools are reluctant to transfer credit from a private homeschool to their public school for the child transferring in. Test scores are something public educators can relate to. Approaching school counselors with test scores in hand may help diminish any hassle the school wishes to dish out. Good test scores can also quiet the homeschooling critics in your family and Uncle CHiN would not hesitate to use them for this purpose.

Young children (under 12) really don't need to take standardized tests. Homeschooling parents know where their children are in relation to their learning. They discover this by talking to their children, working with them on their studies and just by living with them. Uncle CHiN has found that some homeschooled children really want to take tests once they hit their early teens. They aren't burnt out from all the tests their publicly schooled counterparts must endure. So test them and use the test, but don't let the test rule you.

I love to garden, cook, read, listen to music. . . I think I lack the self-discipline to homeschool. The kids would run wild while I was absorbed in a book.

Hmmm...gardening...cooking...reading? Sounds like homeschooling to me. The missing ingredient in your musings seems to be that you would not be able to include your children in your passions. Why not let them play around you while you garden, involving themselves as they feel moved, listening to you talk about gardening as you work? Why not have them help with the cooking? There are few laboratories so rich, fulfilling and accessible as a family kitchen. And besides learning math and science, they learn a laundry list of other skills, too. Reading is the major component of homeschooling. Why not enjoy reading to your children? Soon, if they don't already, they will learn to read and what an example you will have set for them. I see a cozy picture of various family members snuggled up on the sofa together, absorbed in interesting, exciting literature and magazines. Of course, you won't want your children "running wild," unattended. But with love and gentle guidance, it doesn't sound like you would have to sacrifice your life's loves to homeschool. Children love little more than doing "grown up" activities in the company of their parents.

I know testing doesn't prove much, but how else can I know that my children are learning anything?

Oh, how school has trained us not to trust ourselves. While Uncle CHiN does not profess to have a green thumb, he does like the garden analogy. (You know, children are like flowers.) I may plant dozens of flower seeds on a particular day. I must nurture them by giving them water and sunshine (by planting them in the appropriate spot, which I seldom do). I must protect them from pests and weeds. But I also have to trust that they are growing. If I dig up a seed to check its progress, I will hurt or even kill it. After it breaks the surface, I can measure its visible growth and encourage it with plant food, but if I interfere too much I will again harm it. I also cannot determine how fast or how big it will grow, or when it will be ready to bloom. And of course, I can't open the bud to check on the flower's growth. And even though I plant all those seeds on the same day and in the same spot, they will grow at different rates and bloom at different times and be different colors.

Ok, I'll wash off the dirt and be practical. How do you know if you have been learning anything? Well, you probably think about what you were like a few years ago, look at photographs and read your journal, and laugh at that person you used to be. It's even easier with children. Look at those videotapes and photographs. Your kids have grown more than just physically. Look at how those scribbles have turned into drawings and letters of the alphabet. Your children have probably outgrown some toys and books along with clothes. Think of all the different things they have been interested in, sometimes to the exclusion of things we think are important.

Children want to learn, and they do it very well because no one has told them that it is work, that they can only learn if someone older teaches them, and that if they don't learn certain things, they are dumb. It's scary, but we adults have to learn to trust the natural learning process. It works.

My six-year-old daughter is painfully shy. I decided to homeschool her because she was overwhelmed and distracted by the noise in her preschool and kindergarten classrooms. My mother says I'm making a mistake and that she will never become more outgoing unless I send her to school. What should I do?

Forcing a child to socialize before she is ready will not eliminate her shyness; it can actually make matters worse. You are doing the right thing by recognizing your child's discomfort in the school setting. Homeschooling can help her gain confidence and overcome some of the shyness.

You may want to invite one child your daughter feels comfortable with over to your house to play. Find another homeschooled child she likes through your local support group and arrange a weekly play date. Reassure your mother that you are not isolating your daughter, then change the subject.

A shy child will not miraculously become the life of the party with many friends, but that's perfectly okay. Not all of us are social butterflies. Your daughter will develop a few close friends in time at her own pace and in her own way.

I removed my two children from school six months ago. It was a mutually agreed upon family decision. But I am perplexed by what is happening with my children. One of my daughters had many difficulties in school, but she is doing extraordinarily well as a homeschooler. She is learning constantly and is self-motivated. My other daughter was a straight A student, and she is having trouble adjusting. She wants me to "make" her do her schoolwork and play teacher. I am not comfortable with this role and explained to her that I am not the kind of parent who wants to have to "force" learning upon her. Why would the daughter with good grades be the difficult one to homeschool? How can I help my daughter take some responsibility for her learning?

This is more common than you might think. Often, children who rebel against traditional schooling are self-directed, independent learners. They do better being gently guided, rather than dictated to. On the flip side, some children who are straight A students in traditional school are people pleasers. They want to do a good job on an assigned task in order to please their teachers, parents, etc., but need to be told what to do, when to do it and how. This sounds as if it's your daughter's trouble. She needs time to adjust to homeschooling as she will not become an independent learner overnight. Offer her more structure, as this is what she craves, and help her set goals for herself. Occasionally remind her to review her goals to see if she is on track. Continue to tell her that the responsibility to complete her goals, academic or otherwise, is hers alone, but that you will always be available to help when she asks. Let her know that you are proud of her and love her for herself, not her accomplishments. With patience and time she will start taking on more responsibility for her learning.

We withdrew our son from school at the end of this last year and plan to homeschool him this next fall. He wasn't doing well in school. We received several notes saying he "wouldn't listen to the teacher" and "was disruptive." Toward the end of the year the school suggested that he be tested for ADHD and put on medication. What can you tell me about ADHD and do you have any suggestions for homeschooling a child with it?

ADHD (Attention-Deficit Hyperactivity Disorder) is not like the measles or a broken leg. It does not have clear physical symptoms. In fact, it is a kind of umbrella term. Let's look first at how the "experts" diagnose and treat ADHD and then we'll look at some alternatives to mainstream treatments.

Diagnosis of ADHD is based on behavior criteria listed in a reference book called *The Diagnostic and Statistical Manual of Mental Disorders*, DSM for short. There are three patterns of behavior that might indicate ADHD: "inattention," "hyperactivity," and "impulsivity." According to the DSM, signs of inattention include becoming easily distracted by irrelevant sights and sounds, failing to pay attention to details and make careless mistakes, rarely following instructions carefully and completely, and losing or forgetting things like toys, pencils, books or tools needed for a task. The signs of hyperactivity and impulsivity listed are: feeling restless, often fidgeting with hands or feet, squirming, leaving a seat in a situation where sitting or quiet behavior is expected, blurting out answers before hearing the whole question, and having difficulty waiting in line or for a turn.

You might recognize some of these "symptoms" in yourself. Most people blurt out, bounce from one task to another, or are disorganized or forgetful once in a while. ADHD is diagnosed when this behavior is excessive or long-term. The identification of these symptoms in a child is accomplished by having adults close to him rate his behavior on a scale. The diagnosis, in other words, is based on the adults' personal perceptions. One adult might chuckle and say,

"My you're full of it today," or "Do you have ants in your pants?", or "What are you daydreaming about?" Another adult might respond to the same behavior with disapproval and control. By the way, ADHD is diagnosed ten times more often in boys than in girls. "He's all boy," has given way to medicating the active, exuberant child.

The diagnosis ADHD is controversial, because no single cause can be found and diagnostic tools are subjective. Medicating children "diagnosed" with ADHD is also controversial. The medicine is not a cure; it has side effects; its long-term benefit is limited. Consequently, you may want to rule out other possible causes for ADHD "symptoms," before adopting the mainstream treatment. Seek out a sympathetic pediatrician as an ally and explore all the possibilities. As you explore the alternative causes, you might find *The Holistic Pediatrician* by Kathi J. Kemper, M.D., M.P.H. or *Ritalin Is Not the Answer: A Drug-Free, Practical Program for Children Diagnosed with ADD or ADHD,"* by psychologist-professor David B. Stein to be useful. Thomas Armstrong has also written books about ADD, and one of his articles, *Why I Believe that Attention Deficit Disorder is a Myth,* appears on the internet: *http://www.ThomasArmstrong.com/articles/add_myth.htm/.*

Are there physical problems that might lead to your child's behaviors? Poor sleeping at night due to sinus infection, asthma, large adenoids or tonsils can lead to ADHD behaviors. Thyroid problems, high lead levels, undetectable petit mal seizures and hearing or visual impairments can also lead to acting out in frustration. A word to the wise, vision is more than eyesight. When looking into possible visual impairments seek out a behavioral optometrist. A child might have 20/20 eyesight and be seeing double, having trouble focusing or tracking. Consider any special dietary needs. Identify any food allergies or intolerances.

Are there emotional considerations? A kinesthetic learner in a controlled environment will be disruptive. Classroom management techniques that lead a child to feel like a failure might cause him to fight back by breaking the rules. Differences in personality and energy level are not easily accommodated in a group situation. The byproducts of being misunderstood—anger, frustration, insecurity, depression or anxiety, can lead to non-compliance. If your child has been in a stressful situation at school or is a delayed learner, homeschooling may bring an end to last-year's behaviors without medical intervention. While you can benefit from consulting doctors and other health care professionals, the final decision about what to do belongs to you and your child. Trust yourself and him to discover what is best through time and experience.

I Can't Get My Child to
Sit Still and Work!

"Once you understand how your child learns,

you will be able to give him the key

to unlock his talents and abilities."

©Cheryl Maxwell

Making Sense of Learning Styles

By Kate Jimenez

Now that you've decided to homeschool, how will you know which homeschooling approach to take? Will you do unit studies? Will you do school at home with all the appropriate textbooks and worksheets? Will you use a learn-by-doing approach? Many parents will use an approach that corresponds most closely with their own learning style. If they were good readers and studious as children, they will choose that style in their homeschool for their own children. If they are movers and shakers, constantly on the go, they will use a more hands-on approach. That's okay if the parents are learning for themselves. But what happens when your learning style clashes with that of your child?

We can see an example of a clash of learning styles by looking at the children in a public school classroom. The teacher will usually teach the class in the way she learns best and that is conducive to the classroom environment. For most classroom schoolteachers, this way means standing in front of the class lecturing for a majority of the day. The children who don't do well sitting and listening quickly become bored, fidget, fall out of their chairs and are sent to the office or to a corner somewhere. Many are labeled hyperactive or learning disabled and prescribed Ritalin.

You may have one of these children. In fact, this may be the reason you are homeschooling. Perhaps you have taken your child out of school because the school was failing your child and you want to do a better job. The good news is you can do a better job. You can help your child learn to read, conquer math, ride a bike and become a confident life-long learner. Once you understand how your child learns, you will be able to give him the key to unlock his talents and abilities.

One of the best ways to discover your child's learning style is by simple observation. You probably have already noticed many of the unique learning qualities they possess. Johnny is good at jigsaw puzzles. He likes to work them while listening to the radio; it seems to help him focus. His left foot wiggles the entire time he is absorbed in this task. Jenny likes to read. Her favorite place to read is in a tent she's made of sheets in the bedroom. She likes to have her cat for company, but otherwise prefers to be alone while she is absorbed in a book. When you ask her what she was reading, she has a difficult time explaining, but three days later she has written a poem about it or she sees something that reminds her of the book she's just finished and she shares it with you. These children are giving clues to their unique learning styles.

The Seven Learning Styles

Howard Gardner first put forth his theory of multiple intelligences in his 1987 book, *Frames of Mind*. Gardner theorized that there are seven intelligences:

- Linguistic: The use of the spoken word, auditory skills, playing with the sounds of words. These children like rhyming, reading and storytelling, and talking.

- Logical-Mathematical: These kids notice patterns, sort and keep things orderly, use numbers and calculations.

- Spatial: With spatial abilities, children have clear visual images in their minds when describing a story read or a place visited. They are good at puzzles, enjoy drawing, like watching movies and tend to daydream.

- Musical: Enjoy music and often play musical instruments and sing. They remember the lyrics to several songs (these are the same kids that can remember and sing every advertising jingle they've ever heard) and can tell when a note is off-key.

- Bodily-Kinesthetic: Hands on and movement oriented. Good at sports and/or have developed fine motor skills and do well with sewing and crafting. Use gestures when speaking and are constantly moving. As a result they are often labeled hyperactive in school.

- Interpersonal: These are extroverts, people-people. They love socializing and take a deep interest in other people. They like to organize and coordinate people and events.

- Intrapersonal: Tend to be introverted. Have strong feelings and are independent. They don't follow the crowd, but march to the beat of a different drummer.

Recently, Gardner described an eighth intelligence, the *Naturalist*. This is the child who is intuitive with nature and animals.

Dr. Gardner emphasizes that parents and teachers should not pigeonhole children into one category. Most people have strengths in more than one learning style. The trick is to determine where these strengths lie and then to present information to the child in ways he can understand.

Putting the Theory into Practice

Dr. Thomas Armstrong, a former special education teacher who became frustrated with the way special education was taught to children, is a writer and speaker on the subject of learning styles. In his article "Multiple Intelligences: Seven ways to Approach Curriculum" (read the full article at his website, *www.ThomasArmstrong.com*) Armstrong gives the example of teaching a classroom of children how to tell time. He begins by telling a story about a Land of No Time. He describes the people in this land and how frustrated and confused they are because they can't tell time. But a family called the O'Clocks with 12 children help the people of the Land of No Time learn to tell time. Each of the 12 O'Clock children have a little rhyme just for them. After telling the story, Armstrong has the children come up to a large plywood clock face and act out a play of the story. Later the children go back to their desks where they can write stories about the O'Clock family and draw clock faces denoting different times.

The point of these activities is to present the lesson in more than one way so that it appeals to the various learning styles and all of the children will be fully engaged in the activity. Armstrong did this with an entire classroom and was able to incorporate most of the various learning styles in the process. Imagine how much easier it would be to do this with one or two children, zeroing in on their learning styles and presenting the material to them. This is something the homeschooling parent can do that the classroom teacher cannot.

Dr. Dawna Markova, in her book *How Your Child Is Smart*, tells the compelling story of how she helped a boy named Jerome learn to read by teaching in his learning style. Jerome was a 14-year-old sixth-grader. It was believed he would never learn to read and he had been classified as "trainable retarded." Jerome had so many failures that he also told Dr. Markova that it was hopeless and he would never learn. Dr. Markova wasn't ready to give up on him so quickly. She went to the migrant camp where he lived and learned that Jerome was a hero of sorts at camp. He was their champion chess player. She observed how he played chess; he paced back and forth throwing darting glances at the board, then would quickly make his move. Later, Markova questioned Jerome and listened carefully as he described his chess playing strategy. Using what she'd learned, Markova bought a book she thought would interest Jerome and began to help him learn to read it. Jerome would move around the room, his eyes closed while Dr. Markova spelled the words aloud, tracing the letters in his back or his palm. Then he'd look at the words in the book and write them out on paper. It was difficult at first, but Jerome did learn to read.

Children Learn at Different Speeds

Knowing your child's learning style will deepen your understanding and ability to communicate with your child, but it is no guarantee that your child will learn to read at four or be a spelling bee champion at eight. Children learn at different speeds. Even siblings may have startling learning differences that can surprise a parent. One child may be an early reader and seem to excel in everything he does. His brother may take longer and need different kinds of assistance and a longer time frame before he learns to read. The beauty of homeschooling is that parents can tailor an educational plan to their child's needs. Children can take the time they need to develop, mature and learn without the stigma of being labeled. This is by far the biggest advantage to homeschooling and a wonderful gift to the child.

What About the Parent's Learning Style?

In order to gain an understanding of your child's learning style, it is important that you understand your own style of learning. Adults also have favored learning styles, and as we age, these methods of learning become more ingrained. For those of you who like reading there are plenty of books you can find on the subject of learning styles. Those of you who prefer not to read can listen to books on tape, view videos on the subject and attend seminars or use any combination of these approaches to discover how best to tap into information about learning styles and apply it in your homeschool. You can share this learning with your child by reading excerpts from books and viewing videos together. Your child will be able to help you and provide insight into his learning style. It's empowering for children to learn about their unique learning style. It also gives them the tools necessary to be successful.

Homeschooling the Gifted or Accelerated Child

Previously published by CHN, and revised by editor

In an attempt to meet the educational needs of their gifted children, many families are turning to home education to provide appropriate academic challenges. Unfortunately, public and private schools are usually unable and/or unwilling to give these children a consistent daily curriculum that is truly geared to their needs. Schools teach to the average student, and while they will offer special classes for those who learn more slowly, children who learn quickly are considered lucky and without the need of the same level of special attention.

Schools may recognize a child and place them in their gifted program, but that recognition doesn't necessarily mean that the school is adequately teaching that child. A special enrichment class may meet once a week, or sometimes for a week during vacation. The remainder of the time, the children are expected to continue to do assignments along with their class.

Placing children in the gifted program may seem special, but it is not a daily acceleration, and it probably won't meet their needs. This can lead to behavioral problems, acting up out of boredom, or even starting to think too highly of themselves because they know they have made it to an elite status. Or it might backfire, and other children might avoid them because of their gifted label.

At home, families are finding that their children can work at an accelerated pace, as it is no longer necessary to wait for the rest of the class before moving on, and it can be done in a quiet, matter-of-fact natural setting. If the parent so chooses, there need be no labeling of their child simply because the child learns some things more easily than others do. This may be especially important if there are other children in the family with different learning styles. In addition, the student can approach material at his/her own level, from many sources, and with no time constraints, thus permitting a greater involvement with the subject matter. Each child's learning style can be honored and utilized to help the student pursue individual interests. For gifted books and support organizations see page 347.

Schedules: Searching for Order

By Christine Tykeson

First and foremost, a schedule is a tool. Like a carpenter's hammer it can be very useful, provided you have a suitable purpose for it, like pounding nails into wood rather than hitting yourself over the head with it. Schedules are organizing tools. They're meant to serve those who use them. Once we understand this we need to look at what our aims are. What are we organizing for? What are our values? Then we can start to make schedules that serve us.

I assume as homeschoolers, we have many priorities in common with each other. And we're doing something about what we believe, not just complaining or going along with the status quo. I'll list a few of my priorities that guide the way we do business around my house. I want a healthy environment for children and adults to work together. I want to have an environment in which it's easy to learn new things. I want to make it clear what we expect to do at any given time and thereby reduce conflicts between people. I want a premium education for my children, morally, socially and academically. I want a happy and memorable family life. I want a peaceful and respectful environment in which to live. It sounds a bit fluffy, I admit, and the devil's in the details, as always. But if we're way off on some of these targets, my husband and I get together and discuss why we think that's the case and rearrange our schedule towards making improvements. Sometimes I make mistakes and (to use the hammer analogy once again) hit my thumb instead of the nail I'm aiming for. But that's good feedback. Remembering I'm in charge of how I schedule my time, I just fine-tune things so I get it right the next time.

George Burns, when asked why he continued to work well into old age, said, "You have to have a reason to get up in the morning." Work creates meaning for many people. Schedules orient one to one's work. Schedules are commitments one makes to oneself and others about meeting obligations and goals. Much has been said about the importance of play for the healthy development of young children's minds. If all goes well children transfer this passion for play into a desire for meaningful work as they develop into older children and adults. They want projects that require discipline and develop skills. Schedules can help you and your children orient yourselves advantageously to your work.

Well-organized brains create well-organized environments. But, can the opposite be true; does a well-organized environment help create a better organized brain? Jane Healy, author of *Endangered Minds: Why our Children Can't Think*, argues that this is indeed the case. She insists and provides evidence from brain research that the brain is quite plastic and is influenced a great deal by its environment. Order in the environment of a growing child develops better order in his or her brain. Appropriate emphasis needs to be given to work, sleep, rest, recreation, and nourishing.

Schedules imply becoming conscious about priorities. Making a life for oneself is the process of choosing how one allocates one's time. Is it television or storytime? Is it a brisk walk through the park on a windy day or a cozy board game at the kitchen table with hot chocolate? Is it learning math or sleeping late in bed? Is it preparing homemade meals or picking up fast food? It's important to take into account the long-range benefits of any given action, something that's more likely to happen if you consciously schedule your time. I once overheard a woman at a ceramic shop admiring a ceramist at work and despairing that she could never become so skilled a ceramist. The ceramist had been developing her talent for 15 years and the admirer didn't want to start if it was going to take her that long to get good at it. The ceramist wisely said, "Those 15 years will go by regardless. If you start now you'll be a much better ceramist when that time has passed than if you had never started."

Intention is very powerful. It is the spark that focuses thought and moves it into action. Schedules are tools that help execute one's intentions. A regular habit of scheduling your time repeatedly asks the question, "What's your intention today?" The alternative is drifting and defaulting your time (and values and goals) to outside circumstances.

Three Points About Schedules

1. Keep it Simple

   Thoreau wrote, "Simplify. Simplify. Simplify." But, Thoreau never had kids. Life with kids seems anything but simple. The details of life pile up rapidly. With so many demands, how do we make time to do the stuff that makes life sweet and uplifting? First of all, not everything in life is sweet, but some of those sour chores need to be done, or everything begins to smell pretty foul. The point is simply to involve everyone in the have to do chores. Figure out what they are and divide them up. Get them out of the way. Then you can enjoy the fruits of your labors with an easy mind.

The next great enemy of simplicity is (and I think homeschooling parents fall into this trap a lot) overdoing the enriched environment philosophy. There are always good things to spend time doing, as there are good things to spend money on and plenty of worthy causes to support. One can't do every good thing. One has to choose the best and let a lot of other worthwhile opportunities go by. I can't tell you how many learning supplies I bought that provided mere minutes of questionable learning at a high price, or field trips I attended that were noisy and attractively accompanied by lots of stimulating bells and whistles, but which taught much less than a half hour with a well written book from the library would have. Frequently I've found less flashy, simpler materials and activities provide the best long-term value. A parent can become a scheduling maniac, making unreasonably long lists of things to do to the consternation of self and family. It's important to remember that whatever takes time to do alone is more time consuming when done through the dynamics of a family. This is where prioritizing can really pay off. I know I've had a more productive day if I've helped each of my children learn or do two things well than if they've been exposed to five or six things and understood them only halfway decently. My strategy lately is to pick the two most important things I want to help each of my children learn or do each day, plus the two most important things I want to accomplish, put them on my to-do list and do them. Anything we accomplish after that is gravy.

2. The Importance of Wave

This idea I got from my former yoga teacher. She says we don't have enough waves in our lives. When we exercise or engage in hard physical work we are operating on the crest of the wave. When we relax deeply we are in the trough. At the crest we are strengthening our bodies, at the trough we are healing. People frequently get stuck traveling a fairly straight line between these two points. This is where our bodies break down.

I think this analogy can be applied successfully to mental work as well. There are people in the homeschool community who stress the importance of academic rigor, and there are those who emphasize the importance of play, time to reflect, and time to assimilate learning. Both are important. I think rigor is often overlooked. Kids, especially as they get older, want to be challenged, and they want to experience the success of meeting and overcoming those challenges. They want people beside them who believe in them and expect them to prevail, even when they doubt themselves. But rigor needs to be balanced with ample margin time.

Margin time doesn't get a lot of respect in our go-go world. I've noticed if I don't reserve my own time for my own purposes someone invariably comes along with something for me to do. I think you need to schedule margin time. My neighbor schedules margin time into her day by having a quiet time every day for her children to work on projects independently in the afternoon while she catches up on little odds and ends, or sits down to read a book. Another homeschooler I know will take a day off every now and then to do nothing—or at least no scheduled out-of-the-house activities. One of my friends is very selective about how much she schedules for her children to do. Having time available doesn't mean she readily fills her schedule with activities. If her family has done much one day she eliminates extra outside activities the following day. Her children reflect the self-control and serenity of the schedule they keep. Margin time is important for assimilating experience and coming back into balance. Rigor is important for developing, sharpening, and improving skills.

3. Balance Flexibility and Rigidity

    The great thing about homeschooling is the flexibility. You can really individualize education for each child. If something isn't working, it's easy to change it. The best schedules take this into account, but without some rigidity, you don't have a schedule at all. Much of the benefit of a schedule is that everyone has an idea about what to expect on any given day. There is much comfort and freedom in that knowledge. If everything's negotiable, you have nothing to count on; everyone does what they want. These circumstances inevitably create conflicts where doing your thing impedes others from doing theirs. If we remember that schedules are our tools this won't be much of a problem. They need to be firm enough to do the job and flexible enough to be fine-tuned to our specific needs. As our needs change they can be altered.

Feel at Home, Learn at Home

By Estella H. Humphrey

I finally started homeschooling my son, Victor, when he was ten. I had wrestled with the idea for years, especially because I had taught Victor how to read before he ever stepped into a school. I didn't realize it then, but we were homeschooling during his preschool years.

I knew my son could learn more with me, and I felt the relationship we would have was well worth the effort. Exposure did the rest. I read Mary Kay Clark's *Catholic Homeschooling* and made the decision, although I wondered how I'd manage it. A lot of rosaries later, after my office would not revise my work schedule, my husband said he'd take care of the homeschooling while I worked.

That first year, we linked up with the San Francisco Unified School District home education program and were "supervised" by a teacher, who was very supportive. We had to use their lessons, and it was extra work adding my own (like the *Iliad, Odyssey, Aeneid,* long division, etc.). We did not know any other families doing homeschooling.

Then my husband and I got into a nontraditional business, and in the process we joined an organized support group composed of people on the same track. From being barely social beings we came to discover the value of a support network. We thought, if this works for business, think what it could be like for homeschooling. We knew there were homeschooling families out there and we set out to find them.

There were many phone calls, a chance acquaintance at the Marin County Fair, and soon I got in touch with the West Bay Christian Home Educators, and later with the San Francisco Homeschoolers, the Sacred Heart Homeschoolers, and the Regina Pacis group in San Jose. I joined the California Homeschool Network at an Information Workshop in August. I was making sure we would never be alone again. We now know other homeschooling families, real live people who have been at it much longer than we have. We have met different families with different ways of learning at home. We are so relieved to find that we are not alone after all.

For our homeschooling, I had prepared a program from a bunch of Montessori albums that I had amassed over the years. I taught in a Montessori school in Manila (20 years ago?) and have never forgotten the painless way in which kids could just learn, and at an earlier age, too. After I left teaching, I just kept on collecting more information about early childhood education, and it was hard not to try them out on my kids. (Victor is my only child left at home.)

However, working a full time job did put a dent into my efforts, even if my husband was available (flexible business hours, eh?) to be with Victor. But Pichit was not a teacher before, and I'm the one who wants to jump into the fray and take my son's education in hand. Still, we learn to be philosophical. Had I been free from the start to homeschool full time, I might have driven my son instead of allowing him to go at his own pace. Currently, though, I am forced into benign neglect—yet Victor keeps learning, with or without me. He's even leaving me behind.

And we're not alone, either. We've swapped stories with our new friends, and have observed that basically each one uses a "relaxed" approach. There are lessons to work on and activities to engage in, but each mother knows you can't plan a perfect schedule. Diane, mother of five children ages 4-12, has this to say:

"Our 'typical home-school day' varies considerably from day to day because we operate on a repeating weekly schedule. Also, in my experience, a day rarely proceeds according to schedule.

"I have recently come up with a new schedule that incorporates household chores into school activities. Most school subjects for the two older students are studied only once or twice a week, but for an hour or two at a time . . . At other times of the day, the older students do chores while I work with the younger ones, who do every subject (math, reading, and handwriting) in half to one hour periods throughout the week.

"Since we school year-round, any missed day or subject is not cause for concern. We just continue on our schedule as well as we can and take up the missed material the next time the schedule calls for that subject to be studied.

"I have tried numerous ways of scheduling my school day (including not scheduling at all) during the eight or so years we've been at this, and this seems to work best for us. We often can't keep to our schedule perfectly, but having it helps to let me know where we're at and where we should be going. It also helps me to remember all the subjects (and children) and not to miss anything (or anyone!) Before I used a schedule I would often find myself realizing that days had passed without my teaching a certain (possibly lower priority) subject, and occasionally I would notice that the younger kids hadn't been getting my attention on a regular basis.

"An important thing to remember when scheduling, however, is to be realistic. I don't know how many schedules I've written that went down in flames after the first week or two because I'd planned to get up too early. Some people do great at 6:00 a.m., but I'm definitely not one of them! Once I realized that and started allowing for it in my scheduling, things went a lot smoother."

Homeschoolers networking with each other attend meetings, usually once a month. We learn from each other, ask questions, coordinate activities, and have a good time, with or without our kids along. I became convinced that a flexible and open attitude goes a long way when Gail gave a talk at one such meeting, and said she had attempted to institute formal school procedures at home. As she related, in less than a week she "had a pain in the side and was literally limping" because of the added stress. As time went by, Gail received the enlightenment she needed, and now she doesn't mind homeschooling "in pajamas" if that's what works. I like that.

In a similar vein, Vivian, who initiated the formation of the Sacred Heart Homeschoolers, describes an open-ended style that accommodates work and play:

"Our education more resembles the tutorial and seminar approach of a university than the large group management approach of a conventional classroom. The emphasis with our children now, since they are in the primary grades or below, is to encourage their faculty for wonder, train their memories, develop their language skills, and build their moral character. With such a foundation, children are equipped to learn anything.

"Monday through Thursday, between 9 a.m. and noon, we spend some time on the four R's—reading, writing, 'rithmetic, and religion. I spend one-on-one time with each of the two older children, while the other is reading, working, or playing independently. Friday morning we study history together, seminar-style. Of course, with a baby and a three-year-old in the midst of it all, there are interruptions and mishaps. But we manage to accomplish all that is truly necessary, and we even have quite a bit of fun.

"Our weekday afternoons are divided among various extracurricular activities. Both of our older children play team sports, and the oldest takes piano lessons and sings in a boys' choir. We also go on field trips and other outings. Many people ask us, 'What about science?' Between our encyclopedias and our membership at the California Academy of Sciences, there is plenty of material to feed our children's natural curiosity. As the children get older, they will require more formal study of the sciences."

Talk about science, Cynthia discovered how to bring out scientific curiosity and exploration in her children, despite initial fears:

> *"Having been educated in the sciences, I find it interesting, challenging, and rewarding to study various aspects of biological and physical science. It was difficult to impart my knowledge and love of experimentation to my children. When they were very young they had many fears of anything that moved, from the tiniest to the largest creature. So I started out having my son collect specimens of non-living items and then we moved to raising hamsters. He watched his hamster raise her young and learned to handle them. His fears slowly subsided. Next, we raised mealworms. Later, we were given silkworms to raise and after researching about them, we watched them go through their life cycle. With the help of another home-schooled boy, my children captured insects and studied them. Today my son collects wood lice and studies them. He asks questions like: 'Why are some purple?' 'Why do they curl up?' We explore whether they like light or dark, damp or dry, mud or sand, etc. He takes his friends to the yard and has everyone exploring, collecting and studying bugs."*

Cynthia leads a busy life as a homeschooling parent. She takes her children to various activities like ballet, judo, piano lessons, swimming and choir. The relaxed approach also means you don't have to do all the teaching, since you certainly can organize the teaching resources available in the community.

After learning about the experiences of the many homeschoolers that we've met, we feel more at home about it. We see how homeschooling works despite different ways of doing it. And it's so much easier now that we have our support network in place. If you're new to the idea of homeschooling, we would encourage you to check it out. It's okay to feel at home and learn at home.

Native Intelligence
By Christine Tykeson

I once had an interesting friend who had an IQ of 160. His proficiency at mental gymnastics was astounding. He could win arguments without any merit every time. He could create havoc in any environment because his mind sought stimulation relentlessly and at any cost. He was a master at rationalizing any behavior he found himself inclined toward. He attracted interesting people who found him fascinating and lost them when he used them badly for his own amusement. He was clever, witty, amusing, and lived his life stupidly.

Most of us have known or heard about very bright people who possessed certain character flaws or moral failings which caused them to go through jobs and marriages like pistachios and made complete messes of their lives. There's a difference between being smart and living intelligently.

If we mean by success the ability to achieve one's goals, to bring happiness to one's life and the lives of others, then intelligence does not automatically produce success. While above-average intelligence does play a role in success, there are many other characteristics which are at least as important, and perhaps more so: discipline, organizational skills, people skills, integrity, self-knowledge, an appetite for hard work and even physical health.

Even thinking skills do not automatically accompany intelligence. Edward de Bono, a developer of thinking programs sought out by well-known corporations like Shell and IBM, insists that thinking well is not an automatic function of a superior intelligence. He compares high intelligence to a powerful car which can be driven by a good driver with good thinking skills or a poor driver with poor thinking skills. He writes that, "Many highly intelligent people often take up a view on a subject and then use their intelligence to defend that view. Since they can defend the view very well they never see any need to explore the subject or listen to alternative views. This is poor thinking and is part of the 'intelligence trap.'"

Intelligence is a talent, a potential. One's skills and character determine how that talent is used. Some defining is in order here. I've been using the term "intelligence" in its common everyday, highly-esteemed-in-the-schoolroom sense, to mean skill at remembering and recalling information and the ability to reason well. Another perspective on intelligence is that of Howard Gardner who posits seven different intelligences, only two of which, linguistic and mathematical-logical, fit our ordinary definition. Some people have a musical intelligence. Some have visual/spatial skills which they can use to create art or invent or fix mechanical devices. The other three I haven't mentioned are kinesthetic (physical awareness and skill), interpersonal (skill at relating to others) and intrapersonal (knowing oneself and by extension everything else). This expanded definition of intelligence is helpful for looking at how to educate to a person's strengths but still leaves us with the fact that any intelligence, any talent, is only a potential unless qualities of character bring it to flower.

From economics comes an interesting analogy. Economists have found no correlation between the natural resources of a country and its performance economically. How do you explain the success of Singapore, an overpopulated island-nation with virtually no natural resources? The character of the culture of Singapore is the dynamic behind its success. Similarly, a person's character is more important to their success than any "natural resources" they may have.

Exploring further definitions of "intelligence," we come upon another use of the term which has to do with perception. Intelligence in this sense is not a talent but a way of perceiving. It's more akin to wisdom. It is sometimes claimed that education deadens the intellect because it trains it along a certain path, like putting blinders on a horse, and limits the range of a person's perception. It closes the mind by making it learned rather than always learning. To learn about something, you need to be able to see it clearly, and to be able to see it clearly you need to be free of self-deception and preconception. Self-deception is a defense of the intellect. Preconception is a pitfall of the educated. Seeing clearly is a rare phenomenon produced from honesty and humility. Such seeing is an active intelligence worth cultivating.

Certainly children's minds should be educated in math and literature, logic, and geography. Children should know where their strengths lie (how they are intelligent because they are who they are) and we should support them in developing these strengths. But that's not enough. To expand on de Bono's powerful car analogy, we should know the capabilities, the strengths of our vehicle, and we should make sure the driver in command is skilled and alert, looking at everything on the road and making sound decisions based on clear observations. It's more important to cultivate an understanding in our children of what it is to perceive life with intelligence rather than merely enjoying the smug satisfaction of being intelligent.

Trust

By Karen Rafferty

Children are natural learners, curious investigators and would-be conquerors of the world around them. What parent has not heard variations of all of the following? "Mommy, I a big girl now." "Look! Look! See me! I can do it!" "No, no, I do it myself." Homeschooling allows our children the freedom to grow at their own pace, choose their own challenges, enjoy their successes and not be labeled for their transitory failures if, as parents, we can learn to trust each child's chosen direction.

The trust of which I'm speaking is not conditional. It cannot be given or withheld depending on our judgment of the child's choices. It is not based on the child's success in his or her endeavors. It is a trust, which allows the child to fail or succeed while moving erratically toward self-knowledge and self-mastery. Some have labeled this process "unschooling." Others prefer the label "child-led interest education." I call the process life. For me, trusting my son to live his life has been a difficult challenge for my well-schooled soul. We have progressed unevenly over this uncharted terrain. With 20/20 hindsight some of the pitfalls have been revealed as mere dips in the road. We have enjoyed many inspirational points that have given us the courage to continue trusting.

Most of the obstacles to trust are inherent in the traditions—I believe false traditions—of our society. For instance, many believe that responsibility equals control. Just observe the looks and comments when a child throws a tantrum in public. Whispers of disdain abound. "I would never allow that." "What kind of parent is she?" "Why doesn't she put a stop to that?"

So when we accept the responsibility for our child's education, we might unthinkingly assume we must take control of our child's education. But responsibility does not equal control. In *The 7 Habits of Highly Effective People*, Stephen Covey challenges us; "Look at the word responsibility—'response-ability'—the ability to choose your response." (p. 71) We see this clearly in problems that involve our own behavior, but what about problems involving the behavior or misbehavior of others like our children. Mr. Covey has "identified over 30 separate methods of human influence—as separate as empathy is from confrontation, as separate as example is from persuasion. Most people have only three or four of these methods in their repertoire, starting usually with reasoning, and, if that doesn't work, moving to flight or fight." His book goes on to identify new methods of influence so we don't turn to the control response of "shape up or else."

While we are, as home educators, "response-able" for our child's education, we do not need to choose which subjects are tackled or when and how they are approached. If we want our children to grow up to be "response-able" adults—movers and shakers, inventive and imaginative, then we need to trust them. Trust them to want to learn. Trust them to know what to learn. Trust them to know how to learn. Choosing and pursuing their own course leads to self-knowledge and self-mastery—the two traits of a truly well educated man or woman.

That trust can be difficult to maintain unless our children choose a conventional course. Some children love to read, to write stories, and to pursue other recognized school subjects. Others choose a more unconventional route, but one that is validated in our society, through art, dance, music. Then there are the children who choose mudpies, Mutant Ninja Turtles and Legos for their curriculum. Parents of these youngsters might become desperate enough to believe that, "Children don't know what's good for them" and, the unspoken corollary, adults do.

My own son fell into this last category. With regularity I would privately lament to my husband, "I believe children learn best what they love most, but couldn't our son be interested in just one subject that is socially acceptable?" Fortunately before my trust dwindled completely, he started to read, but he would resist reading aloud if he believed I was checking up on his burgeoning ability. You would think that his mastery of reading would have temporarily satisfied me, but as I wrote in my journal at the time: "Why do I continue to be concerned when he is obviously reading? There are two answers to that. The first hinges on the assumptions about learning to read I gleaned from *Why Johnny Can't Read*. I was so convinced by Flesch's thesis that I have suggested an abbreviated course in phonics, but Andrew has no inclination to follow my advice in this area. My second source of disquiet comes from deep within my well-schooled soul. In spite of all the literature I have read that supports my experience, I continue to be amazed that Andrew learned to read without a teacher explaining how to do it. Andrew's learning to read and my hesitant embracing of his accomplishment reveals to me that, while I intellectually face the open door of child-initiated learning, my school-imprinted, emotive self is reluctant to cross the threshold." Fortunately this self-revelation aided me as I struggled to trust him to master other traditional educational subjects. At almost 13, he has turned to writing stories—fresh, innovative, delightful—which satisfies the emphasis of the maternal side of his family and to computer programming, which pleases Dad.

It is also difficult to trust that learning can be fun in a society that believes learning is not supposed to be fun and that all children need to experience drudgery. "Drudgery builds character." The drudgery approach might bring competence, but it will not result in self-knowledge or self-mastery. In the long run it just doesn't work. Recently in the checkout line at our local library, I felt a breeze as a man whisked past us and toward the door. "Do you have anything to check out," the librarian shouted after him. He turned, laughed derisively, and said, "Who me? Are you kidding? I haven't read a book since high school!"

Finally, it is hard to trust when the educrats reinforce the idea that there are certain ways to learn that are better than others. Unfortunately some homeschooling "experts" fall into the trap of teaching the "one and only" way of doing reading or math. Several years ago the big emphasis in homeschooling circles was math manipulatives. I bought into the arguments and purchased a program. My son, who had grasped enough math to figure out to the penny how far his allowance could be stretched at Toys R Us in the Mutant Ninja Turtle aisle, patiently put up with my experimentation for about an hour. Then he explained to me, "I don't learn like that. I hate these things. They are confusing."

I do want to clarify that by trust I do not mean abandoning a child to his own devices. Trust does not mean you step back and have no interaction. Trust means your interaction is not coercive or manipulative. Trust means respect.

Trust is not violated when you share your own passions. When my son was small, I shared with him my love for animals. For two years we purchased an annual zoo pass. We went to the zoo several times a month. He knew kudus from zebus and could answer all the questions in the docent-led workshops. When his interest ended, we exchanged the zoo passes for tickets to the Hollywood Bowl.

Trust encourages modeling valued behavior. I am not speaking of the kind of modeling that is a veneer for friendly coercion—do as I'm doing or you're in big trouble. I'm speaking of being a leader. A good leader sets the highest example. Contrast that to the school system where the teacher is paid to be a good manager. Management's purpose is to direct. It necessitates keeping the underling submissive with hall passes and classroom rules. Leaders have a passion for equality. The manager, on the other hand, views equality as counterproductive. Promotion, perks, and privilege are everything. Managers need paperwork, inflexible adherence to rules, and vigilant watch over attitudes. The leader says, "This is my vision. If you believe it, you will follow me." The manager says, "If you know what is good for you, you'll follow me and not make a lot of waves." Managers never promote individuals whose competence threatens their own position, which is why mediocrity thrives under management. Leaders act as guides, pointing out possible alternatives, encouraging development of the individual, and rejoicing in the success of others.

Trust means sharing information and skills when asked, which is usually before you deem the child ready to learn. My son begged to do the dishes when washing sharp knives and breakable containers was an exciting challenge with an uncertain result. As his ability increased, his interest in the task diminished. During these seasons, when he has grasped for abilities just beyond his reach, I have reflected on the story of the rancher whose sons did a sometimes less-than-adequate job. His neighbor queried one day, "Why don't you hire someone? Your ranch would be more successful." The rancher replied, "I'm not raising cattle; I'm raising boys."

Trust cannot exist without respect. While you might respect children, many adults dismiss the abilities and seriousness of the work of children. Respect permits advocacy. My son was recently involved in a project to promote organ and tissue donation. I was pleased and grateful to the adults who took his desires and abilities seriously. Some adults, however, were totally dismissive. At that point, my husband or I stepped in to assure them that he had adult backing. This assuaged their fears and opened up the opportunity for him to prove his worth.

Finally, trust encourages allotting free time for self-discovery. A child does not need to be busy every moment with quantifiable goals. John Taylor Gatto has pointed out that this is one of the biggest problems with schools. He says, "Don't be fooled into thinking that good curriculum or good equipment or good teachers are the critical determinants of your son's or daughter's education. All the pathologies we've considered come about in large measure because the lessons of school prevent children keeping important appointments with themselves and with their families to learn lessons in self-motivation, perseverance, self-reliance, courage, dignity, and love and lessons in service to others, too, which are among the key lessons of home and community life." (*Dumbing Us Down*, pp. 20-21) Daydreaming, volunteer service, introspection are your child's springboard to self-knowledge.

When I recently asked my son what he wanted to study next year, he chose Latin, the great European composers, algebra, and computer programming. Fickle mother that I am, I momentarily regretted he no longer wants to make me a "cherry" mudpie or launch a sneak Mutant Ninja Turtle attack while I'm doing the dishes in the kitchen. But, I trust he knows what's best.

Thinker's Apprenticeships
By Jackie Orsi

Author's Note: THINK is a national magazine for educators. It focuses on methodologies for teaching critical and creative thinking in the classroom, and includes reproducible worksheets with thinking exercises for children to do. For their February-March 1997 issue, THINK asked me to write an article telling how we homeschoolers "teach" thinking. So I did, and if I caused their readers some discomfort, I am not the least bit sorry.

It seemed like a natural for the THINK editors to beckon an article out of America's burgeoning homeschool movement for an issue devoted to "thinking in the home." Homeschooling has a small, provocative track record in the matter of thinking. I found three studies in which the thinking processes of homeschooled students came under the lens of academic research.

A study by de Oliveria, Watson, and Sutton in 1994 [*Differences in Critical Thinking among Students Educated in Public Schools, Christian Schools, and Home Schools*, Home School Researcher, 10:4] found homeschoolers performing well in the critical thinking dimension, while Williams [*The Relationship of Family characteristics and Instructional Approach to Creativity in Home School Children*, Home School Researcher, 1990, 6:3] located even more admirable results in creative thinking.

The most arresting findings came from a 1988 study [Home School Researcher 4:3], which revealed the *Reasoning Abilities of Home-Educated Children*. Quine and Marek investigated the intellectual development of a group of homeschool children using the Piagetian model. They measured the pace at which the children proceeded from preoperational thought to concrete thought to formal thought. They concluded that "The data from this study seem to suggest that students taught at home move into formal thought between the ages of 10 and 11, whereas the 'national average' is between 15 and 20 years."

All these results nestle compatibly next to the far larger body of research that shows homeschooled kids outperforming institutionally schooled kids on all manner of achievement tests. We see that, on the whole, homeschool kids learn well, and now we have some data that say they think well, too.

Quine and Marek also showed, at least in part, how homeschoolers are developing such extraordinary thinking skills. Curiously, all their findings with respect to homeschoolers were serendipitous. Their objective at the outset was to chart the intellectual strides of the students of Pathways School in Texas as they completed a tightly formulated Piagetian learning cycle designed to accelerate them into the stage of formal thought. The homeschool sample in the study was meant to be a control group against which the Pathways progress would be compared. To Quine's and Marek's utter surprise, the two groups of children kept pace with each other, and both made the leap to formal thought at the young ages of 10 and 11. They had to ask, "What gives here?"

They found, "Although the research design was sound and appropriate, we discovered that the students in the two groups were experiencing similar treatments. The students in the experimental group [Pathways] received instruction utilizing pre-written activities which promoted intellectual development and the students in the comparison group [homeschoolers] had the same kind of experiences even though the activities were not pre-written learning cycles." The homeschooling parents, it seems, unconsciously designed a Piagetian program for their children as they "1) redesigned traditional curriculum, 2) provided extensive field trip-type learning experiences, and/or 3) allowed their children to explore their environment during extended free time."

Thinking is Not a Homeschool "Subject"

My daughters have learned at home for seven years now, and during that time I've been very active in the homeschool sub-universe as a writer, researcher, and consultant. I know homeschooling well from the literature of the movement, from the talk, formal and informal, that takes place at conferences and support group meetings and afternoons in the park, and which products are hot on the homeschool market and which ones are not. I know for a fact that basic educational skills—reading, math, writing, science, and history—are diligently taught by virtually all homeschooling parents, though they go about it with a fabulously diverse array of methods and philosophies. What I can also say with equal conviction is that hardly any homeschool parents teach thinking, per se.

If Quine and Marek had come to me, I could have told them they had the wrong kids entirely for their control group. I would have also boldly asserted that if children are given freedom to go looking for meaning in their lives, they do not need formal instruction in thinking.

I realize that this may be a heretical statement to make in a magazine that serves the teaching of thinking, but I do believe that it is correct. Certainly neither Ben Franklin, Thomas Jefferson, Agatha Christie, Winston Churchill, Margaret Mead, Abraham Lincoln nor Thomas Edison had any classes in how to think, but somewhere in their growing up, each must have enjoyed the kind of conditions that permit and promote the development of sound thinking skills. Learning to think was integrated into their experience of life.

So it is with thousands of homeschooled youngsters today who learn to think throughout the day in the course of living and growing. A homeschool offers an ideal apprenticeship for becoming a skilled thinker.

By failing to teach thinking purposefully and systematically, homeschoolers run the risk that their children's learning will be haphazard, but whatever learning does occur will be genuine and practical. As John Holt, the intellectual parent of modern homeschooling, wrote, "When we try to teach a child a disembodied skill, we say in effect, 'You must learn to do this thing in here so that later on you can go and do something quite different out there.' This destroys the continuum of experience within which true learning can only take place."

Terms of the Apprenticeship

The three conditions named by Quine and Marek that distinguished the learning environments of homeschools are duplicated in nearly every home I know of, and I can name several more conditions that allow a child to learn to think.

Yes, homeschool parents "redesign traditional curriculum." Rank beginners typically clutch formulaic teaching materials for the first few months, but when they begin to see how homeschooling really works, they do indeed tend to improvise, usually arriving at highly individualized instruction. The guiding star of homeschool pedagogy is, "Is she or he learning?" Any method or textbook, which isn't bringing about good results is abandoned for something that will.

Yes, homeschoolers go on lots of field trips. In fact, the name homeschooling is a misnomer. The homeschoolers I know don't stay home much. There are concerts, museums, volunteer work, community groups, classes, tours, jobs, and all kinds of things happening. The world is our classroom.

And yes, yes, yes, homeschooled kids have lots of time, glorious time—and this, more than any other condition allows a kid to learn how to think. Homeschools are highly efficient, you see. The book and paper work of traditional schooling rarely consumes more than two or three hours a day, and even when music lessons, sports, scouts or other structured activities are scheduled in, I would estimate that the average homeschooler gets about five hours a day more free time than the child whose day is consumed by prepping for, transporting to and from, and enduring school, with hours of homework thereafter.

When I say free time here, I'm talking about time being free. In their natural state, kids are perfect learning engines, and learning to think inevitably becomes a part of what they do. You can always tell when a child has made the adjustment to homeschooling because she stops turning up at her mother's elbow to whine, "I'm bored." The evolved homeschooler has come face to face with boredom, wrestled it to the ground, and risen victorious. My daughters haven't been bored in years, and they don't expect anyone or anything, including TV, to entertain them.

All Kinds of Time with Nothing to Do (Ha!)

Of course, their five hour daily bonus of free time allows them to leap into some wild and hairy inquiries. Within reason and within our budget, I just stand aside and see what comes. Janelle, who is now 17, has over the last six years plunged head first into mineralogy, astronomy, photography, nanotechnology, stock market investing, archaeology (which led her to join a Mayan dig in Belize), composing and arranging music on computer, web programming, and ethnomusicology. She digs out her own resources, informs herself, conducts her own experiments, deals with their outcomes, and moves on to greater levels of mastery. Janelle is in perpetual motion.

On the other hand, sometimes children who are stretching their brains fail to show visible signs of…well…life! My daughter Caroline has perfected the art of dreaming. When she is deep into her spell, I am tempted to hold a mirror to her nose to see if she's breathing, but I trust that some vital brain work is in progress, so I leave her undisturbed. She comes by her dreaminess genetically from me, but I went to school, so I had to hone my dreaming skills on the fly and on the sly. I'm glad she can take large chunks of time for those all-important conversations that are happening in her head.

I'm glad, too, that my daughters have long periods of time to converse with other thinkers through the medium of reading. They can and do spend hours absorbing the themes of literature, the compelling ideas of history, and modes of reasoning that become the raw material of good thinking. If my kids want to spend all day with their heads in books, that's fine with me. No bell is going to ring around here. Lucky them; John Goodlad's 1984 study (*A Place Called School*) of how time is spent in the nation's schools found only 1.9% of a student's day in high school devoted to reading.

Just Goofin' Around

Give a child time and freedom, and they'll go off and invent all kinds of thinking exercises for themselves. Any thinking they do on their own in order to satisfy their own curiosity far surpasses what we can elicit with workbooks and gimmicks. Their self-imposed assignments are at once more creative, more ambitious, more sophisticated, and often more consuming than anything we would demand of them. Our five-year-old homeschooled friend David put two kiddie chairs back to back and suspended a model of the Golden Gate Bridge made from string, straws, paper and tape, conceived and executed entirely on his own. Who would ever imagine that as part of the kindergarten curriculum? David, obviously. I taught my daughter Janelle about binary number systems one day when she was eleven, ended the lesson, and I went about my housework. She spontaneously went to work developing a base-six number system, which she presented to me with great elaboration hours later. Had I assigned her the task, I promise you there would have been groaning, resentment, and a half-baked result not worth her time or mine. Homeschoolers have a word for the kinds of spontaneous, creative, inspired, mind-stretching tasks David and Janelle performed; we call it "play."

For love or money, whichever, play can turn to serious study, problem solving, and hard work when something real and desired is at stake. When our homeschooled friend Bert was 11 he set himself to learn Latin sufficient to understand the nomenclature of taxonomy. How else could he move forward with his passionate love of ornithology and communicate clearly about the species he was identifying? At age 15, Bert was awarded an internship normally given to graduate students at the Big Sur Ornithological Lab, and serves as a Field Naturalist on pelagic boat trips out of Monterey Bay.

Rachel, who loves to work with her hands, tried her first home business making scarves at age nine, but found she couldn't add enough value to charge adequately for her time. For the next two years, she prospered somewhat more making clothespin angel Christmas ornaments, but still wasn't getting the return she hoped for when she factored in her time and materials. Now at 13, she's making a killing in the English Toffee market. Genuine motivations lead to genuine thinking lessons.

Taught in the Act

Homeschool parents don't teach thinking on purpose, but they do it all day long in the context of their children's questions and interests. When Caroline was 12, she found a recipe exchange on the Internet. She announced her intention to cook a meal including sauerbraten meatballs, noodles, spinach au gratin, muffins, and apple-lemon tort—an ambitious meal even for an experienced cook. She had to take stock of supplies on hand, assess quantities, and develop a shopping list; she had to analyze the steps of preparation and break them down into a plan which would get all the food to the table, cooked and on time. Sure, I hung around near the kitchen, made a few pointed suggestions, and gave consultation about whether the muffins were done, but the evening and the glory were all hers.

Homeschool parents also teach thinking by demonstration, by simply living. We've read maps because we wanted to go places, we've learned how to fix a piano because it was busted, we've rolled up our sleeves to advance our causes and spread our charity, and we've spoken of spiritual matters in times of loss and joy. My daughters have had a front-row seat on my sometimes messy life for seven years now. Everything I do as household manager, writer, volunteer, employee, coworker, citizen, neighbor, sister, daughter, wife, and friend—all have been open to their view. It is rarely necessary to speak in hypothetical terms, because real life offers enough didactic opportunities by itself. We link our beliefs and values to our decisions, and our decisions to their consequences, and sometimes reassess our beliefs and values in light of consequences. We are directional, we hope, each of us moving toward completion, maturity, and the development of better selves. In this way, I believe my daughters have learned not merely to think critically, but to think morally.

Not the least of all the lessons my husband and I have taught comes from our very choice to homeschool. What more powerful way to convey to our daughters how much we care about them and how highly we value education? What more obvious way is there to teach that an individual must do what she believes is right, regardless of what other people think? And since we have persisted in the face of some legal harassment by school authorities, what more compelling way to demonstrate that our convictions sometimes require courage? In homeschooling, the medium is a message. Maybe *the* message.

No "Honor Students" Here, Only Honored Children

Finally, homeschooled kids get all of the above opportunities in the shelter of people who love them, protect them, and who would never let them truly fail. As Maslow told us, give physical health and safety, emotional security, unconditional acceptance, and respect for accomplishments, and an individual will reach very far.

A homeschool comes as close to a natural apprenticeship for thinking as one could hope to devise. The children supply the spark, and parents must simply create the conditions in which the spark may kindle and glow. If my children and their homeschooling friends do not convince you, then perhaps the examples of Franklin, Jefferson, Christie, Churchill, Mead, Lincoln, and Edison will. Each of them was homeschooled, you see.

7

Where Do I Begin?

"There is no one right way,

or one required book for educating."

©Cheryl Maxwell

Approaches to Home Education
By Cafi Cohen

If I were to interview one hundred homeschooling families, I would hear one hundred different versions of learning at home. Home education is idiosyncratic—as individualized as education can get. It varies according to family and community resources, parents' educational philosophies, and interests and goals of the children. In practice, homeschooling approaches seem to fall into one of four categories:

- Traditional education, also called school-at-home
- Unit-study approach
- Interest-initiated learning, also called unschooling
- Eclectic education

School At Home

The traditional approach, also called school-at-home, is just what it sounds like. It is structured, with lesson plans, textbooks, quizzes and tests, subject-specific projects, and grades. Usually the core program includes four subjects—language arts (English), science, math, and social studies (history and geography). In most cases, children study every subject every day. Electives (optional courses) may be added, such as music, art, religious studies, physical education, and foreign language.

Students following a traditional approach also participate in extracurricular activities. Examples are 4-H, sports, music lessons, church youth groups, and volunteer work. While parents using traditional materials consider these activities vital, these families have decided to emphasize textbook learning. "Yes, you can go to your martial arts class if you have completed your math."

Educational philosophy behind the traditional approach is, I-teach-you-learn. You, the parents, decide what is best for your sons and daughters, and they complete the assigned material.

The principal advantage of the traditional approach is that parents know the drill. Most likely you attended school and were taught this way. Students work out of textbooks, reading, doing problems, and answering questions. At regular intervals, they take tests, write papers, and do related projects. Parents or independent-study schools evaluate the work, usually grading the work. Many beginning homeschooling moms and dads find comfort in the familiar sequence: read and write, test, grade.

Some parents use a school-at-home approach because they like knowing that, in their words, "We have covered all the bases. Our children are learning what they are supposed to be learning." In addition, some families say their traditional methods work well for children who like school-type structure. Students motivated by grades, probably 10% or less, enjoy school-at-home. At the high school level, teenagers may teach themselves using traditional-approach resources, that is, textbooks and study guides. This relieves parents of the necessity of re-learning geometry or biology—unless they want to.

Why doesn't everyone use a school-at-home approach? Consider the drawbacks. First, school-at-home can be the most expensive way to homeschool. Costs for textbooks alone may exceed several hundred dollars per year.

Second, as schools prove on a daily basis, text-based learning can make watching paint dry look interesting. Boredom creates burnout. Often, I meet parents who feel overwhelmed by homeschooling. They complain about too many bookwork hours each day and say, "I have to push my children to do everything." On questioning these parents closely, I almost always learn that they use an exclusively traditional approach.

Avoid traditional instructional materials if you have a school-phobic child who sends the message, "If it looks like school, I can't do it!" These children do poorly with school-at-home because, to them, textbooks, work sheets, tests, and grades spell failure. They learn better with hands-on, real-world experiences.

Finally, the traditional approach can lead to over-dependence on teachers and programmed instructional materials. Students learn how to play the game, but they never learn how to learn or how to take advantage of community resources. Additionally, families may spend so much time covering the material that their children have no time to develop talents and to pursue interests.

Unit Studies

A second approach to home education, using unit studies, is popular with home-schooling families. To do a unit study, children investigate a topic in depth. The topic may be academic or non-academic. Examples are: Astronomy, Japan,

Classic Film, Nutrition, and Horses. In exploring the topic, the student eventually covers most school subjects (math, science, social studies, language arts).

As an example, let's say your son or daughter finds birds fascinating. You might plan the following learning activities:

- Read and write about birds, famous ornithologists (language arts, science)
- Diagram and outline life cycles, habitats, ecology of birds (science, math)
- Reconstruct a chicken skeleton (science)
- Study the aerodynamics of flight (math, science)
- Diagram the migration pathways of birds (geography)
- Go on a field trip with the local Audubon Society, and subscribe to their magazine (science)
- Sketch birds (art)
- Cook birds (home economics), and so on.

The unit study approach is more open-ended than school-at-home. Children work on units for a day or a week or a year. Unit studies prompt more interaction with the real world and involve hands-on projects more often than school-at-home. Generally, instead of textbooks, children pursuing unit studies will use a variety of sources: libraries, magazines, newspapers, people, computers, and so on.

From the standpoint of educational philosophy, children doing unit studies work from real world specifics to general concepts. They learn the Pythagorean theorem from squaring up a building project. They study biology in the context of caring for horses. The word "discovery" applies here. Instead of being told what to learn, unit studies encourage teenagers to draw their own conclusions.

Like school-at-homers, families using a unit study approach may involve their children in a wide range of outside activities. Some of those activities can be a part of the current unit study. As an example, volunteering in a veterinary clinic might be a portion of a zoology unit.

Many home educators believe that unit studies encourage curiosity and independent thinking more than traditional materials. Children often find unit studies more involving and entertaining than a steady diet of texts and tests, leading to greater retention, not only of facts and figures, but also of the deeper significance of those facts and figures.

Unit studies often motivate children to go beyond the planned unit. In the process, your child may become an independent learner. This clearly provides an advantage for a high school student wishing to pursue a topic in which the parents have no expertise or interest.

Unit studies are not for everyone. They do not work well in families where parents have no patience with the discovery approach to education. It is harder to know if children are learning, in the words of some homeschooling parents, "what they should." Unit studies can require the frequent use of outside resources, like the library, and may not be a good choice for those with limited time or transportation.

Unschooling or Interest-Initiated Learning

Unschooling or interest-initiated learning is a third approach to homeschooling. In contrast to children in families using traditional and unit study approaches, children in unschooling environments select and direct their own projects and activities. Unschooling parents facilitate more than they teach, helping their children learn about the world around them rather than subjects listed on a suggested course of study.

Your unschooler may spend weeks or months with computers or art projects or even auto repair. Conscientious unschooling parents help when asked—supporting their children by planning collaboratively, assisting with expenses, and networking for resources. Most unschooling families only buy curricula if they and their children determine that using traditional materials will help them achieve their goals.

Unschoolers often participate in community activities. They volunteer at the library, spend time with local drama groups, work at hospitals, and stuff envelopes for political campaigns. Many hold paying positions in various settings.

In unschooling families, student-selected activities and real life comprise the core of the curriculum. Running a small business is consumer math and bookkeeping and language arts. Gardening is science. Reading the newspaper is social studies. Planning and preparing dinner is home economics. Parents sometimes help translate interest-initiated learning into educationese, the language of school course descriptions, when needed. Often unschoolers describe the curriculum after, not before, the curriculum has been completed.

Clearly, the educational philosophy behind unschooling differs from the traditional and unit-study approaches. "Students learn best when their interests direct the learning," probably sums it up best.

Advantages of unschooling are many. With community activities and everyday life at the core, interest-initiated learning can be inexpensive. Unschooling is flexible and hands-on, a boon for school-phobic students. Most importantly, because unschoolers assume responsibility for their education, they, the students, often become self-directed learners. Interest-initiated learning works well for children with a deep abiding interest or hobby as well as for students with clearly delineated goals.

You have probably already thought of the primary drawback of unschooling—it does not look like school. This makes parents nervous, relatives nervous, and neighbors nervous. To get the most from unschooling, most parents have to restructure their thinking by reading a great deal about interest-initiated learning to overcome their previous conditioning. For those without previous homeschooling experience, this can be a tall order.

Other drawbacks? Some say that unschooling results in educational gaps, holes in a student's knowledge. Children who spend hours each day programming computers, for example, may not find time to read Shakespeare. There is a trade-off. Unschooling families have decided, up front, that self-direction is more important than imparting a broad, arbitrarily selected spectrum of knowledge.

So, interest-initiated learning does not look like school, and it may contain holes. Yet many unschoolers have become computer wizards, successful business operators, published writers, inventors, and so on. This makes them very attractive to selective colleges, and many unschoolers have excelled there.

The Eclectic Approach

A fourth method of homeschooling, the eclectic approach, combines traditional materials, unit studies, unschooling time, and anything else that works.

The eclectic approach emphasizes flexibility to tailor educational experiences to the student, without an overlay of educational philosophy. Parents respond to changing student needs in an ad-hoc fashion. Students, especially teens, are given a lot of freedom. Without the philosophical constraints of unschooling, parents also feel free to impose subjects they deem essential.

143

With the eclectic approach, a balance exists between the traditional and the innovative, a balance with which most parents and children are comfortable. Students not only learn how to learn—due mostly to the unschooling component of this approach—they also learn how to handle traditional materials and in-depth projects or unit studies. Together with their parents, students discover how to locate and evaluate educational resources in the community.

Our son and daughter enrolled in a diploma-granting, independent-study program. Still we considered ourselves eclectic home educators. Why? Both Jeff and Tamara, in completing 16 units with American School, worked with traditional materials one to two hours daily. They devoted most of each day to activities they planned: flying practice, reading, art, music, hiking, volunteer work, and other pursuits.

The primary disadvantage of the eclectic approach is that parents may lack the confidence to work cooperatively with their teenagers to put together such a program. Additionally, the constant communication between parent and student and the resulting readjustment of studies and activities makes some families uncomfortable.

Which Approach?

Traditional-approach home educators say that children learn best with texts, schedules, and grades. Unit study aficionados say that children learn best with thematic projects. Unschoolers say that children learn best when their interests direct the learning. Eclectic home educators say that there is no one way that all children learn best all the time.

All these methods are effective. In practice, most homeschooling families do not fit exactly into one of four neat categories. Linda Dobson, in *Homeschooling: The Early Years*, points instead to a continuum of homeschooling practice, from structured and traditional to unstructured and child-led. In addition, families often switch gears. As needed, they adopt different approaches to get the job done.

Why specify four approaches then? These categories can help you articulate what you do and why you do it. An overview of the four categories also begins to illustrate the wide range of successful homeschooling practice for those new to the idea of home education.

In deciding among overall approaches and in selecting materials, you will make mistakes. As my father is fond of saying, "The only people who don't make mistakes are those who don't do anything." Remember, compared to government schools, you have an edge. When you detect a mistake, you can fix it immediately. You do not have to wait for a new teacher or until the end of the school year.

In deciding how to homeschool, you have expertise right in front of your nose. Ask your child what he thinks about various options and programs and resources. You may have to ask more than once, but I guarantee that eventually most children will tell you.

Proceed with what best fits your situation. How can you decide what fits? Try the following checklist:

- Know and understand your options
- Educate yourself about resources
- Discuss student's goals and priorities
- List parents' goals and priorities
- Think of your own formal and informal educational experiences; describe what you believe about how people learn best (This is the exercise of determining your educational philosophy)
- Rely on your sense of what "feels right" for your family

Then go for it. And if you need to change course, you can. One reason homeschooling works so well for so many children is that parents are free to experiment to find out what works best, not in theory, but in practice.

Choosing a Course of Study
By Karen Rafferty

Many parents are excited by the creative possibilities of teaching their children at home, but puzzled about just what to teach, and when. Veteran homeschoolers also struggle with these issues at various times. Since homeschooling is a process involving growing children, the answers must be discovered over and over again.

What am I Required to Teach?

The first concern is "What am I required to teach?" A quick scan of the statutory requirements (see Education Code §51210 and §51220 in the appendix) reassures that the private school option selected by homeschooling parents when they file the R-4 offers a relatively free hand in choosing materials, methods, and pacing of instruction. There is no one right way, or one required book for educating. Note, moreover, that although there are state-mandated courses in grades 7 – 12, the law stipulates that they shall be "offered" by the school, but not necessarily chosen by the student. The "what, how, and when" is going to be up to you and your child if you have established a private school (see Chapter 3). Enjoy this freedom to customize your child's education! Parents who homeschool through a public school usually have more limitations, and they may be given a predetermined course of study, or they may be asked to select a curriculum that meets district approval.

Three Steps to Identifying a Workable Curriculum

Choosing a curriculum is one of the most intimidating tasks for new homeschoolers. They have many questions. Should they choose a packaged curriculum or tailor-make one from a variety of resources? Should a curriculum be activity oriented? Is a cross-curricular approach better? What can they do with a child who is great at math and poor in English? What inexpensive resources are available that fit a limited budget? What exactly is unschooling and who was Charlotte Mason?

The vocabulary of curriculum and the array of resources can be overwhelming. Added to the monumental task of filtering resources, is the anxiety that if we don't choose the perfect curriculum, our children are going to suffer the rest of their lives. If you've just pulled your child out of school, there is also the nagging thought that you must decide rapidly so that the family can get on with the business of learning.

The curriculum monster can be tamed. There are only three steps to identifying a curriculum or a homemade course of study that will work for your family. There are resources to help you decide what to teach when. There are curriculum reviews. And finally, there are experienced homeschoolers willing to share the wisdom derived from their successes and failures.

Start by discovering your educational philosophy, then learn about homeschooling approaches (curriculum), and finally match it all up with your child's learning style.

1. *Educational Philosophy*

Having an Educational Philosophy is the first step toward being a wise shopper in the market of ideas. What are *your* expectations? Author David Guterson wrote, "If you are going to keep your children out of school you had better decide what an education *means* because no one is going to do it for you." Indeed, it's hard to make choices about what, when and how your child should learn if you do not have a vision of what the learning is for.

One way to come up with philosophy is to write your own educational history. How did your learning take place? What elements of education were the most helpful to you: factual knowledge, concept building, thinking skills, value identification or a combination? How important are academic results or meeting standardized test requirements? What has been the main purpose of education in your life? What did you like and dislike about your own educational process? This exercise will help you define what educational success means to you and how learning has taken place in your life.

Time spent in contemplation to discover your educational philosophy is a sound investment. Without it you will be forever questioning other people's ideas about what your child should learn, how they should learn it and when they should learn it.

2. *Homeschooling Approaches*

Once you've defined your idea of educational success, it will be easier for you to choose among the many strategies or approaches. Be aware there is an overlap in homeschooling approaches. For instance, you can combine Charlotte Mason's ideas of living books with a unit study approach. Also remember that homeschoolers sometimes start out with one approach and then shift to another. Your educational philosophy might indicate that young children learn better from an unstructured, hands-on curriculum or through unit studies that integrate subjects for good understanding. At the same time you might believe that teens benefit from a more traditional approach to prepare them for college. One of the benefits of homeschooling is being able to switch approaches as your children's ages, interests, and goals change.

3. *Learning Styles*

Before you can actually choose a homeschooling approach, it is best to discover a bit about your child's learning styles. David Guterson wrote in *Family Matters: Why Homeschooling Makes Sense*, "The finest possible curriculum is precisely the one that starts with each child's singular means of learning. Instruction and guidance are best provided by those with an intimate understanding of the individual child and a deep commitment to the child's education." A terrific benefit of homeschooling is that your curriculum can be tailor-made to your child's learning styles.

The Way They Learn by Cynthia Tobias is an excellent overview of various models of defining learning styles. Her book is a composite of the five most useable theories of learning styles. It is written so that parents can begin to identify and maximize the learning strengths of both their children and themselves. The volume has several exercises that are fun for the whole family. Her book also has an interesting section on learning environments. She has published a companion volume entitled *Every Child Can Succeed: Making the Most of Your Child's Learning Style,* which shows parents how to utilize a learning styles approach to help their kids live up to their potential. Other highly regarded books on learning are listed in the reading list in Chapter 15, and include authors Thomas Armstrong, Dawna Markova and Sharon Hensley.

The bottom line of all these books is that every child is capable of learning and has potential. All of us have different strengths and weaknesses; it makes sense to capitalize on our strengths.

What Do I Teach and When?

After identifying your educational philosophy, you may not even be worried about what to teach when. Many parents, believing that education is a lifelong pursuit, are not concerned with covering specific topics in their homeschool, or following the public school plan closely. Other parents are more comfortable when their homeschool has a detailed course of study. Outlines of what to teach and when come by various names: scope and sequence, grade-level expectancies and typical course of study. Many publishers put out a scope and sequence for the curriculum they are selling. Each school district in California has published grade-level expectancies. Many homeschool catalogs offer scope and sequence books. The *What Your __Grader Needs to Know* is a series for K to 6th grades, by E.D. Hirsch. World Book offers a publication, *Typical Course of Study*. This pamphlet lists, by grade, the typical subjects covered by students in classrooms across the nation. Call toll-free 1-800-WORLDBK or visit their website: *www.worldbook.com/ptrc/html/curr.htm/*.

Curriculum Reviews

As you review curricula, you might ask yourself the following questions:

- Is it flexible or does it have strict lesson plans?
- Are parental demands high or is preparation minimum?
- Is it activity oriented or will there be a lot of seatwork?
- Does it address many different learning styles or a single intelligence?
- Does it help develop reasoning or is it based on rote memorization?
- Is it fun or does it tend to be dry and in need of enrichment?
- Does it have a cross-curricular approach or is each subject taught separately?
- Is it fluid, catering to multi-level abilities, or is it graded?
- Does it emphasize literature and living books or does it use text-books or readers?
- Is it inexpensive or very costly?
- As you ask yourself these questions, remember that your definition of educational success and your child's individual learning style will dictate the characteristics of the curriculum you choose.

Some homeschoolers want to see and touch before purchasing. Some publishers provide sample lessons on the Internet or by mail. A support group family already using the curriculum may bring it to park day for viewing. Curriculum fairs and vendor halls at conferences also give you the opportunity to personally evaluate resources. If you are willing to rely on reviews, there are books and magazines that evaluate curriculum. Or you can ask for opinions on an e-mail list such as CHN's state list (*http://groups.yahoo.com/group/CaliforniaHS*).

Non-Traditional Curriculum

Rather than follow a school-at-home approach, some homeschoolers do things differently, looking for unusual, interesting ways to teach. Perhaps a better description is that they provide the setting or resource that allows the child to learn. What do potatoes, goo, games and dirt have in common? They are just a few examples of the many successful alternatives to sitting at a desk and learning in a traditional style.

The Spud Curriculum
By Karen Rafferty

Over our years of homeschooling, some of our most enjoyable interludes have been prompted by mundane events. Our spud curriculum started at the dinner table while piling various toppings on Idaho bakers. Where did potatoes come from? What exactly was the Potato Famine? Are they good for us to eat? I even reminisced about the potato prints I'd made in elementary school. Over the next weeks we researched the answers to our questions and found even more avenues to pursue.

Where did potatoes come from? The "Irish" white potato was born in the Andes and was a staple in the diet of the Aymara Indians. The Aymaras developed a method of freeze drying the potatoes for long-term storage. During the frosty Andean nights, they spread their potato harvest on the ground and during the day protected it from the sun by covering it with straw. After several nights of frigid temperatures, the potatoes were ready for the next step of processing. The women and children of the village would trample on the potatoes to squeeze out the moisture and scrape off the peel. Then the potatoes were put in a stream for a few weeks to wash out the bitter taste and, undoubtedly, excess toe jam. Finally they were dried in the sun for a couple of weeks. The processed potatoes were preserved for up to 4 years.

Potatoes were a significant part of the Ayamaras' culture. They had a potato god. Potatoes were used to divine truth. Potatoes were used to predict weather. The Ayamaras even measured time by equating it to how long it took to cook a potato to various consistencies. Can't you just hear the dad of the family saying, "I want that field cultivated to mashed potato quality in half-baked time?" They also had the precursor to Mr. Potato Head. Much of their pottery is potato-shaped. To the lifelike potato eyes, some potters added tiny heads.

So how did the spud end up in Ireland in time for the potato famine? Early Spanish conquistadors might have failed in their efforts to find Au (gold, for those of you who've forgotten or never took chemistry), but they found sunshine neatly packaged in the potato which saved many a Spanish sailor from the plague of scurvy.

When potatoes arrived in Europe, they faced a public relations problem. The plant was recognized as a relative of the nightshade family which is poisonous. But the spud had a powerful ally. Frederick the Great of Prussia told his people he'd cut off their noses and ears if they did not plant potatoes. Sounds a bit excessive, but he hoped that the potato, a dependable crop, would stave off recurring bouts of famine. His threats were quite effective and less than 100 years later the spud had a place of honor in the Prussian diet. Fortunately for future potato connoisseurs, Augustin Parentier, a French agriculturist and chemist, was introduced to the potato while a prisoner of war in Prussia. He marketed the spud to King Louis XVI and Marie Antoinette. While King Louis and Marie lost their heads, Mr. Potato Head survived. Voila—potatoes au gratin, pommes frites (French fries), and lots of other yummy potato dishes were developed.

In the meantime Sir Francis Drake was out confiscating property from Spanish galleons and procured some well-traveled spuds. He generously passed them on to Sir Walter Raleigh. Raleigh wasted no time in planting the new crop on his estates in Ireland and, later on, in Virginia. I'm not sure whether it was a visa problem or not, but the roving spud didn't successfully transplant to North America until the early 1700s. Irish immigrants smuggled them into New Hampshire and eventually they became the second largest crop in North America. Idaho became the home of the Russet. Washington State became known as "Potato Country U.S.A." Wisconsin, known widely for its cheese, is also a great potato producer. I'm guessing it was some innovative Wisconsin farmer's wife that first mated the potato with a cheddar cheese topping.

Meanwhile back in Ireland, the weather turned nasty. Rain poured out of the skies and spurred the growth of Phytophthora infestans, a fungus that rotted the potato crop while it was still in the ground. Over a million Irish citizens died and almost 2 million emigrated, many to the United States, institutionalizing the Irish cop, Irish whiskey, St. Patrick's Day, and generations of drunk or dumb Irish jokes.

Are they good for us to eat? In the 1950s the diet industry gave Mr. Potato Head a black eye by claiming he was fattening. Nutritionists came to the rescue and restored his reputation by explaining that the potato, when not smothered in cheese, sour cream and other delectables, is nutritious and low fat.

Potato prints? Sure! You can make your own gift wrap for an occasion. All you need is a roll of plain white shelf paper, potatoes, and different color ink pads. Cut a potato in half, and then carve out the design(s) you want. The design should be the raised portion of the cutout. Then you stamp the potato on ink pad and then paper. Even those of us who are not particularly artistic can be successful with this one. Imagine how attractive something simple like alternating colors of triangles, squares and circles can look.

There's even more I can learn about potatoes? Absolutely.

Language Arts: I'd start with one of the following books depending on the ages of your kids. Kirkus gave a rave review to Kate Lied's book, *Potato: A Tale from the Great Depression*, for ages 5-8. It relates how a depression family picked potatoes in Idaho for two weeks and how this experience enabled them to survive. A witty history for older kids would be Larry Zuckerman's *The Potato: How the Humble Spud Rescued the Western World*.

If you are really curious, you could search out the origin of phrases like "hot potato" and "couch potato."

Science: If you are more science-oriented, try *Potato* by Barrie Watts (from the Stopwatch Series) which explains for kids 4-8 how potatoes grow. How about growing your own potatoes?

There are science experiments using potatoes. Learn about osmosis using the spud. Fill two dishes with water. Slice a potato lengthwise into several pieces so that each piece has two flat sides. Add about two tablespoons of salt to one of the dishes. Put half of the pieces into the plain water and the other half into the salty water. Wait 20 minutes. What happens and why? Well, through osmosis the water moves from the areas of low salt concentration to areas of high salt concentration. Adding salt to the water creates a higher salt concentration in the dish than in the potato, so, water in a potato that is soaking in salt water migrates out, leaving behind a mushy potato.

A bit more complicated is building a food battery. For directions see *The Mad ScientistNetwork* at *www.madsci.org/experiments/archive/889917606.Ch.html/*.

Cooking: Recipes to enhance skills in this domestic art can be found in any cookbook. For those dedicated to the culinary arts, refer to the potato recipe collection at *www.cs.cmu.edu/~mjw/recipes/vegetables/potato/pot-coll.html/*.

You can learn history, geography, nutrition/cooking, politics, advertising, economics, science, art and more—all from the spud. We even covered family history spurred by the surname Rafferty on my husband's line and McGarey on my maternal grandmother's. We ended with a mini-unit on party planning by organizing a spud and topping party for our homeschool support group. What a yummy way to maintain our energy while we were digesting all the food for thought provided by our research.

Don't like potatoes? Well, try out "The Food Timeline" web page at *www.gti.net/mocolib1/kid/food.html/* and pursue your own gastronomic favorite—bread, popcorn, rhubarb, peanuts and many more are featured.

The Cell, or How to Make a Dry Subject Gooey
By Terri Williams

I like to start my study of the cell with an egg toss. One thing you will learn from this is how well a cell flies, or how it feels when it lands. An egg yolk is one cell. In fact, the largest single cell is an ostrich egg yolk. A bit expensive to throw around, but you get the point. So for starters invite the family over for a cell picnic. Include an egg toss, an egg and spoon race, egg juggling, push-the-egg-with-your-nose race and my all time favorite—egg toss volleyball, where you toss the egg to the team on the other side of the net and score when it breaks on them. Sorry, spiking is forbidden in this version. You have just covered Physical Education for this unit. You can also include a picnic lunch centered around the egg theme—egg salad sandwiches, deviled eggs etc., but make sure to tell your children that virtually everything they eat is made of cells. Everything that was or is alive is made of cells. And not just cells, but stacks of one cell atop another, like Lego blocks. In fact, ask your children to name what they are eating that isn't made of cells. Hmmm, the salt?

The history of the cell is closely tied with the history of the microscope. In 1665 an Englishman, Robert Hooke, was looking through his microscope at cork and was the first to notice the rectangular building block structure. He named these blocks after the rooms or "cells" in a monastery. My sympathy to all monks subjected to these living conditions. What he was actually seeing were just the cell walls that once surrounded the living cells. Several microscope revisions and about 200 years later scientists discovered that these cells were the basic building blocks of life and by the end of the 19th century they proposed the cell theory which states that 1) All living things are made of cells and 2) Cells can only come from other living cells. This being true, Jurassic Park scientists will never be able to repopulate the planet with dinosaurs or we will have to rewrite the second part of the cell theory to state that cells must come from other cells, dead or alive.

So, is the cell just a bag of goo to toss at Aunt Minnie? Actually, a cell is like a small community or business, so full of parts, called organelles, that it can function on its own. It has 1) a security system, *the cell membrane*, to keep out danger 2) a cafeteria, *the mitochondria*, to process food 3) trash men, *the Golgi body*, to transfer waste to the outside 4) a boss, *the nucleus*, that gives orders and runs the show 5) a planning commission, *the chromosomes*, in charge of reproduction and growth as well as 6) storage areas for food, water and waste, *the vacuoles*. They also have a nucleolus, nuclear membrane, ribosomes, endoplasmic reticulum and lysosomes, which may be included depending on the maturity of your kids. In the case of plant cells, they also have a cell wall to connect one cell to another and chloroplasts to make food from the sun. I tell my children the functions of the cell in plain terms like this. Next, we discuss these jobs in terms of their dad's business or our kitchen or whatever they happen to be fascinated with that week, such as the fire station. I then have them do a collage on a paper plate. Using pictures from magazines they cut out anything that does the same job as that organelle, and paste it onto the plate where it would be in the cell and then label it with the organelle name. For instance, the "security system" would be on the outer edge of the plate and labeled "cell membrane." You can also do the same thing using different occupations, for instance, border patrol might be the cell membrane and Mom might be the nucleus (in my dreams). Actually I'm more of a chromosome type, I guess. I'm the one in charge of reproduction and family growth. This distinction has more to do with bringing home stray dogs, cats, etc., than what you are probably thinking.

Now I have to make my plug for a microscope. I love mine and I haven't met a child yet who doesn't share this love. Yes, I know they are expensive ($100 - $300 for a decent working model) but I bet your children will get a lot of use and enjoyment out of one. The easiest cells to see under the microscope are onion cells. To get a thin (one to two layers thick) section of onion, take a slice of an inside ring and bend it forward (towards the inside of the ring). It will snap, leaving a very thin film of onion on the inside. Place this on a slide, unfolded, in a drop of water mixed with a drop of iodine. Iodine will stain the nucleus (and your clothes), making it easier to see. Another great thing to look at is the tip of one of the leaves from the very top of an anacharis (or Elodea) plant. These are live plants that you can buy from fish stores. Place one in a drop of water on a slide without stain. You will probably be able to see "cytoplasmic streaming" of the chloroplasts as they flow around the nucleus. Other hits on the microscope:

1. Cheek cells (RUB inside of cheek GENTLY with a toothpick. Mix with water and iodine on slide).
2. Potato (starch stains so you will see huge vacuoles in the cells where the potato is storing starch).
3. Of course, don't forget the pond water that contains many living things that are made of only one cell. Not only will you see cells, but you will see them moving around in a number of cool ways.

Also, how about the bacteria in your yogurt, one strand of bread mold or tomato skin with the "meat" rubbed off. You can even see blood cells streaming through a goldfish's tail, but be careful to keep the rest of the fish moist and covered with wet cotton, and don't look too long or you will be at the pet store trying to find an exact match before little Susie wakes up. The possibilities are endless as long as you remember your goal is to find living tissue that is so thin light easily passes through it.

One cell process that most of us studied in school was osmosis. You don't have to have fancy equipment to show osmosis; a potato and small scale will do just fine. Cut two slices of potato about 6 mm thick. Weigh each and record the weights as "Weight before." Keeping track of which is which, place one slice in a dish with distilled water and one slice in a dish of salt water solution. (These are my exact scientific measurements to make the proper salt water solution: get water, add so much salt it doesn't want to dissolve anymore. Stir. Perfect solution every time.) After about 30 minutes, remove slices, dry on paper towel and re-weigh. Water should move into the potato from the distilled water, making the potato grow. It should move out of the potato in the salt solution, making it shrink. This is often obvious even without the use of a scale, as the potatoes will feel different after the experiment is done.

I conclude my study of the cell with another party. Of course, any excuse for eating cake serves my needs. Have your children make food that looks like a cell. A cake decorated with gummy worms (endoplasmic reticulum), jelly beans (mitochondria) and the like, Jell-O with floating tangerine (nucleus), banana slices (vacuole) etc. and whatever food your heart desires. I like to have them label the parts with the frosting that comes in a tube, or with little flags stuck in with toothpicks. They also have to prepare for the party by completing the engineering section of the curriculum: the dropped-egg saver, the egg catapult and the egg-mobile. The dropped-egg-saver is any container that will protect an egg in the event of a fall from the roof (which of course will be tested by a parent at the party). The egg catapult is a device that launches an egg as far and/or as accurately as possible. It's fun to set up a target at a distance and see who can get the closest. The egg-mobile is made from two pieces of paper, eight straws, four toy wheels (with a hole big enough for a straw to go through), and tape. The participants make any "cart" that will hold an egg and can go when blown. You can include whatever cell games your heart desires and enjoy your studies.

The Game Curriculum
By Carolyn and Martin Forte

Note: The Game Curriculum is a project of Carolyn and Martin and their homeschooled daughters. A booklet, written by Tenaya and Carolyn Forte, is available by contacting Excellence in Education at 626/821-0025 or visit their website: www. excellenceineducation.com/.

Our family loves games and our children are allergic to workbooks. So, not being prone to swimming upstream, we found or devised games for nearly everything. Games are a fun way to drill. They get the job done in a fraction of the time with better results because children seldom have to be coerced into playing a game. Our daughters, Tenaya and Tylene, started Fun-Ed in 1993 to sell the games they had enjoyed using for many years. In the ensuing years, many people asked for our curriculum, so Tenaya and her mom, Carolyn, wrote *The Game Curriculum* in the hope that it would help make the homeschooling years more enjoyable for others.

It is possible to teach every subject with games. We also love books—except textbooks—and recommend that you select good, real books to complement *The*

Game Curriculum. Together, it is possible to have a complete learning program that is fun, challenging, and interesting. As with all curricula, we suggest that you take what you need and leave the rest. Our suggestions are only examples to get your creative juices flowing. If you like the textbook method, you can use the games to vary your program and take the pressure off when you hit a hard spot. You can integrate the games with a unit study curriculum quite easily, or you can use *The Game Curriculum* as a complete program for the early years. Here is a sample of what you will find in *The Game Curriculum*, second grade:

Math: Math-It, Math War, Dominoes, Blisters, Additions Songs, Match'Em, Mancala, Fruit Salad.

Other Suggestions: If your child can count backward from 20 with his eyes closed while tying his shoes, he is ready for Math-It. This is a game-like math program that will take you through 8th grade math at whatever speed works for your child. You needn't hurry because there isn't really much to learn. The educationists have managed to stretch about a year's worth of study (for a mature student) into nine full years. You can't teach this to the average seven-year-old in a year, but a 12-year-old who is interested could do it easily. So relax and take it at a reasonable rate. If you don't push too hard, your child will probably finish Math-It and Advanced Math-It well before 8th grade. To practice his or her math skills your child can use problems you make up (not too many) or a simple math workbook such as the McGraw-Hill *Spectrum* Series. Once the basic math facts are mastered (games will do this) only about 15 minutes of practice a day will give your child fluency in math problems.

Language Arts: Smart Cubes, Alpha Animals, Phonogram Fun, Phonics Game, Geo-Safari Phonics Pack, Geo-Safari Reading Games.

Other Suggestions: You don't need all of the above to teach reading. Choose what you want or need to get the job done. Learning to read is extremely easy when the student is ready and it is extremely difficult when the child is not ready. Just because your child is smart does not mean he is ready to learn to read. If you get massive resistance even with games, your child is probably not ready. Read *Better Late than Early* by Raymond and Dorothy Moore. Children's eyes do not finish developing until they are about eight years old, so many are not ready to focus on printed matter until after that. Games that use large letters can help you get the basics of phonics to your child so that when he is ready, reading will come easily.

Physical Education: Jump rope, jacks, Chinese jump rope, U Can Do Subtraction, ball games, hop scotch.

Be sure to get plenty of physical exercise. Children will do this naturally if not distracted by television and video games.

Science: Somebody, Animal Rummy, animal card games, IQ Animals of the World, Nature Bingo, Science Bingo, Geo-Safari Animal Packs.

Other Suggestions: There are lots of great animal picture books. Usborne's The *Great Animal Search* is a fun way to learn to identify a lot of animals. *The Great Undersea Search* will teach your child about plants and animals of the ocean. If your child enjoys coloring there are scores of educational animal coloring books available. These are available with audiotapes for those who are not yet fluent readers. For those who like to draw freehand we would suggest some how-to-draw books from several publishers.

Don't forget the zoo, the aquarium, the lake, beach, river, urban park or whatever wild areas you actually see in the real world. If you can't stand to learn without a book, get a book of flowers, trees, birds or whatever to take out with you to identify things you run across. We might also suggest place mats with animals, insects, etc.

Welcoming Dirt into the Curriculum
By Karen Taylor

My son has loved dirt ever since he was old enough to toddle out to it. Back in those early days, he would throw it in the air, and scuff through it over and over. He never tired of watching the patterns the dirt made in the air. When he could talk, he explained the kicking and throwing was to "make smoke."

Well, it is one thing to have a preschooler play in the dirt. After all, they are little and having fun, but what do you do when your dirt-loving children grow up and really should be inside learning like other respectable youngsters? Hopefully, you will silence the urge to speak out and let them go play in the stuff!

Most of the time I am fairly relaxed about homeschooling and it is clear that my son is indeed learning. There have been times, however, when I thought about calling him into the house to do something that would be considered more conventionally productive—a worksheet, perhaps? Later, when I learned what he was up to, I was glad that I had not interfered. Yes, I can think of several instances that have convinced me that dirt play, like all play, is important, and that it is fortunate that I refrained from acting on any impulse to call him in for "real learning."

So, what can a child do with dirt, besides track it back in the house? By keeping my adult notion of cleanliness to myself, and watching and listening, I have observed many things.

One day, I discovered he was not only digging, but adding water. Gee, did he have to play in the mud? He was making such a mess! I was not only thinking about missed worksheet time or other ways I could impart knowledge, but I was also thinking LAUNDRY! Oh, how I wanted to call him in, but I refrained that day. He was busy for hours, contentedly playing alone on a beautiful sunny day. Before he came in, he invited me to come take a look at the "Snake River." We had been reading about the Lewis and Clark Expedition, and he was following up on parts that had interested him with this mud play. He wasn't merely playing. Due to an aversion to muddy laundry, combined with a sincere interest in teaching my child, I had almost stopped some true learning. It was a close call.

Another time, he made adobe bricks, using his own invented recipe. Once again, he was following up on a story. He pulled out some scrap wood and managed to independently build a rough form and then filled it with his mud concoction. He had a few failures, and worked on improving his recipe. We had hard bricks all over the yard for awhile.

He also tried digging to the center of the earth once. That is pretty typical kid stuff, and he gave it a good try. There was quite a hole in the back yard! In typical homeschool fashion, he didn't stop there—he wanted to read more about the core of the earth to learn how deep his hole would have to be. And, he wanted to look at the globe to determine if the proverbial China was indeed where he would end up (no it wasn't).

Another huge project took months of dedicated earth moving, and the final product had extended paths for the flow of water. Yes, water again, and he used a lot of it for this project. And yes, I had to refrain from asking him not to "waste" water. He was trying to figure out different ways water can move, what happens to the surroundings, and how one can change the flow with barriers. It looked like some erosion experimentation had been going on too. After awhile he made a little wooden boat to sail down the waterway. I imagine he now knows much more about water flow, dams, and erosion than if I had introduced a formal science experiment, or read from a book.

Then there was the "loafing" incident. He was just kind of kicking around. Clearly loafing—the kind of loafing that can make a parent think of the bedroom that needs cleaning, or the weeds that need pulling. He explained later that he was drawing math problems in the dirt. He had read that Archemedes used to do that, and he wanted to see how well it worked. Given that he was going through a less-than-eager math phase, this was indeed interesting information.

There is nothing quite like kid's play. It's worth standing back and allowing a child plenty of unstructured time to learn on his own, without adult intervention. And in our household, the medium of choice is frequently good, old, readily available...dirt.

Advice from Experienced Homeschoolers

Fit The Curriculum To The Child, Not Vice Versa

You know your child, her special talents and her particular stumbling blocks, her courage and her trepidations, her needs, her indifferences, and her dreams. Bring this wonderful insight with you to every homeschooling day, let it color your every decision about what she needs to learn and when. Above all, remember that your child knows herself even better than you do, even though she may not always be able to express what's going on inside her head. Listen, observe, adjust, and prepare to sometimes change direction totally as she grows and changes.

Seek Joyful Learning

You surely want to preserve, or reawaken, as the case may be, the boundless curiosity and zest for learning that so dominated your child's character when he was a toddler. Remember how he would shake, rattle and roll whatever he found until his curiosity was sated, and then he was off like a shot to tackle the next challenge? He also knew enough to quit when he was overloaded and he would let you know, sometimes at the top of his lungs! Recapturing that undiminished drive and fearless approach to finding out is an educational prescription for our times. We're so often told these days that one must become a lifelong learner to keep up with our fast-changing world. To be a lifelong learner, one must have skills, energy, and desire for learning—to be a toddler at heart!

Homeschooling is More Than "Schooling at Home"

You know that when learning is made to be drudgery, it is seldom truly learned. Rote instruction, especially when combined with harsh criticism and humiliating comparisons, dissipates energy and kills the desire to learn. Avoid, if you possibly can, duplicating the worst failings of institutional schooling in your homeschool. Homeschooling is about preserving the fragile and wonderous spirit of our children. Homeschooling gives you the freedom to be in all ways more personal, more lively, more attuned to the needs and interests of each individual.

More Than An Educational Choice, It's a Lifestyle

Your homeschool should also correspond to who you are as a family. Your deeply held values and beliefs, your vocations, geography, and living space, your daily, weekly, and annual schedules of work, relaxation, and play—all these elements are yours to shape and control as you design your child's learning experience.

Your Homeschooling Style Will Develop Over Time

Families new to home education typically stick pretty close to the shore at first, using traditional materials and a structured schedule because formal "school" is all they know. For some, it continues to be what is right for their families, and for others, after some months or perhaps even years of experimentation and adjustment, they may start leaning toward more spontaneity, less structure, and fewer conventional teaching materials. As you search to find what suits your family in the vast array of curricula and materials, don't be afraid to make some unconventional choices. Enjoy the freedom and flexibility that homeschooling affords you. Trust your own sense of what is right for your child.

Some Final Tips From Old-Timers

Are you still wondering, "What if I make the wrong decision about curriculum?" Fortunately, whatever decision you make is yours to change. There is no homeschooling bureaucracy; there are no committees to pass judgement; there are no forms to fill out in triplicate. If you find your initial decisions aren't working out, you can modify your program. Don't forget that learning is a dynamic process. One of the compelling reasons to homeschool is that it allows for change and growth over time. It also allows for individualizing so that you can speed up or slow down in order to match your child's developmental readiness in various subjects. If you will consider your curricular decisions as temporary, recognizing that they may shift as your understanding grows or your child's needs change, the weight you are feeling will be lifted considerably. We offer some final advice from old timers, followed by the reflections from a long time homeschooler whose children are now grown:

- There is no such thing as *the* perfect curriculum.
- Don't panic about choosing a curriculum. The rule of thumb is that for every year your child has been in school they need one month to decompress. Use that time to decide on your educational philosophy, learn about your child's learning strengths and evaluate some of the available resources.
- Curriculum choices change as your children grow up, change interests and develop educational goals.
- You will make mistakes. You will buy materials that you later wish you hadn't. Making mistakes is part of the process. The corollary to that is that you will make some great choices that work well for your family.
- Some resources are perfect for one child and disastrous for another. Be sensitive to learning styles.
- Curriculum is a tool, not an obligation. This does not mean that you should not set goals, but be willing to be flexible. Don't write your lesson plans in ink. Don't be a slave to your curriculum. Adapt. Enhance. Keep an eraser handy.
- Involve older kids in planning: What do you see yourself doing in 2 years? 5 years? What have you always wanted to do that you haven't had the opportunity to do yet? If nobody were telling you what to do, how would you spend your next week? Month?

Nine Lessons I Learned in Ten Years of Homeschooling
By Jackie Orsi

Lesson #9: Don't listen to anyone too much, including me.

Be wary of experts. You left the experts behind at the public schools, so don't rush to sit at the feet of homeschooling experts. Be the expert on your own life. Figure homeschooling out for yourself. My nine lessons are not mandates, but points to ponder. I hope to challenge your thinking so that you will go on to create your homeschool. They represent my honest discoveries gleaned over ten amazing years. Some of them are paradoxical; you won't expect them. Some of them you may not agree with, and that's okay, too.

Lesson #8: You need a dream.

You need a vision of the people you want your children to be, intellectually, socially, and morally. Don't dream your worst fears, dream your fondest hopes. Homeschooling is all about imagining and then making it so. We homeschoolers can dream our dreams and live out our realities with remarkable congruence between the dream and the reality. My dream, my vision, is an expression of my values, just as your vision will be your values translated into a story about how your family would like to be, now and in the future.

Reality is messy, of course. It won't always follow the beautiful vision as you hope it will. Sometimes it presents you with tough choices you as a parent have to make based on your values. Sometimes you are faced with a great deal of uncertainty. When your powers of reason can't guide you, your vision can. Your vision becomes your intuition. It helps to give you those gut feelings of how to raise your kids.

Don't make your story too modest, and don't be afraid to dream a big dream of who your child will be. You can identify your child's gifts and urge him to follow his own dreams. Dream big. Don't be afraid of excellence as a vision.

Lesson #7: You need to be a little lazy.

Our homeschool only began to click when I got lazy. In the first year of homeschooling I was really involved and really busy. It's only when I stopped scheduling and planning and testing and measuring and worrying, that my kids began to grow. Thanks to my lazy streak, we enjoyed the true genius of homeschooling.

You see, when I was busy being teacher and principal and curriculum planner and super mom all rolled into one, I was standing in my children's way. All my good intentions and extraordinary efforts meant that I was using my creativity, and my ambition, and imposing my discipline. All they were learning was how to please Mom.

Now don't misunderstand me. I didn't disappear altogether. What I did was to turn the job of learning over to my daughters. I selected out my highest priorities—math and vocabulary, and said, "Do a unit every day. Here's the answer key. If you start getting less than 80% right, back up and go over the material again. Come to me if you get stuck." The rest was their own.

The bottom line is that my efforts to educate my kids, enthusiastic and well intentioned though they may have been, were external control. Learning is an internal process, it can't be imposed. And self-discipline can never take root and grow where external discipline is firmly planted. So be a little lazy on purpose.

Lesson #6: Forget about socialization.

You know, the "But what about socialization" question. What an overblown big deal about nothing! Just never mind. Kids don't need massive exposure to other kids to grow up healthy and happy. Kids need exposure to all kinds of people to grow up healthy and happy, and a lot of parental guidance in the process. Being stuck in a schoolroom all day with 30 other seven-year-olds under the rule of one adult is hardly what I would call adequate socialization. Homeschooling, on the other hand, lets you give your kids a healthy panorama of social experiences. It's not that hard to give your children varied social experiences in which they can learn to be polite, respectful, considerate individuals. It's really relatively easy to teach your kids how to get along with people.

But here's the real gift of homeschooling. Homeschooling allows your child to learn to get along *without* people. Loneliness, like boredom, is a state of mind. It is a state of dependency on other people. A child who is not every moment of every day trotted around in a crowd of other kids gets the opportunity to learn to enjoy his own company and the pleasures of solitude. It is a powerful thing to be alone *and* content. When you are not capable of loneliness, when you have become immunized against loneliness, you are a powerful person. You get the courage to be able to walk away from a crowd when you don't agree with it. You know that you will be okay even if the crowd sneers at you. You can reject them, they can reject you—and either way your world doesn't come to an end.

My kids had a lot of alone time in the ten years they homeschooled. The effects are evident. They are indifferent to peer group pressure. They are fully self-accepting and don't need other people to tell them how to dress and how to act. They are socially self-assured—able to go anywhere in the world on their own. The blessed isolation of homeschooling gave them the quality of being socially independent. Yes, I said isolation.

Lesson #5: A smooth, harmonious homeschool is a dead homeschool.

If your family is perfectly happy, if family members never squabble amongst themselves, if you aren't really worried about some aspect or another of your child's character, if your children never give you sass—then something is seriously wrong with your family.

Conflict is a necessity in raising kids, because growth is frequently a reaction to stress—and helping them grow is what it's all about, yes? They help us grow, too. It's natural for parents and kids to take turns pushing each other and hanging back during this long process of moving a child from the wholly dependent infant to the wholly independent adult he or she becomes. It's a messy business. To grow a child you need a slow evolutionary process punctuated by revolutionary periods. Don't be quick to suppress conflict. Don't be embarrassed by it. Don't feel that you are a failure if your homeschooling experience is full of ups and downs, and bad patches, and disagreements. A certain amount of conflict is natural and normal and it's alive.

Lesson #4: Do it the hard way.

Homeschooling has changed radically in the ten years my family has homeschooled. When we started there were hardly any support groups, conferences, or homeschoolers' days at amusement parks. All that has changed, especially the vast marketplace of curriculum and learning kits, and instructional videos, and classes, and tutors, and so forth. I'm not so sure that all of these developments are good ones. In fact, I'm sure that taken as a whole, they are not. Increasingly, homeschooling has become something you purchase. I see people buying products that I call "Homeschooling In A Can." Open the can, plop it in a bowl and set it in front of the kids.

Sure, it seems like a plan to pop the kids in the car and haul them from the science museum classes, to the ballet school, then back around to the library reading program. So many wonderful choices that weren't available to homeschoolers even five years ago. But though they sound wonderful, give a little thought to what might be missing. When you are old and gray like me, you will think back on your time when the kids were little, and all of your memories will be of sitting in the car in traffic, or sitting in parking lots waiting, while someone else enjoyed your kids.

Don't buy your homeschool. Don't hire an expert to take care of things for you. Don't attempt only the safe and traditional subjects. I am telling you to think outside the box, and better yet, make the box. Create your own standards and methods. Think through for yourself what it means to be an educated person, and then put together the elements of your children's curriculum. Then the pacing, the content, and the approaches will be exactly right for each child. It will be whole and it will make sense. You and your children will feel a sense of ownership of the process. Doing things for yourself empowers you to do more for yourself. Do it the hard way on purpose.

Lesson #3: Enjoy the fact that homeschooling is unpopular and misunderstood.

It's a plus that works in our favor. Decades ago Marshall McLuhan pronounced that "the medium is the message." That is certainly true of homeschooling. Right now, while you still have every other mother-in-law thinking it's outrageous what you are doing to your kids, and the lady across the street sniffs with disdain at the mention of homeschooling, and the school bureaucrats pontificate that homeschooling parents are neglecting their kids' needs—be glad for all of them.

Our unpopular choice to homeschool taught my daughters many lessons. Choosing homeschooling said to them, "We care about you so much we will do this extraordinary thing." It showed them just how important a value we placed on their education that we would risk social disapproval. In California, where school officials run around saying homeschooling is illegal, going ahead and homeschooling anyway taught them the importance of standing up for what you believe in. It said, "Don't let people in authority take away your right to do what your heart and mind says you must do." Homeschooling in an unaccepting world set my principles in harsh relief. I had convictions, but the climate made me have to have the courage of my convictions, too. The medium was the message.

Lesson #2: Don't worry about them. Worry about you.

You can get so caught up in homeschooling that you can forget that you, the parent, have a life too, or at least you're supposed to. You may think that putting your life on hold is a noble sacrifice for the kids, but I think it may be a case of throwing the baby out with the bath water. Who you are matters more than who they are for two reasons:

1. *You really can't control who they are.*

    The whole world will be better off when we finally get it through our heads that people don't want to be controlled, can't be controlled. You can't control kids, but you can hold them, kiss them, soothe them, show them, talk to them, listen to them, provide for them, and in the process you can hope that you inspire them and lead them.

2. *You can control yourself.*

    Kids learn about life from their parents, and they know hypocrisy when they see it. You can't hope to turn them into eager learners unless you are an eager learner. You can't hope that they will have the courage of their convictions unless you do. Homeschooling shows children their parents' life; 99% of American kids are sent away to a place where they can't see real life. My kids had a front row seat on my life for ten years. They were right at hand to see how I played my roles as a wife, a mother, a sister, a daughter, a friend, a co-worker, a volunteer, a neighbor. They saw me deal with all kinds of life's joys and trials—family financial matters, the formation of friendships and the dissolution of some, my attempts to build a career as a writer, and many bureaucratic tangles. They saw how I take criticism, how I take praise, how I lead and how I follow, how I deal with difficult people, how I face a life-threatening illness, how I got through the death of my parents. Did I do everything right? Hell no. But I promise you they saw it all, and that's why I say, *pay more attention to who you are than to who they are.* The one follows the other.

Lesson #1: Stop—just stop—thinking about how the children will be when you are finished homeschooling.

Slow down. Live in the moment. Take it from someone who can't homeschool anymore because she hasn't any little kids anymore: This is the time of your life. Enjoy it.

Why Aren't You
in School Today?

8

"We grow, thrive, live and learn together

in the warmth and comfort of our home..."

©Bill Taylor

Life Happens

By Charlotte Monte

Life does happen. Like gravity, life doesn't care if this is a bad day for the toilet to overflow. It doesn't matter if you have a big party on Saturday, and the oven goes on the blink on Thursday. Life happens, like it or not. How you cope with it is an entirely different matter.

For homeschooling families, life's diversions can actually be easier to handle than for families with two parents working outside the home. For the dual-income families, it is even harder to find the time to drop off the car for a brake job. When Johnny gets sick, who is going to miss work, Mom or Dad? Wondering how to help Cassie with her homework when you absolutely, positively must get your manager's report in tomorrow by 8 a.m. and the electrician can't figure out why your electricity is out, would probably drive just about anyone over the edge.

Homeschoolers, like anyone, suffer from many of life's arbitrary dealings. Life can get quite "in your face" when you are having your children with you practically 24 hours a day, seven days a week. Recently, exasperated by the demands I had made in my life (to pick up the bulk food order, to write that particular article by that particular deadline, to keep my dental appointment an hour's drive away, and so on) I despaired of ever getting around to educating my children.

Being in charge of my children's education is a big responsibility that, in my view, can't be put on a back burner, regardless of educational approach. But instead of despairing of the valuable "study time" we were losing, I was able to sit back and take stock.

Realistically, I can take a day or a half-day off every now and then. I am not a schoolteacher, tied down to a particular curriculum that must be covered by a certain time. My children will not be tested Friday on that week's material. In fact, education can look a lot different from "schooling." That's where the beauty of being able to deal with life's ups and downs comes in. On days when I know I won't be sitting down with my children in the mornings to cover math, phonics, handwriting and so on, I can transform the day into a learning adventure.

Our car might become our classroom. I flip on the tape of *Johnny Tremain*, and we are spirited back in history, transported instantly to 1770's Boston, enriching and reinforcing the previous year's study of the American Revolution.

As we drive to keep such and such appointment, we might find something interesting to see on our way back. Mission San Jose (Fremont) is only a few miles out of our way as we return home from the dentist. It is a wonderful field trip and California history lesson. We learn so much more by walking through the musty halls than by just reading about it.

In fact, it's great to get "out of town." Our long drives to Alameda brought us to Coyote Hills' Ohlone villages and the salt marshes at Don Edwards State Park. We toured the visitors' centers, looked at the museum exhibits and took long hikes and walks in the natural surroundings of the marshes.

And, on those days when there truly seems to be no "learning" going on, I can catch up on reading to my children in the evenings. I snuggle with them on the sofa, extend their bedtime a bit, and carry us all away with the glory of books.

Really, there is no day that "learning" doesn't happen, in spite of the third visit by the plumber for the same problem, the cat needing to go to the vet, and the electrician scratching his head over the power outage. Watching plumbers at work is fascinating; have your children watch. Wonderful conversations have been struck up in the waiting room of the vet's office. Don't overlook the value of observing an office at work. We've even practiced homeschooling public relations on visiting technicians, one of whom commented, "You know, people almost don't blame you these days!"

Homeschooling does not alleviate life's occasional turmoil, but neither does it cause it. Sending your children to school may keep your house cleaner and neater, but it won't necessarily give you respite from "life happening." Don't get the impression that homeschooling will end all your troubles, but it just may give your family greater leeway to cope.

A Day in the Life of a Homeschooling Family
Six homeschooling parents were asked to give an inside view of what daily life is like for their families.

Family #1: Using traditional studies while balancing the needs of three children. *By Charlotte C. Monte*

The children have risen early, and are outside rollerblading. I call them in. We begin at 8:30. The breakfast dishes are cleared, the table is wiped off, and the floor is swept. Michael, 10, and Maria, 7, gather their backpacks, pencils and I my record-keeping book, and we begin with Spiritual Studies. I thumb through a book of inspirational sayings from various sources, and together we pick an appropriate passage or two to copy down in our notebooks. I'm hoping that the children will create keepsake books that they will take with them through their lives, occasionally rifling through them for a needed word of inspiration or guidance. Meanwhile, Steven (4 1/2), is either drawing at the table, or playing with his cars or toys in the living room.

By 9:00, Maria is ready to do some Saxon math, and Michael will practice handwriting. After about 20 minutes, we switch, and Michael pulls out his math, while Maria works on handwriting or language skills.

It takes Michael an extraordinary amount of time to work through his allotted problems, so I make a note to switch his math time to the end of the day. Then he can work through it at his own pace (and probably faster, because he'll look forward to his free time when he's all through).

After math, the kids get a 15-minute break.

When we reconvene, we move from the kitchen table to the living room sofa. There, we curl up with a phonics book, a grammar primer, timelines and our current history or social studies books. We spend about twenty minutes doing phonics and grammar, then spend the rest of the hour reading, looking at the atlas, and filling in our timelines. Sometimes, one or the other of them will want to read a story to me. Then it's time for lunch.

After lunch, depending on what day of the week it is, we may head off for science class, art class, or music class. If it is Park Day, we head for that month's meeting place for our homeschool group. If it is a day when no classes or activities are planned, we might do any one of the above at home (a science experiment, practice piano, or do some art). On nice days, we might take our Nature Notebooks out into the garden to sketch. If our library books are due, we'll return them. Often, we'll have a friend or two in tow.

The children are free from about 1:30 onward on afternoons when there are no outside classes planned. That's often when I'm able to catch up on my projects.

We usually have dinner around 6:30. By 7:30 we are ready for stories, and we read lots of books and stories till bedtime at 8:30. I count this evening reading time as very important, crucial homeschooling time, and it's the time that I enjoy the most. We often read books related to our current history project, or our *Children's History of the World*, by Hillyer.

No two days are the same. Some go more smoothly than others. Sometimes we need to do a lot of housecleaning or picking up, but we are in charge of the what, why, where, when and how of our days. When problems do present themselves, the solving of them is often just as important as bookwork. We grow, thrive, live and learn together in the warmth and comfort of our home, with all the joys and trials. We are a homeschooling family!

Family #2: A mom balancing a job outside the home with homeschooling.
By Sydney McCurdy

It's 8:20. Get up and exercise for 45 minutes, wake up the kids, have them make their beds and get dressed while I take a shower. Head downstairs, have breakfast, throw a load of clothes in the washer, clean the kitchen and sit down at the table at 10:30 for the broadening of our horizons. Either Samantha (age 9) or Michael (age 7) goes first while the other plays with their younger brother Will (age 5). We spend a couple of hours together doing science, social studies, math, grammar, phonics, spelling, reading, handwriting, etc. (Michael is not yet doing all these subjects).

At noon we break for lunch. We eat, clean up, finish the laundry, and then sit back down to finish up with the second learner. By 2:00 or 2:30 we're finished, we put everything away and I get ready for work. If it's Monday, Tuesday or Thursday, then Sam will pack a dinner and her dance clothes as she will be heading to work with me at the local dance studio I help manage. We leave at 3:00 to pick up their older sister from high school and then drop her and the boys back at the house. Lindsay (age 15) watches them for me while I'm at work (except for Thursdays—they go with me).

Around 8:00 I'm heading back home. The kids get baths, have snacks, we clean up the house, feed the animals, I do more laundry then collapse in my room with some form of dinner at 9:30. I drag myself out of my chair to read some bedtime story and put them to bed. It is now approximately 10:30. The rest of the night is mine. I usually end up reading, quilting, writing letters, working on scrapbooks, researching curriculum, etc., during this time.

All the nitty gritty stuff gets saved for the weekend when my husband is home and can lend a hand with the major house cleaning, grocery shopping, meal planning, yard and car maintenance, etc. I plan the schoolwork out for the entire week on Sunday afternoons. I plan field trips and art projects for Fridays since I don't work that day.

It is a lot to do. With the help of my three older daughters during the week and everyone pitching in on the weekends it all seems to come together. The emotional support I get from my husband is the icing on the cake.

Family #3: Homeschooling one child, using the relaxed year-round approach. *By Karen Taylor*

We are the parents of two; our oldest is an adult who attended school, and our youngest is a 10-year-old who has always been homeschooled. Although not an only child, he has been the only child in residence since infancy.

Although I am the parent home during the day, my husband and I share parenting/teaching, and our son eagerly looks forward to evenings spent reading and talking with Dad. Our days reflect our philosophy that looking for ways to learn every day of the year should continue to be as natural as it was during the preschool years when we weren't under pressure to be teaching. As parents, we are opportunists—grabbing the moment before that window of opportunity is gone. With one child, it is easy to do that, although I know some large families accomplish it also.

What happens day-to-day can be influenced by so many variables. Tangents are important in learning, and easy to accomplish with just one child. Perhaps there is an interesting article in the morning newspaper, or something we read or see at the library makes him want to learn more. He has plenty of unstructured time in the day, and it is for a reason. I have general goals for the year (such as improving cursive writing), and also goals for the next eight years (preparing for college and adult independence), some of which will be met when conditions are optimal, rather than trying to force learning in the traditional order required of schooled children. We are not concerned with mass education standards, trusting that he is right on target for himself, and progressing in many ways.

As many homeschoolers will claim, we also have no typical day. He awakens around 8:00, often shares something he has been pondering, then wanders to a bookshelf to select something of interest for some independent reading. He likes to read, and he is often digging up some answers to questions he has been thinking about. My presence somewhere in the house is sufficient for now. It's a good time to do household chores and answer e-mail.

Around 9:00, we decide to eat some breakfast, and we make it together. While we eat, I often ask him questions from our supply of trivia cards that we have acquired from different sources, primarily thrift stores. They are all hodge-podge questions on many subjects, and he enjoys them. A question might be easily answered, sometimes surprising me that he knows the answer, or it might be more difficult and lead him to ask many more questions. Sometimes, he heads for a book, or he checks his wall map for further information. Sometimes he decides it is time to quiz me. It's a fun way to learn. These questions often lead to more in-depth reading and learning, and sometimes we agree to wait and let Dad help answer something when he gets home.

The next segment of our day varies, depending on whether it is going to remain a stay-at-home day, or if we will be leaving for a violin lesson or park day. We are relaxed eclectic learners, somewhere between traditional schoolers and unschoolers. I have collected some learning materials from various sources—what I consider the best of the best for him, rather than purchasing a standard grade level curriculum. One favorite is *English From the Roots Up*. He thinks Greek and Latin words are fun, and I marvel to myself about this because he is joyfully learning without the prejudices that some schooled children carry with them regarding what is boring.

Some days, he is either reading or so deeply involved in projects of his own making, that I respect his independent learning, and try not to disrupt it. Other days, I may ask him to do a page of Daily Grams (another favorite of his), and some things like handwriting, phonics and math. I might also just ask him to look through our collection and pick out several things he would especially like to do. None of this takes long, but the skills learned will help him accomplish other things. They are important, but they can be fit in around other interests and activities. Since we do this all year long, there is plenty of time. This extra time means you will always find us at park days and field trips, since they are important too.

Does he have enough social contact with other children? That's a common "only child" worry, although not one I share. I can worry as much as the next mom about some things, but I 've never worried about keeping him entertained, so he looks to himself for ideas rather than to me or the TV. Some days he plays with neighbor friends when their school is out, once a week he meets with homeschooled friends, and some days we're home by ourselves. Whether with friends, or alone, he finds something to do, and remains content. I believe the independence he is gaining by not having me overly plan his day is beneficial.

Homeschooling is such a natural part of our family. We're enjoying learning together, and even more important, we enjoy being together every day, all day.

Family #4: An unschooling family learning in rhythm. *By Tammy Rousso*

I didn't start out to unschool our children. But sometimes life sends us lessons that lead to answers we hadn't considered. I've learned to trust the children because any unschooler will tell you there are no typical days. Although our day has no structure it does have rhythm. Here is a glimpse into the rhythm of our day.

6:30: I'm up to care for our four dogs and enjoy a cup of coffee in the morning stillness. The children are late risers, so I'll have 1-2 hours to catch up on e-mails and read.

8:30: Jacob, our 5 year old, awakens. We snuggle and I grab some books to read to him. Before we can read, he shows me the spaceship he and his dad built out of Legos last night. After he thoroughly explains about his droids, energy source and ship radar we are ready to read. I read a couple of fun stories to him and simplify *Yankee Doodle, A Revolutionary Tail* by Gary Chalk. (Yes, it is tail and not tale. The illustrations are of mice.) It is a story of the American Revolution written for upper elementary age children.

9:00: Time for breakfast. I put on Celtic music. I like to expose the children to many different styles of music.

9:10: Kalee, age 9, is awake. She spies *Yankee Doodle, A Revolutionary Tail*, and sits down to read it. Jacob asks to have the futon couch made into a bed. He climbs aboard with his Lego spaceship for a space adventure. I hear the sounds of rockets blasting and whispered dialogue. The roots of written language arts are in progress.

9:30: Kalee reads all 16 verses to the Yankee Doodle Dandy song found in the book, and calls me over to show me how the song matches history. We discuss the Declaration of Independence. The book quotes *"We hold these truths to be self-evident; that all men are created equal; that they are endowed by their creator with certain unalienable rights; that among these are life, liberty, and the pursuit of happiness."* Kalee is curious what those words really mean and I help her break it down into understandable chunks. The book also mentions the role of Native Americans in the revolution and Kalee wants to know more about that. She spends the next 20 minutes reading and asking questions about the revolution.

9:50: Kalee feeds the fish in her aquarium. Tropical fish are her hobby. She has spent the last month watching the classified ads to find a larger aquarium that is within the budget set by her dad. In the meantime she is researching various fish to put in the aquarium and determining which ones require the same water conditions and match temperamentally.

10:00: We eat breakfast and do clean up. Afterwards the children have a few minutes to wrestle and play.

10:25: I ask Kalee if she would like me to read to her. She does. Even though she reads quite well, we still enjoy a good book together. We are reading a wonderful story called *From Anna* by Jean Little. It is the tale of a family leaving Nazi Germany and immigrating to Canada. Even more, it is the story of a child who is a misfit in her own family. It has opened up some nice discussions about how to treat others. As we read today, Beethoven is mentioned in the story as a German composer. I make a mental note to myself to play a Beethoven CD later in the day. As Kalee and I sit down to read, Jacob finds a journal that a friend gave him for Christmas a couple of years ago. It has been months since he showed any interest in it, but today he decides to write "words." He writes down a scramble of letters and asks me what "it says." Initially I try to give him the phonetic blend because, of course, it doesn't really say anything. He delights in the silly sounds and continues to add letters until it becomes a bit cumbersome for me to read. I begin using the sounds to produce a Native American type chant. This really excites him. He can't wait to show other family members how he writes "songs," and spends the next 30 minutes practicing writing letters—oops! I mean writing songs. That done, Jacob heads outdoors for some water play and Kalee and I finish reading.

11:30-12:30: We run errands. Back home, I bring out centimeter cubes made for math manipulatives. That is not what we are using them for. The children spend the next 40 minutes building with them. At some point in their development a question will come up that is answered using the centimeter cubes. When that happens I want the cubes to seem familiar and comfortable.

1:45: We subscribe to an e-mail service called Krampf's Science Experiments. Kalee reads through them and picks the ones she wants to do. Jacob joins us.

3:00: We do two experiments and start a third one. In the process, we talk about inertia, cloud vapor, and copper acetate. Kalee continues making clouds in a bottle.

The rest of the day is spent in play and following their interests. At bedtime, their dad reads them a story. The current favorites are Greek myths.

This is how our days go. Nothing structured that looks like school. Just the rhythm of time spent together engaging in activities that stimulate us. Some days it seems geniuses must live here and other days, well, let's just say "trust the children" becomes my mantra. Unschooling becomes a life style—a lifestyle of living life and learning as we go. It fits our family perfectly.

Family #5: A working dad looks for ways to contribute to homeschooling.
By Morgan Rogers

As a full-time and away-from-the-home employed father, the duty of homeschooling falls primarily with my wife. Five days a week, I'm out of the house before the kids wake up. When I return home in the late afternoon, it's time to play a little with the kids, get ready for dinner, eat dinner, clean up after dinner, go through the mail, do a few chores, and then get the kids to bed. There isn't much time for me to help with the formal homeschool lessons. However, I still want a role in my children's homeschool education. There are many roles for the homeschool-supporting father.

I think my most important role in homeschooling is in teaching the children some of the practical lessons of life. I don't just mean teaching moral lessons like honesty, integrity, working hard, etc., although those are certainly important whether homeschooling or not. I mean the lessons of taking care of yourself and being self-reliant, like how to fix a flat tire on a bicycle, how to stop the drip from a leaking faucet, how to replace the flushing mechanism in a toilet, or how to do maintenance on a hot water heater. Often while in the middle of a repair project, I'll call the kids to show them what I'm doing. At the same time, I try to introduce the mechanics and physics of the situation. Find the leak in a flat bicycle tire by increasing the pressure inside the inner tube above atmospheric pressure (i.e. pump it up) and holding the tube under water to see the higher pressurized air bubbles escape to show the leak location. Show how to use a siphon to pump water out of a toilet water tank. Explain how the rubber washer in a faucet is used to create a tight seal to prevent water leakage.

Or, after showing them the corroded sacrificial anode rod from the hot water heater, explain the concept of corrosion and how the anode rod helps keep the hot water heater from corroding. I love working on my house, so the possibilities for practical lessons are endless. Repair people are not usually welcome at our house.

Next in importance, or maybe even more important, is giving my wife a break whenever possible. After spending most of the day with the kids, she can use some time to herself to catch up on some personal business, relax, or just get away from the house for awhile. Whenever I run some errands, I'll take the kids along with me. Even if I just take our three-year-old son and leave my seven and 10-year-old daughters at home, that gives my wife a little more free time to do other things. If I'm at home, I try to involve the kids in what I'm doing so they don't interrupt their mother. Although my wife has accepted the sacrifice of her time in order to homeschool the children, it is important that she be given some time back whenever possible.

I try to call home once a day from work and talk to each child. Part of the conversation always comes to the homeschool lessons and how they're doing. I always emphasize the importance of their education and that they have to help make it work. We try to keep the motivation positive but sometimes we have to hold their fun activities over their head, i.e. if their lessons aren't completed, no dance class, no sleepover, no etc. It is their decision to do the work or lose some privileges. I always tell them how lucky they are to be homeschooled and how I wish I had been homeschooled because I would probably be a lot smarter.

Minor and occasional roles I'll play include standing in to finish up a lesson started earlier by my wife and act as a sounding board for lesson plans and book purchases.

We have accepted homeschooling as an important part of our lives and have dedicated ourselves to that endeavor. While I'm not the primary teacher in our homeschool, I want to be a part of the homeschooling experience for both my children and my wife.

Family #6: Singularly Triumphant: A single mom raising and educating her child alone. *By Tana Bevan*

Homeschooling reminds me of a tapestry with strands of colored thread interwoven this way and that. When all goes according to plan the result is a beautiful picture or design. Looking closely, you notice not every strand of thread is beautiful. Some are indeed dazzling, others however are muted and on occasion even ugly. Such is the homeschool life. Some days can be good and productive—bright and vibrant. These days validate everything you're doing. They are worth remembering and sharing with others, especially the doubters. Other days are quiet and introspective, giving muted and subdued colors. Those days can be restful and don't tend to stand out in your memory. They are best described as "just there." Some days are frustrating and it seems nothing goes right or is accomplished. Those colors are ugly. On those days you wonder if the nay-sayers are right and you question your sanity for homeschooling. You don't tend to share those days with anyone not sympathetic to the cause. Over the course of time, the days weave themselves together to yield a colorful, complex, rich picture of your homeschooling life. Looking at just one day, or one week, or even one month misses so much. Every so often, remember to step back and look at the whole picture—see where you've been, where you are and where you're going.

In my utopian homeschool fantasy we are home as much or as little as we want to be. The "home" in homeschool presupposes actually being at home—such a misnomer! We are never at the mercy of a clock and no alarm clocks enter our little world. We lead rich, full lives, without time structure stresses. We somehow magically and serenely go through the days that blend into weeks, months, and years, accomplishing wondrous homeschooling feats of depth and breadth. I love the fantasy, but it's definitely NOT my reality!

Welcome to the world of a single homeschooling mother.

Mornings ALWAYS come sooner then I want. I am NEVER, EVER ready for them. The sun ALWAYS rises well before noon! (Can you tell I'm not a morning person?) My first thought on hearing the alarm go off is "It can't be morning already!" My next thoughts are, "What day of the week is it?" and "Where do we need to be?" I envision a Rolodex with cards showing the days of the week. I mentally flip through them as I try desperately to wake up and jump-start my brain cells.

Monday. We begin the day with yoga at our local YMCA. I used to volunteer there and now have a scholarship. After class my daughter goes with her piano teacher for a lesson. She is a wonderful woman who loves music and approached her about the lessons. It was through our yoga teacher a piano was found and given to my daughter. I then head off to work for a few hours. To accommodate my daughter's schedule, I freelance. Where I'm working now is a godsend. I work part-time [20 hours a week], hours I choose and child comes with. When necessary I take time off. I don't get paid for hours not worked, but considering my daughter is accepted as part of the package deal, I'm not complaining. This one's known as a "keeper." I bring my daughter back to the office after her piano lesson. She eats and does her work. Math and Hebrew I require of her. She's good about covering the rest on her own. Then we're off to ballet. (Grandparents pay her ballet expenses. I chauffeur.) After ballet we come home, usually around 5:30 p.m.

Tuesday. Food Share to pick up our box of food for the week. (Humbling. Very humbling.) Run a couple of errands. Unload the food at home. Go to the office. We then head "over the hill" (about 30 miles away) so she can go to Hebrew school. She's in her fifth year. My on-site sweat equity covers her tuition. When I sign up for classes, to learn something about our religion of which I know very little, we get home between 10 or 10:30 at night. Otherwise, we return home around 7:30 p.m.

Wednesday. A yoga, work, ballet day. Wednesday is my daughter's long ballet session—2-1/2 hours. That gives me about two hours to run errands, straighten up the house or do laundry (single moms know how to have a good time!) before picking her up. We're usually home by 6:30 p.m.

Thursday. I like Thursdays. We get to cuddle together and talk before going to work. We again head "over the hill" for Hebrew School. We'll be home around 7:30, if I have no classes. The weekend's getting closer and that's a lovely thought.

Friday. A yoga, work and ballet scenario with a variation. On Friday nights we welcome the Sabbath into our home. (Kabbalat Shabbat in Hebrew.) We come home for a wonderful Kabbalat Shabbat ceremony. Once those candles are lit there's time to breathe, to be quiet. We haven't quite gotten the Shabbat to carry over the entire 25 hour period, but at this point even the few hours with no phones or scheduled tasks, offers a respite and rejuvenates. A very special time.

Saturday. Home. A wonderful treat. I won't work on Saturdays. Often we go to our terrific local library. We can (and often do) spend hours there. Many times we'll go to the beach afterwards. Play tag with the ocean. Build sand castles. Beach comb. Play in the playground by the Pacific Ocean. Life is always good when looking out across the ocean. Hearing the waves crash does wonders for my soul.

Sunday. If I have a project (income generating) to work on at home that gets done. (My daughter's father contributes nothing to her care, so I take work in, as well as work outside, the house.) If there's no work and we aren't scheduled to be somewhere else, I try to catch up on my household maintenance chores. My goal in that department is to keep things "down to a dull roar." Sometimes my daughter helps and sometimes she does her own thing.

My daughter has daily responsibilities she tends to: taking care of her cat, practicing piano, helping me with the mundane—dishes, laundry, housework, yard work, and whatever else needs to be done. One of the reasons homeschooling works for us is because we work as a team toward our common goal.

My daughter blossoms and is very productive with time to call her own. Because of this I try to carve out as much time for her as our hectic schedule permits. Regardless of all the running around (we've already cut the "fluff," what's left is extremely important to one or the other of us) there are always those magical moments which make it worthwhile. I don't care how busy I am or what I'm doing, there's ALWAYS time for a magical moment break. It can be when we hug and I remember how special she is to me. It can be that she has written something she wants to share with me, or remembered an incident she wants me to know about. She may have discovered something new or done something for the first time. It can be any one of many little things of import to her. That's what keeps my batteries charged—those magical moments.

Our lives are far from my ideal. Even with that, I have the most important thing of all—I am rearing my child. No, I am investing in my child with my time and energy. She sees daily the decisions I make, and she knows emphatically how important she is to me. Asking for help and receiving help are not easy. It doesn't get easier with time. However, my belief that what I am doing is right by my child makes it bearable. So too does the conviction my time will come when I can return (many times over) to others those kindnesses we've received.

Tears of frustration are a part of the package, but then again so are tears of joy. Our lives are what they are. Money may be an extremely scarce commodity in this household, but love isn't! Every night I tuck my daughter in. I remind her of how much she is loved, kiss her and wish her pleasant dreams.

Homeschooling Moments

Each homeschooling family experiences unexpected moments which ease our minds, warm our hearts, and help us remember that homeschooling works.

Recognizing the Big Picture
By Monica Cardiff

Many of my homeschooling moments are times that I realize I have learned something through homeschooling that I may not have learned otherwise. Of course there are the actual academics—some obscure point in grammar that I never absorbed the first time around or a major era in history that was either neglected in my schooling or was lost in a boring presentation. But more important are the lessons in life that I am learning.

From planning our schedules, I've learned that one person can't do everything, no matter how good and worthwhile it is.

From good intentions gone awry, I've learned the importance of accurate communications.

From observing my toddler master difficult skills, I've learned the value of small steps.

And I've learned that homeschooling helps me see the Big Picture.

Recently, I visited some friends who had just moved into a gorgeous 3500 square foot dream home in the mountains. I felt not so much envy of their prosperity, as a materialistic desire for something similar. I immediately started scheming how to afford this luxury. The obvious way would be for me to return to my career outside the home.

Then I began to think about what I would have to give up to make that a reality. I could have an incredible house, but little time to enjoy either it or my family. Or, I could continue to homeschool—enjoying the privilege of being with my children daily in our comfortable home, helping to build their minds and characters. And their lives, in turn, will affect many others. Put that way, it's an easy choice.

Homeschooling my children gives me perspective, when I just open my eyes to see it.

Life's Important Lessons
By Kate Jiminez

There are days when all of our best homeschooling intentions go awry. We had one of those days when I decided we weren't doing enough academic work. It was a day I was determined to make some progress teaching Angela to read. She was 8 years old at the time and reading very little. I'll admit it; I was beginning to get scared. The ugly mother competition, you know the my-baby-was-potty-trained-by-2 or walking-by-9-months kind, reared its head and claimed another victim when a friend called and bragged about how wonderful her daughter was doing in school. It left me wondering why my children weren't brighter, talented or gifted.

So we took out the phonics cards and began our lesson in earnest. After twenty frustrating minutes I resorted to hollering and Angela began crying. I put away the phonics cards, apologized for my bad behavior and we went out into the garden to pull weeds. A lesson was learned.

Epiphanies of Homeschooling Life
By Monica Cardiff

The sun was sinking as my friend Mary drove wearily across town yet another time to complete her last errand. She just wanted to get home to finish some schooling, but her baby made it clear—as babies often will—that a stop was in order.

Mary pulled into a deserted church parking lot. Melissa, her 5 year old, hopped out of the car to play under a nearby tree. Mary watched while nursing the baby and lamented the lost math lesson.

After the baby fell asleep, Mary stepped out of the car to join Melissa. On the ground at the base of the tree, Melissa had sorted 40 sticks from longest to shortest and numerous rocks and leaves according to size and shape. Independently, while her mother had been taking care of the baby, Melissa had completed a math lesson on her own.

A Mom's Homeschool Lesson
By Karen Taylor

I vividly recall the day—no the moment—that my son taught me how to homeschool. He was five, and it was our first official year homeschooling, and although he was continuing to stay home with me as he always had, it felt different. I regularly vacillated between being overly concerned, and reasonably relaxed. I recall that I felt the need to prove I had made the correct choice in homeschooling, and that I didn't want to make a mistake and ruin his life. I felt the societal pressure of how much more important things were now that he was old enough for kindergarten. Typical beginner emotions, I've since learned.

We were visiting his grandparents that day, and they suggested going to a museum. What could be better than a field trip? It was another opportunity to experience the advantages of homeschooling. I was ready!

As we walked through the exhibits, I carefully pointed out things because it now seemed important that he not miss anything. After all, his peers were in school—this was the big league now, and I felt the pressure to "do it right." We moved on to an antique car. Knowing his interest in mechanical things, I wanted him to view the simple engine so he could learn something. I knelt down and suggested he join me to look under the old car. Then I looked up and saw that he was still standing and patiently pointing to a large floor mirror that I had not noticed. It was directed at the underside of the vehicle, and he was busy observing the engine details, only from a more comfortable standing position.

At that moment, I received the greatest lesson of the day. I learned to relax and trust my son. He didn't need me to tell him how to learn! I stopped pointing out everything, and began trusting that he had the ability to see these things for himself.

These days, he's the one who shows me things that I might otherwise miss, and I'm pleased to accept his help.

A Conversation, a Revelation
By Kate Jimenez

Angela has a school friend who comes to our home before and after school while her parents are working. Her name is Sally; she is 11, and Angela is 9 years old. One day, Sally pulled her math book out of her backpack and began to work on a long homework assignment. Angela decided this would be a good time to work on her math, too. She took out her math book and some paper and began to work alongside Sally.

"I hate math." Sally grumbled. "It's boring."

"I love math." Angela replied.

"You won't love it once you get to fifth grade." Sally responded.

And so went the conversation with Sally telling Angela what she hated about school, the various subjects (except reading which they rarely had time to do), the mean kids, the long day, and getting up early.

"How late do you sleep in on Saturdays?" Sally asked.

Angela said, "I get up early every day."

"Why would you want to do that?" said Sally.

"Because I don't have to go to school." Angela replied.

As I listened to this conversation I was reassured about our decision to homeschool Angela. It brought home to me how school can turn perfectly interesting subject matter, like math, into a drudge and hated chore. And because Angela is free to plan most of her day herself, she looks forward to getting up every morning.

But there was also a feeling of sadness when I listened to them talk. I felt sad that Sally couldn't be home educated, too, and I felt for all the children who hate math, or reading, or science, or life in general after a long day at school.

Learning In Their Own Way
By Monica Cardiff

A friend, Lori, homeschools her five children. During the afternoon, Lori was trying a creative approach to language arts with her active son, Micah. Micah, a kinesthetic learner, was frankly not interested in any formal academics or book learning. Lori wisely forced none on him.

Instead, Lori played her guitar and sang songs while Micah danced—a way of learning which delighted both of them. When they finished, Micah raced off to play with his friend Max.

In the course of their music sessions, Micah had memorized the "A-B-C Song," but Lori had no idea if he had absorbed anything beyond that.

Lori knew Micah had made a breakthrough when a little while later he burst through the door and said excitedly, "Mom, every letter in Max's name is in the alphabet!"

An Unplanned Unit Study
By Monica Cardiff

My friend Barbara has two children that my girls describe as "wild, snake-lovin' boys." These active boys make Barbara's life an adventure—she doesn't know what each day will bring.

One morning, Neal (9) and Jeremy (7) found and captured a bunch of grasshoppers, collecting them in a big box. They didn't know what to feed the grasshoppers, so they decided to do some research in the World Book Encyclopedia. They first needed to figure out how to spell "grasshopper" in order to find it. They successfully found that grasshoppers eat leaves and plants. They also discovered that grasshoppers can jump twenty times their body length.

This led Neal and Jeremy to find a tape measure to measure themselves. Then the jumping began. The boys (and the grasshoppers) tried to jump for distance. Neal and Jeremy marked and measured. The boys were trying to jump twenty times their lengths, which would be about 85 feet. Came pretty close too!

In the course of the project, the boys covered reading, spelling, reference work, math, physical education, and science. The unplanned day turned into a great unit study.

Being Available When Our Children Need Us
By Monica Cardiff

One night I was reading a bedtime story with my then six-year-old Katherine. The book was called *A Bargain for Frances* and at one point the main character is deceitfully tricked by her "friend."

Honesty is highly valued in our family, so it took a little while for Katherine to comprehend the deception. When it finally sunk in, Katherine looked up at me with wide eyes and said incredulously, "She LIED."

Her loss of innocence was quite evident, and it pained me greatly, but I was glad I could be with her to help her through it.

As homeschooling parents, we get to experience the joyful, "Aha!" times of discovery with our children as well as the painful growing-up hurdles. There is no way to prevent the loss of innocence in our children. However, we can be with our children in a very real way during those crucial moments that happen unexpectedly at any hour of the day.

Lessons Learned in the First Year
By Bj Darr

It is hard to believe that it has already been one full year since our family started this radical experiment called "homeschooling." It is even harder to believe how much we have changed and grown as a homeschooling family in that short time. But, perhaps, what surprises me most is not what my children learned this year, but what I learned about my children, myself, and education.

Lesson Number 1: *Give yourself and your child time to make the transition away from public/private school and into homeschooling.*
When we first started this adventure last summer, I thought my daughter, Letha, could end her four years at her private school and that we would just smoothly continue the educational process with her at home. I was taken completely by surprise by Letha's need to "debrief" from her institutionalized schooling days and her need to put that time in perspective.

Lesson Number 2: *It takes time to "get acquainted" with all the curricula, resources, and options available. Eventually, though, it will start to look familiar.*

The next surprise was discovering that we had choices, lots and lots of choices, about curriculum. In fact there were so many choices it overwhelmed me at first. How could we ever make good choices when the possibilities seemed so endless?

Lesson Number 3: *You are not alone in your homeschooling venture unless you choose to be.*
While you are trying to make sense of it all it helps to realize that there is a lot of support out there and many homeschooling families who are willing to spend time helping you. Find these people. You don't need to reinvent the wheel.

Lesson Number 4: *There are "bad days" in homeschooling, too.*
After our family had settled the basic questions about approach and curriculum and we had settled in, we then discovered that we had some days and weeks when nothing seemed to go right.

Lesson Number 5: *Homeschooling may be the best choice for your child, but it is not perfect.*
Gradually I learned that when we had a bad day it was better to take that day off and start fresh. We had high hopes and perhaps some unrealistic expectations as we began homeschooling. Flexibility has been a huge advantage when working and learning with our children.

Lesson Number 6: *The decision to homeschool should be an ongoing choice, and not a static decision.*
You need to be willing to accept the limitations and shortcomings you find and work with them. Otherwise, when you hit these potholes, you may erroneously decide the whole road is impassable. We found that our family needed to evaluate our trip under these "road conditions" toward the end of our first year. That is, it was important to our family to reevaluate the choice we had made to homeschool and to renew our commitment to educate our children in this way.

Lesson Number 7: *Homeschooling is taking responsibility for your child's education, and making a personal commitment to your child's learning.*
Finally, as our first year of homeschooling came to a close, I realized that I was beginning to understand what homeschooling really meant. At the start of our adventure I had thought that it was something we could "get" if we could just wade through all that information about curricula and pick the perfect one. The process, as I had seen it, was similar to shopping for a private school—read the literature, sign the enrollment papers, and drop 'em off.

Our family has renewed its commitment to homeschooling, and we are now at the beginning of our second year. We are grateful for all that we learned our first year and how it made us grow and stretch. For us, it has truly been the best choice we could possibly make with our children and in spite of all the potholes and occasional wrong turns, we had a wonderful year together. I can't wait to find out what a second-year homeschooling family learns.

Homeschooling? Get Real!

By Janelle Orsi

When I was in public school I could think of millions of reasons why homeschooling would be a dumb idea. It seemed quite evident to my naive brain that it would be impossible to get an education without going to school. I was also sure that all homeschoolers must be "social morons," obviously because they are isolated all day long. Since then I have de-brainwashed those notions and come to see the reality of it all.

Real Life Education

I've now been homeschooling for seven years and I can think of millions of reasons why homeschooling is the best thing that has ever happened to me. The first and foremost of these is that I've had the freedom to live a real life. While most of my peers are being marched through depressing hallways and spending hours in uncomfortable classrooms, I have been out experiencing interesting things and meeting interesting people. While other teenagers have been sleeping through 4th period history, I have been learning about Andean music, experimenting with astrophotography, designing webpages, and going on archaeological digs.

Through most of my teenage years I have been given the freedom to manage my own time and education. Many people hear that and assume that because no one is forcing me to learn, I'm spending my time watching TV and goofing off. Quite the contrary. By being homeschooled, I think I have developed an attitude toward learning that is not shared with many of my peers: I love learning!!

So many times I have stood with a group of (non-homeschooling) adults and listened to them carry on about their three and four-year-olds who are so enthusiastic about learning. I stand there quietly and wonder why they never say that about their seven-year-olds. Is there any reason why most kids over age six lose enthusiasm for learning? There is only one: school.

When I was in third grade (public school), I didn't understand why I was supposed to get an education. All I knew was that it was a fact of life, so I didn't question it. My attitude was that learning was a task through which I must suffer for six hours per day. For me, when school got out, learning ended. As far as I was concerned, learning played no part in the rest of my life.

Now, at the age of 17, I can sincerely say that learning IS my life. What I finally figured out was that there is a purpose and a place for everything I learn. I now know that the more I learn, the more I will be able to understand the world in which I live—quite an exhilarating feeling.

Part of the problem with the formal education system, in my opinion, is that it makes kids sit for hours as teachers feed them a constant flow of information. The kids memorize hordes of facts but are not given the opportunity to organize them into something meaningful. With the freedom and flexibility of homeschooling, I have been able to step back from my studies and consider why I am learning a certain thing, how it relates to other things I'm learning, and how I can apply it to my life and understanding of the world. That's what makes learning fun and exciting.

Here is a recent observation I made in my "Art of the Americas" class at Skyline College: After our class watched a video that gave a general introduction to the civilizations of Teotihuacan, the Maya, and the Aztec, we were given a list of questions pertaining to the video. In the days before our answers were due, many students came up and asked me to help them answer the questions. Most of them had watched the video and picked up specific facts that they thought they might have to know, such as specific pieces of artwork and archaeological sites, but many failed to pick up on the general concepts and information essential to the overall understanding. THREE students asked me to give them the answer to a question, which read, "Name two countries discussed in the video." I was astonished that they couldn't answer this most basic question! I want to know how these students are planning to use the information learned in this class when they don't understand it in context. I wondered if they'd believe me if I told them the Maya lived in Tanzania; would they just memorize that fact without thinking whether it made sense of not?! I suspect that this is the way many students approach education; it basically shows that they don't know why they are learning in the first place.

Real Life Socialization

Have I done enough ranting about education? I could go on for hours but I won't because I've yet to do my ranting about socialization. Socialization is a touchy subject among homeschoolers. Every homeschooler has had to smile and politely answer that naive, but so common question, "What about socialization?" I recall a situation at my weekly orchestra practice in which I was casually conversing with a group of adults when one of the women found out that I was a homeschooler. She immediately asked me whether I "missed getting the socialization." As my insides resounded with laughter I resisted the urge to yell "What on earth do you think I'm doing right now?!!" Of course I stayed calm and satisfied my skeptical inquirers with the assurance that my days are filled with activities involving other kids, college students, and adults. And no, I am not isolated.

Some time I want to respond to that socialization question by making the inquirer explain exactly what is so great about public school socialization. I want to know what I'm missing. I think back to some of my "social" experiences in school.

I remember a situation in third grade. During the middle of the school year a boy named Ted moved to town and entered our class. Probably by the end of his first day, everybody in the class had decided that they didn't like him. This was for no particular reason that I could see; Ted seemed to be bright and friendly, but nevertheless his classmates decided to devote their lives to making his miserable. Over the next few months they started insidious rumors, refused to sit with him at lunch, and threw dirt at him on the playground. Even some of the nicer kids in the class were able to justify this with the mentality that Ted was something less than human. They forgot that Ted had feelings that could be damaged by having mustard put in his backpack or having his belongings stolen.

I shudder when I try to imagine how it would feel to spend every day with 30 kids that hated me, with no allies for support. In third grade I was overweight, something that a couple of kids had to remind me of quite frequently. It's not fun to be made fun of. However, what I experienced was far from the worst of brutalities that kids experience every day in school.

Shucks! Is that what I'm missing? I'm failing to see what is so great about that kind of socialization. If anyone would like to come forward and explain it, please do! In the meantime I'd like to paint a more cheerful picture: In my observations of homeschoolers I have seen what I would call "real socialization." Picture this: 15 homeschooled kids at a bowling alley. In this group there are varied ages, sizes, religions, ethnicities, opinions, and clothing styles. The difference in this situation is that everyone is treated like a human, no matter who they are. Most homeschoolers I know treat other people with respect and courtesy. They don't feel as much need to compete, make fun of people, and resort to physical violence in order to gain the esteem of their peers. In my opinion, this is the kind of socialization that is essential to maintain a moral and peaceful society. Maybe homeschoolers should be asking the public-schoolers whether they're the ones that miss socialization.

The Real World

Having been out of school for seven years, I've been able to stand back and see the problems with our country's education system. I also see that many people have yet to notice these problems. Most people still hold the view that in order to produce well-educated and moral citizens, we must send our children to school. Most people are so used to this assertion that it's very difficult to question it, but I'm hopeful that more and more people will try to see that there is something better. This is something I'm assured of every time I watch a homeschooled kid get excited about learning or when I see a group of children playing peacefully together. I'm also assured every time I look at my own life and see everything that homeschooling has taught me. There is no doubt in my mind that my current attitudes towards life are largely the result of having the freedom to explore and experience the real world through homeschooling.

Your Teenager Isn't Going to High School?
Just How Long Are You Going to Homeschool Him Anyway?

"Homeschooling families have various options

for educating high school students at home."

©Luana Holzer

Homeschooling High School

At one time, high school was a time for putting homeschooled children back in school so the teens would receive what worried parents perceived would be a higher quality education than they could provide for those last few years. The notion that a child can't be successfully homeschooled through high school has since been dispelled, and many now plan to homeschool through high school, while others begin homeschooling during this time when they become frustrated by social problems compounded with a lackluster education. In this chapter, you will hear from experienced homeschooling parents, along with homeschooled teens. You will read about some options open to teens. The news is good!

Graduation Options

Homeschooling families have various options for educating high school students at home. As a private, home-based school in the State of California, you may issue a high school diploma to your students. Families for whom graduation from a state-accredited high school is important have the option of enrolling their students in an accredited correspondence high school program. Students in these programs receive a state recognized high school diploma upon completion of graduation requirements. Other homeschooling students choose to earn the legal equivalent of a diploma by taking the CHSPE or GED examination.

California High School Proficiency Examination (CHSPE)

The CHSPE was developed to provide a means by which qualified individuals could leave high school early. Examinees who demonstrate their proficiency in the basic skills (reading, writing, and mathematics) receive a Certificate of Proficiency, which by law in California is equivalent to a high school diploma [EC §48412]. The CHSPE is open to anyone meeting one of the following requirements:

1. Sixteen years of age or older
2. Completion of at least one year of enrollment in the tenth grade
3. Student has "been enrolled in the second half-year of the tenth grade since the beginning of the semester in which that test date occurs."

Homeschooling students younger than 16 may take the CHSPE if the teacher (in a home private school, that would be the parent) verifies the student's mastery of 10th grade level work. There is no penalty, other than paying another $50 fee, to take the test more than once.

By passing the CHSPE, students 16 and older have graduated from high school and are exempt from California's compulsory school law. Children younger than 16 who pass this test, although having graduated, are still required to comply with the compulsory school law until age 16 and therefore should continue to homeschool using one of the four options described in Chapter 3.

The CHSPE is normally given two times a year, in November and April, and there is a $50 fee. Test registration and information booklets are available from your public library or the CHSPE program. Test preparation books are published by ARCO and Barron, and there are also sample questions at the website. Information about the CHSPE, including the registration form, can be found at www.cde.ca.gov/statetests/chspe/, or by calling 916/319-0330.

The GED

The General Educational Developmental Test (GED) is deemed by California law to be a high school diploma for purposes of employment by all state and local public agencies [EC §51420-51427]. Examinees must be 18 years of age or older. The GED purports to measure a student's ability to comprehend, apply and analyze information in: literature/arts, writing skills, history, math, and social studies, or, as closely as possible, the outcomes associated with four years of high school instruction. GED classes are offered through local school district and adult programs. For information, call 202/939-9490 or visit *www.acenet.edu/calec/ged/intro-TT.cfm/*, or contact a local school district.

The California High School Proficiency Exam: A Teen's Experience
By Brianna Cardiff

The California High School Proficiency Examination (CHSPE) is an exam designed to test the basic life skills of tenth grade and older students. California law states that the Certificate of Proficiency "shall be equivalent to a high school diploma." The reason for taking this test is so you may go on to higher education, which for me was a wonderful incentive. All institutions controlled by California law that require high school diplomas must accept the certificate as satisfying those requirements. It is not the same as going through regular high school course work, and, military services may or may not accept the certificate.

I took the CHSPE on a rainy Saturday morning at a local high school. After showing my school ID card I was assigned to a seat. Once everyone was signed in, and the tests were passed out, we wrote our names in about 10 different places. Then the first part of the test began: writing an essay. We had a choice of two essay topics. Then we had 30 minutes to write our essay. The next part of the test was answering 100 multiple choice questions. We had 2 1/2 hours to complete this, and there was no penalty for guessing. The questions were on reading comprehension and basic math skills (percents, measurements, etc.). Once done with the test I was allowed to leave early. Then came the hard part—waiting a month for the results. Finally they sent me a letter with my score of "pass" and a Certificate of Proficiency.

Here's what to do to prepare for taking the CHSPE. My first advice would be to practice, practice, practice. You can get a book full of practice tests at B. Dalton or other bookstores.

Next you need to register. They have space constraints, so the earlier the better. On the registration sheet they ask for a school code. We put "Private School Without Code."

If you are under the age of sixteen, you must have the school counselor (your mom or dad) sign that you are doing tenth grade level work. You will receive a ticket that you must bring to the test.

You also must show sufficient identification, such as: school ID card, driver's license, passport, or if none of these are available, a parent's driver's license is accepted. They do not accept social security cards or birth certificates. My mom made me a school ID card by printing a small (the size of a business card) paper with the name of our school, my name, and the date. She then glued on my most current school picture and had me sign my name on the card. We went over to a copy store and had it laminated.

Approximately one month after taking the test, they will send out the results. They score pass or not pass; no grades are given.

Now that I've passed, watch out Junior Colleges, here I come!

Designing a High School Course of Study

Excerpted with permission from *Christian Home Educators' Curriculum Manual: Junior/Senior High*
By Cathy Duffy

Old ways are not necessarily better, but our present educational system is obviously missing something important. So much of the material is repeated over and over again from elementary grades through high school. Much time is wasted, and children's talents and gifts that fall outside a narrow academic range are ignored. We need to take a hard look at our course of study in terms of what is best for our teen.

If there is a possibility that our teen will enter a regular high school sometime after his freshman year, ensuring that course work parallels that done in the school becomes important. Accredited correspondence courses are more likely to be accepted than our own self-designed course, but we can still put together courses with widely recognized textbooks covering the typical course content.

Confidence will definitely influence the decisions we make about the choices confronting us. There are many different ways of planning a high school course of study. The more confident we are, the more freedom we are likely to exercise in determining how we will proceed.

For both philosophical and practical reasons, home educators will have diverse ideas about what they consider essential course content. Let us look at some of the ideas that might shape our course of study.

Cultural Literacy

In his book, *Cultural Literacy, What Every American Needs to Know*, E. D. Hirsch, Jr. states that people must practice effective communication to function effectively, that effective communication requires shared culture, and that shared culture requires transmission of specific information to children. That specific information comes primarily from books which have been widely recognized as having had a significant impact upon society's thoughts—books such as the *Bible*, Plato's *Republic*, and other great literary and philosophic works. It also comes from the arts and languages.

In defining cultural literacy, Hirsch says, "It is the background information, stored in their minds, that enables them to take up a newspaper and read it with an adequate level of comprehension, getting the point, grasping the implications, relating what they read to the unstated context which alone gives meaning to what they read." He concludes that general cultural literacy is necessary for people to learn about new ideas, develop new technology, and deal with events and challenges. Hirsch believes that people trained in narrow vocational educational pursuits rather than with broader tools of learning will have difficulty expanding their learning or dealing with new situations.

Charlotte Mason

Charlotte Mason, a proponent of home education more than sixty-five years ago, promoted ideas similar to those of Hirsch. Her reasoning differed only slightly. Mason's description of a liberal education is in close accord with what Hirsch promotes—an education that consists largely of reading acknowledged, influential literary works. She says, "…one of the main purposes of a 'liberal education for all' is to form links between high and low, rich and poor, the classes and the masses, in the strong sympathy of common knowledge." Mason further believed that a liberal arts education (as she proposed it be taught) would enhance each person's intellectual ability, attention, and power of recollection—boons to both the intellectual and business worlds.

Liberal Arts or Classical Education

In centuries past, education for older levels consisted largely of reading and discussing great books—the liberal arts (sometimes called classical) education similar to ideas of both Hirsch and Mason. The idea of using workbooks would have seemed ridiculous. Children were expected to have accumulated a great deal of factual information through study and memorization at younger levels. When children reached their teens, it was time to begin the real thinking and application of knowledge.

Many people have been promoting a return to some form of classical education. Proponents would have students concentrate on a liberal arts education in high school and college, learning additional skills in college and after graduation, but there is by no means universal agreement about what specifically constitutes a classical education. Generally speaking, it would include literary studies of recognized classical authors from most periods of recorded history. Some think specifically of Greek and Roman writings and their pagan civilizations as the source for classical education, but few, if any, modern-day proponents concentrate solely, or even primarily, on these roots. Classical education in its popular revival stresses writing and communication skills, and, generally, a foreign language (preferably Latin). Study of history, philosophy, world religions, and the fine arts are incorporated for the light they shed on other subjects.

Principle Approach

The Principle Approach provides a solid, well-developed philosophy of Christian education, although the methodology is challenging. The Principle Approach can encompass a classical education, Charlotte Mason's ideas, cultural literacy, and other ideas described here, because it outlines a foundation that answers the questions about why we do what we do in education. It operates at a more fundamental level than do most of the others.

The principles are described slightly differently by various persons using this approach, but the following list from Rus Walton's *Fundamentals for American Christians* is typical. The principles are identified, studied, and used as a foundation for further learning. The principles are based on the following ideas:

- God's sovereignty
- Individuality
- Personal property
- Self government
- Family government
- Stewardship
- Local autonomy
- Voluntary association

Unschooling

The idea of letting children follow their own inclinations in their education has been called "unschooling." The philosophic ideas behind this approach are most often associated with John Holt, author of numerous books such as *How Children Learn* and *Teach Your Own*.

Many home educators support these philosophic ideas to varying degrees and have allowed their teens to follow their interests in putting together a course of study to fit their career goals. In general, those following an unschooling approach allow teens to choose what, when, and how to study, according to their need for knowledge or proficiency in different areas. For instance, a person interested in becoming a veterinarian can work part-time with a veterinarian, similar to an apprentice. On his own he can read books related to the subject. If the intent is to go on to college for further training, the student would study whatever subjects he needs to pass college entrance exams.

Unit Study

While many families feel comfortable with unit study in the elementary grades, they often turn to more traditional approaches in junior and senior high. However, with the advent of some of the comprehensive unit study packages being developed and marketed in recent years, unit study for the teen years is becoming increasingly popular and practical.

Practical

Some home educated teens want to work in construction, farming, plumbing, or another trade that will not require college education. They want a practical course of study that will prepare them to begin work as soon as possible. They do not want to waste time on subjects they never expect to use. Such a narrow course of study has limitations which might present problems in the future if the original career goal does not work out. However, if a teenager has made up his mind that he will learn only what is important to him, we can waste our time and energy trying to force him to go beyond his self-imposed limits. If the original goal has to be scrapped, it is always possible, although it might be difficult, to return to school and learn something else or pursue another career.

"James Madison High School"

Former Federal Secretary for Education William Bennett has promoted what he calls "James Madison High School." This is a model for a high school course of study which emphasizes the basic academic subjects while allowing choices that take the individual needs into account. Bennett's concern has been the increasing percentage of courses consisting of physical education, health education, work experience, remedial math and English, and personal development which have displaced core academics.

Following Bennett's ideas, we would plan a course of study that remains somewhat traditional yet allows for emphasis on an educational area. For instance, for students interested in one of the scientific fields, the course of study would be weighted towards math and science, communication skills would have next priority; and history, philosophy, and the arts would be covered more superficially.

Traditional

The majority of home educators stick (to some extent) with traditional courses of study which include standard courses in math, language arts, history, and science, plus electives. There is more security in conforming to standard expectations, especially when students plan to go on to college. Beyond that, such a course of study does provide a fairly balanced education. The questions home educators raise about the course of study challenge the underlying assumption that "one size fits all." There are thousands of subjects that students could be studying, yet the traditional course of study limits the choices to a small handful. For example, biology and chemistry are the standard science courses, but there is little that makes either inherently better than geology, botany, oceanography, or most any other scientific topic. Algebra is justified for all students because of the logic and thinking skills it uses, yet some people question if there are not more practical ways of teaching those skills.

Concocting Your Own Course of Study

Many veteran home schoolers end up creating their own courses of study that draw from any number of the above-described approaches combined with their own ideas. For example, Robin Scarlata, in her book *What Your Child Needs to Know When,* describes her "Heart of Wisdom" approach which is sort of a unit study approach based on the Bible, but which stresses strong language arts development (shades of Charlotte Mason's ideas here). Some traditional texts round out the study, and teens are encouraged to incorporate development of practical life skills.

The beauty of home education is that we have the freedom to determine what is best for each of our children. We need not determine which, if any, of the above approaches is best for everyone, but only what works for our children.

CHN member Cathy Duffy is a popular speaker, and the author of numerous books and articles on home education. For more information, visit her website: http://www.grovepublishing.com/.

Dropouts? No! Homeschoolers? Yes!
By Jackie Orsi

In recent generations, we've come to sort all teen-agers into two, and only two, groups: good kids and dropouts. We've bought into the supposition for generations now that good kids dutifully attend high school until graduation day. A dropout, by contrast, is a lout, a loser, and quite likely, a reprobate.

These moral extremes don't admit much tolerance for individual needs, for deficiencies in the schools, or for any other variable that might yield an exception, but they are a necessary result of the logic of compulsory school attendance. The thinking goes: if we force children to go to school, then it must be good for them, right? And therefore, if they reject school, they must be bad children, right? So it is that society wags a shaming finger at dropouts while truant officers patrol the streets. All in all, it's a fairly successful formula—nine parts moral coercion and one part legal constraint—enabling us to herd the vast majority of kids into the schoolyards with a minimum of effort.

Of course, we pay a price for this either/or arrangement. The millions of teens who don't fit the high school mold languish and suffer, trying to hang on till their time is up and a diploma is dispensed to them. If we're lucky, they merely grow passive during their captivity. Despite the social pressure to hang on, other kids drop out as soon as the law allows, deciding that the stigma of "dropout" is easier to take than a single day more in a place that is meaningless, suffocating, and humiliating to them. High schools are full of dropouts-to-be, waiting to reach the legal age of liberation and haunting the halls like the living dead, restless and defiant. Shamed for failing or hating school, they league together in a subculture that promises to validate their self-worth, a gang that calls it "cool" to be bad. The cruel dichotomy of diploma vs. dropout has estranged countless millions of our youth.

Until now. There's a blessed new choice on the scene. In my role as a homeschool activist, my phone rings all day long. I'm witnessing an incoming tide of teens and their parents who are turning with hope and relief to homeschooling. Teens are the fastest growing segment of the nation's fastest growing educational movement. Significantly, in the majority of these cases, it is the teen who initiates the discussion by asking mom and dad to please consider homeschooling.

Because homeschooling exists, and because it's gaining stature as a valid educational choice, teens and their parents are sitting down together, communicating, and solving problems in ways that would have been unlikely even a decade ago. Increasing numbers of parents are willing to consider the possibility that their child's frustration/fear/boredom/alienation is not just willful perversity, but might just be an Outcome Based on Education, to use the system's own buzzwords. A growing number of teens are discarding the "dropout" label and calling themselves "unique individuals" instead. Working together, families at all income levels are finding creative new ways for their young person to continue on a learning course, adapting to his or her needs in a way no institutional school, public or private, can.

Take Ben for example. He's a 15 year-old charmer without a scholar's bone in his body. Schoolwork was so meaningless to him that he grew hostile, started to "hang out" and "get in trouble." Now in homeschool, he's studying to pass the California High School Proficiency Exam and apprenticing in an auto mechanics shop. This sensible and challenging plan put together by mother and son has restored Ben's good nature. His mother now says, "I've got my son back."

I hear that phrase often. Homeschooling defuses a lot of anger and salves a lot of psychological wounds. It puts parents back on their kid's side again. America is full of good kids who have sound individual reasons to leave school and go about their own ways of growing up. There's 17-year-old Mark who knows his life's work is to be a classical musician and who wants to dedicate more of his time to that accomplishment. There's Trisha who desperately wanted away from her seventh grade peer group's dive into sex and drugs. There's Laura, a plain 15-year-old who needed release from relentless teasing in high school, and delightedly found acceptance and challenge studying at a museum. There are dozens more I could tell you about, all of them needing out—and not a lout, loser, or reprobate among them!

Homeschooling is a small door punched in a far back corner of the solid public high school edifice. Kids are leaving one by one. It's a promising start.

Modern Day Apprenticeships

By Jackie Orsi

This bookish inclination at length determined my father to make me a printer. . . I stood out some time, but at last was persuaded, and signed the indentures when I was yet but twelve years old. I was to serve as an apprentice til I was twenty-one years of age, only I was to be allowed journeyman's wages during the last year. In a little time I made great proficiency in the business, and became a useful hand to my brother.

- The Autobiography of Ben Franklin

Just What is an Apprenticeship Anyway?

Homeschoolers use the term often, referring to it as a desirable alternative open to teenage students. What exactly do they mean? "Apprenticeship" is a word with a rich historical meaning, but in today's context an apprenticeship system like Ben Franklin described would be looked upon as tantamount to child slavery. Homeschoolers may have some traditional notions, but even we aren't that retro!

Today, certain livelihoods use the designation "apprentice", but what they mean is not really what homeschoolers mean. Our young people aren't necessarily ready to commit to career training, nor be narrowed in on construction trades, either, although they certainly are a part of what we have in mind.

Homeschoolers have revived the term "apprenticeship" because it more nearly describes a kind of experience we would like to make available to our kids. We don't want to use the word "job" because what we have in mind is not exactly a job (though an apprenticeship may involve paid employment). We don't want to call it "volunteering" because what we have in mind is not exactly volunteering (although the young person may apprentice without compensation). The primary motivation for a job is usually to earn money. The primary motivation for volunteering is usually to serve and support a worthwhile cause. The primary motivation for an apprenticeship is to learn. It may involve learning for a future career, or it may involve a temporary interest, or it may simply involve a desire to experience the world from a new perspective.

Homeschoolers have apprenticed in stores, in libraries, in insurance agencies, in auto mechanic shops, in computer businesses, in publishing houses—all sorts of things have happened, and virtually anything is possible. There are some formal community programs that provide apprenticeships and internships for teens, but most of the apprentice relationships homeschoolers have enjoyed have been arranged individually by the teens and their parents. Some apprenticeships are deliberately created: teens and their parents have spotted a field of interest, sought out reasonable people in these fields, and asked politely for the opportunity. Sometimes a young person with extraordinary potential gets a chance to move beyond his initial limited role as a volunteer or part-time employee. Other apprenticeships have evolved unexpectedly out of chance meetings.

It is true that society contains many people who are skeptical about homeschooling, and some who are much opposed to it; at the same time, there are growing numbers of enlightened individuals who are supportive of homeschooling. When it comes to apprenticeships, we are encouraged by the many adults who have been generous with their time and expertise. The apprentice relationship seems to appeal to something in all of us that wants expression and fulfillment; a real satisfaction comes from sharing one's knowledge with respectful, well-mannered young people who show genuine desire to listen and learn.

An apprenticeship is about learning in the world of work. A young person must expect to work hard and to shoulder a share of tedious tasks or downright dirty work, as the case may be. The apprentice's work contribution balances out his employer's economic costs for training him, and in many cases, is enough to turn the relationship into a win-win for both parties.

Three Contrasting Experiences

The following true stories reveal some of the potential joys and potential problems of apprenticeship.

Case #1: "Amy"

Amy, at age 13, thought she might want to be a veterinarian. With her parents she approached a vet in her hometown to ask for an apprenticeship. He said she could try it. He warned her that she would have to do hard, unglamorous work like mopping, cleaning cages, and so forth, but she would also be permitted to observe in surgery and all other aspects of the practice. Amy worked hard for no pay for a couple years, and then was put on the payroll as an assistant. Now 18, she is still working there part-time, while she attends community college and works toward a career in veterinary medicine. She is fully trained in lab work and routine procedures. She handles patients and their anxious owners with confidence and a gentle touch.

Amy's apprenticeship is perfect: she has received a marvelous education in a field where hands-on experience is absolutely necessary if one wishes to pursue professional status. (Too many tenderhearted animal lovers used to find themselves in the wrong profession; veterinary colleges will no longer admit students who have not had first-hand experience with the grim realities of illness and death that are a part of a vet's day.) In return for her learning, Amy exchanged something of value—cleaning, carrying, and doing whatever task was assigned to her. In time, her value grew to such extent that the veterinarian knew she was as good a worker as the paid assistants were, so he rewarded her accordingly.

Case #2: "Linda"

This same veterinarian was so impressed with Amy, that he allowed a second homeschooler, age 15, to come into apprenticeship on the same terms. The outcome was entirely unlike Amy's success. Linda showed up only half the time and when she did, she wasn't an eager worker. He eventually "fired" her. The obvious lesson: the young person needs to bring a good work ethic to his or her apprenticeship: dressing appropriately, appearing on time, paying attention, and showing responsibility and good nature.

Case #3: "Jen"

Fifteen-year-old Jen heard about Amy's success and wanted the same chance. She and her family asked a vet in the town where she lives. The vet consented at first, but then got nervous. He told Jen to get a work permit, despite the fact that she was not asking to be paid for her work. The vet said his insurance agent insisted on it, saying that liability insurance wouldn't cover her otherwise. Despite her misgivings, Jen went to the local high school to inquire about a work permit; the school official there erroneously told her that she did need a work permit, and then began to dispute the legality of Jen's homeschooling through a private independent study school. Jen wisely gave up on the whole apprenticeship plan.

A Successful Apprenticeship Experience

Amy's and Jen's stories illustrate how undefined the concept of apprenticeship is. One vet felt free to create a new position just for Amy. If he even thought about negative outcomes, he set them aside and focused on Amy's willingness and her potential to give something of value to his practice and ultimately to the veterinary profession. Jen's vet got caught up with worst-case scenarios, the very thing insurance agents dwell upon. To compound matters, the school official in Jen's case was the proverbial Bureaucrat From Hell, inventing laws and sticking her nose where it didn't belong. Work permits are not required for volunteer work. Volunteer workers who get hurt are usually covered under workman's compensation plans, but the fact that Jen was under age 16 may have disturbed the insurance agent. Meanwhile, there was another scenario to consider: whether damages caused by a volunteer would be covered under the vet's errors and omissions policy. All these are valid questions, but the answers are not clear, mainly because of the unusual nature of the apprenticeship Jen proposed.

The good news is that Jen's disappointment is unusual. The overwhelming majority of homeschooler's apprentice arrangements come together smoothly and do not require the involvement of outside parties. It is good to be aware that the issue of work permits and liability may cloud the horizon on occasion.

Another issue to think about is that some people might see a teen working in a business setting and wonder why the young person isn't in school. Homeschoolers sometimes avoid problems by scheduling their apprentice work during nonschool hours, or just keeping their public visibility low.

If you would like an apprenticeship, go into the quest with a positive point of view. Don't be like the vet who worried about the bad things that can happen; be like the one who made something truly wonderful happen. Apprenticeships, like homeschooling itself, are a new and creative development in the education of young people. Lacking official definition and regulation, they can be individually tailored to the mutual rewards of employer and apprentice, and provide unlimited learning through experience.

Homeschoolers and Employment
By Jackie Orsi

Note: The laws governing child labor are extensive and detailed. This is an attempt to summarize the major conditions of child employment, and it should not be viewed as a complete and comprehensive review of child labor law. Furthermore, nothing in this section is intended to be the giving of legal advice.

The growth of the homeschooled teen population naturally means that more teens are combining employment and home education. This means dealing with the work permit bureaucracy and sorting through the complex child labor laws. In some locales this is still a relatively new frontier, both for homeschoolers and for bureaucrats. When any government bureaucracy meets up with homeschooling, things can sometimes get a little tense. The area of employment law is no exception. It's important to approach the matter of obtaining a work permit carefully. Things will likely go smoothly if you come into the process well informed, well organized, and with a positive, courteous attitude.

The employment of minors is heavily regulated by the State of California and the Federal Fair Labor Standards Act (FFLSA) in order to safeguard children's health, safety, and morals. Additionally, employment is not permitted to interfere with children's education and compulsory school attendance. Whenever the state and federal laws are in conflict, the law which provides the greater protection to the minor employee prevails. A minor is defined as someone under the age of 18.

Steering Clear of the Government

There are some strategies that allow teens to be legally employed without the hassle of obtaining a work permit. One strategy is to seek a job in a field that does not require a work permit. The following situations qualify:

- Performance of odd jobs like yard work and baby-sitting in private homes
- Sale or delivery of newspapers, if the minor is a self-employed, independent contractor
- Any job in which the minor is self-employed
- In agricultural, horticultural, viticultural, or domestic work on premises owned, operated or controlled by the minor's parents or guardians
- In certain employment situations among family or friends.

A minor does not need a permit to work in a family-owned business or a business owned by someone else who is "standing in the place of his parents" (for example, a close friend of the family, perhaps). However, these businesses may not be "manufacturing, mercantile, or similar commercial enterprises," or involve occupations which are forbidden to all minors [Education Code §49141]. Additionally, California Labor Law Digest (1993, p. 108) states, "work permits are not required for minors engaged in…Family-owned business if work is done on a casual, nonscheduled basis."

A second strategy to avoid government entanglement is to meet the educational requirements that free the teen from needing a work permit thereafter. A work permit is not required if the minor of any age "…who has been graduated from a high school maintaining a four-year course above the eighth grade of elementary schools, or who has had an equal amount of education in a private school or by private tuition, or who has been awarded a certificate of proficiency…" [Education Code §49101].

Freedom from work permits is a strong incentive, possibly the most compelling incentive, to accelerate the student's academic work so that he or she can pass the California High School Proficiency Examination (CHSPE) or graduate early. It's a surprisingly attainable goal. Many homeschoolers have passed the CHSPE at early ages—14, 13, even 12 years old. Not only are CHSPE "grads" exempt from the work permit hassle, they may also work the same hours as adults, and must be paid the same wages as adults when working the same hours as adults. (Information about obtaining a certificate of proficiency by taking the CHSPE, is at the beginning of this chapter, pages 197-198.)

Labor Laws: Restricted Occupations

There are many picky little statutes that apply to specific occupations and situations, such as restricting the hiring of minors under age 16 as messengers in cities having less than 15,000 inhabitants, or permitting minors to participate in horseback riding exhibitions without permits. In general, you should be alert to possible laws restricting minors from occupations in manufacturing, heavy industry, construction, or any other field where potential hazards to health, safety, and morals exist (for example, selling alcoholic beverages; in a pool or billiard room; around chemicals and poisons; any use of mechanical equipment). Be aware also that many restrictions surround the door-to-door sales and sales to passing motorists. Also, non-parent-owned agricultural businesses are subject to different laws than parent-owned farms.

Age 15 Days to 12 Years

Only the entertainment industry permits formal employment of small children, and then only under rigorously governed conditions. "Entertainment Industry" is defined as using the services of a minor in motion pictures using any recording format; photography (modeling), recording, live theatrical productions, publicity, rodeos, circuses, musical performances, and the like.

Ages 12-13

While the State of California allows minors ages 12 and 13 to obtain work permits, federal restrictions narrow the opportunities available to youth of this age to agricultural, domestic and entertainment industry occupations. Hours of employment for this age group are similarly restricted especially when school is in session.

Ages 14-15

Generally, the wider world of work is open to minors ages 14 and 15 with some restrictions on type of employment. Federal statutes apply:

When school is in session: Student may work a maximum of 3 hours on school days, with a weekly maximum of 18 hours. Federally sponsored Work Experience and Career Exploration Programs (WECEP) programs are excepted, permitting a maximum weekly of 23 hours per week.

When school is not in session: maximum 8-hour days; 40 hour week.

Hours: 7 a.m. to 7 p.m. From June 1 till Labor Day, youth may work till 9 p.m. Public messenger service limited to 6 a.m. to 9 p.m. On days preceding a non-school day, student may work till 12:30 a.m.

Ages 16-17

State statutes apply:

When school is in session: Four hours per day maximum; on days before non-school days, 8 hours of work is permissible. Students in "work experience programs" may work 8 hours on any day.

When school is not in session: Students of this age group may work the same hours that govern adult employment.

Hours: 5 a.m. to 10 p.m. Public messenger service limited to 6 a.m. to 9 p.m. On days preceding a non-school day, student may work till 12:30 a.m. Wages: All minors must receive at least minimum wage. Overtime must be paid for more than 40 hours per week or more than 8 hours in a day, except when the minor is employed by his parents.

Some other items worth noting:

- A day of rest from work is required if the total hours worked per week exceeds 30 hours, or if more than 6 hours are worked on any one day during the week.
- Under dire circumstances where a family needs the earnings of a minor due to the death, illness, injury or desertion of parent, a minor between the ages of 14 and 16 can be issued a permit to work full time. Education Code Section 49130 et seq.
- When a minor works two jobs, the total hours per week cannot exceed the legal maximum for his age group.
- The permit must be issued before the minor does any actual work for the employer.

How to Obtain a Work Permit

1. Before applying for a work permit, the minor must first be offered employment.

2. Next, the parent and minor determine who manages the work permit process in their public school district. The superintendent of each school district has the legal authority to issue work permits, and to designate other personnel to issue work permits. In some areas, the county superintendent of schools exercises this authority. Generally, private school students (which includes homeschoolers so enrolled) must obtain their work permits from the designated personnel in the public school in which they reside. The student's private school principal (that is, his parent) should investigate to find out how work permits are handled where they live. A phone call to the school district administrative office would be a good place to start.

(Exception: Children in the entertainment industry—actors, models, dancers, and the like—receive their work permits through one of the branch offices of the Department of Industrial Relations, Division of Labor Standards Enforcement, not through public schools.)

3. The issuing authority gives the student a B1-1 form, *"Request for Work Permit and Statement of Intent to Employ a Minor"* to be completed by student, parent or guardian, and employer. The youth will need to bring his social security number, and documentation such as a birth certificate or other official document that indicates his birthday. A designated person in your local public school district, usually a guidance counselor, looks the form over and issues a B1-4, *"Permit to Employ and Work."* (In some areas it is customary for the blank B1-4 to be given to the minor at the same time as the B1-1, and he or she is asked to have both filled out by the employer, then return with both to have them reviewed and signed.) The employer must have copies of the forms on file, or be liable for misdemeanor charges involving fines and or jail time. Work permits are specific to each actual hiring arrangement. If the youth gets a second job, or a new job, he/she must seek a permit to cover each circumstance. Work permits expire five days after the opening of the next succeeding school year; a new permit must then be sought.

Problems Obtaining a Permit

In some instances, public school personnel do not know they have a responsibility to handle private school students' requests for work permits. It has been necessary to politely instruct these persons about their obligations by pointing to Education Code §49110, *"Issuance; jurisdiction"* and §49110.1 *"Private school pupils; issuance."* The latter section indicates that school superintendents may designate private school personnel to issue permits, but by implication, where no such designation has been made, the private school student must apply to the issuing authority at the public school.

The individual who issues work permits—often a high school guidance counselor, or other administrator, does have discretionary authority to withhold a permit, or revoke a permit if they feel that the employment interferes with the student's education.

Unfortunately, sometimes when homeschooled students approach public school personnel to request a work permit, the school authority uses the opportunity to question the validity of homeschooling. It is most important for the homeschooled student and parent to avoid volunteering information, which may incite problems. The very term, "homeschool" should be avoided. They should use the correct term, "private school," to describe their legal schooling arrangement, and be firm, courteous, and well informed about their legal rights. The student in a private school with an enrollment of one should expect and receive the exact same treatment as private school students of any size enrollment.

Still, it sometimes happens that a homeschooler is denied a work permit. Legally challenging the denial of a work permit might risk much more than the opportunity to hold a part-time job, since misinformed school authorities might widen the matter to include truancy charges against the student and family. Going around the problem is probably a more sensible response. It may be possible for the student to locate and temporarily enroll in a private ISP that issues work permits, or to seek a job that does not require a work permit, or to exempt himself by passing the CHSPE.

Driver Education and Training
By Paige Smith

The information in this article is not meant to be, nor should it be accepted as legal advice. There are several sections of the California Education Code and California Code of Regulations that apply to driver education and driver training. It is your responsibility to become familiar with and to interpret these laws (and future revisions), and to make any necessary legal decisions regarding your choice.

Who Needs It?

To obtain a provisional driver's license before age 18 in California, drivers must have passed approved courses in driver education and driver training.

What are the Options?

Courses in driver education and driver training may be taken from public and private secondary schools and from professional driving schools. Students interested in taking these courses have several options. If they are enrolled in a secondary school that offers approved (see "course content" below) courses, they can enroll at that school. Or, if their school offers only driver education but not driver training, students can take driver education at their school and driver training from a professional driving school. If their school offers neither approved course, students can take both courses at a professional driving school.

Which Method is Best?

There are pros and cons to all methods. On the plus side, if you choose to offer the courses to your students, you will have control over the content of the courses and will have the opportunity to supervise your students as they learn. Also, you will know how well your students have been trained and how well prepared they are to drive.

On the other hand, you might decide it's worth the cost to have your students take these classes at a professional school, sparing you the time of designing and teaching the courses and the stress of teaching beginning drivers. For homeschoolers who are used to running their own schools with little interference by "authorities," dealing with the DMV can be a frustrating experience. The DMV personnel don't customize or make exceptions to their rules and they expect us to follow those rules to the letter. If dealing with bureaucracy is not what you do best, you may want to opt out.

The costs of taking these courses at professional schools vary, depending on the courses taken and where you live, but a few calls to local driving schools will give you an idea of the expense. Often, the courses are offered at a lower price through a local high school's adult education program.

Teaching Driver Education and Training at Your Private Secondary School

There are three steps to teaching driver education and training in your private secondary school: one, acquiring the materials you will need from the Department of Motor Vehicles; two, planning your courses and acquiring the instructional materials you want to use; and three, teaching the courses. All of these steps assume that you have a private school affidavit on file with the state of California and that your affidavit shows secondary students in attendance. If not, then you'll need to file your affidavit before you start.

Acquiring Materials from the Department of Motor Vehicles

All of the necessary forms and a booklet explaining how to fill them out (*Secondary School DE/DT Handbook*) are available free of charge from the Department of Motor Vehicles. Materials may be ordered at any time during the school year, but may be ordered only once each school year, so it's important to plan ahead.

Getting a Requisition Form

To order materials from the DMV, you must use their requisition form. To obtain the requisition form, write a letter of request on your school letterhead to: Department of Motor Vehicles, Occupational Licensing Branch, PO Box 932342, Sacramento, CA 94232-3420. Ask them to please send a *Requisition Form (DL 396)* for the current school year. If your school has not been issued a California Department of Education CDS# and you have five or fewer total students (including elementary school students) on your affidavit, we recommend that you send a copy of your affidavit with your request.

The requisition process has been subject to controversy and change in recent years and represents a compromise between the DMV and small private schools in California. As of January 2001, small private schools will receive the forms and materials they need if they have complied with the DMV's rules and regulations, but you should be prepared to spend some time and effort assuring that compliance. As you begin the requisition process, it is vitally important to keep in mind that you are a private school administrator, and to refer to yourself as such, rather than as a homeschooler. It is best to conduct your communication with the DMV in writing and to avoid telephone conversations with DMV employees. If you have questions about the requisition process that are not answered here, please contact CHN first before calling the DMV. This will help avoid confusion and potential confrontations, and will provide us with valuable feedback for the next edition of *The California Homeschool Guide*.

Filling Out the Requisition Form

In general, you will want to order materials for each secondary student on your private school affidavit who will be taking driver ed/training, with a small margin for mistakes. You also will want a student examination (practice test) and a *California Driver Handbook* for each student, and a copy of the *Parent-Teen Training Aide* and *Secondary School DE/DT Handbook* for yourself. The requisition form is accompanied by specific instructions on filling it out that should be followed carefully.

Before sending in your form, you will need to have received a letter from your county office of education on their letterhead, verifying that you have filed your affidavit for the current school year (since the county does not normally send a confirmation, you will have to request it). If you have filed your affidavit with Sacramento rather than with your county, and you don't feel comfortable requesting the letter of verification from your county office, you may contact the office in Sacramento with which you filed your affidavit. This written verification is only required the first year you request materials from the DMV.

If you have requested materials from the DMV for the previous school year, then for the current year's request, you will need to send a copy of your affidavit, but will not need the letter of verification. However, you will need to send in your DMV Completion Certificate Logs for the previous year when you make your request. (Each completion certificate has a number at the top and when you receive the certificates, you will also receive a log on which to record the following information about each student who is issued a certificate by your school: certificate control number, student's full name and address, student's birthdate, and the certificate's date of issue.)

Section 7 of the requisition form refers to the criminal record summary or teaching credential requirement and asks that you check the box that applies to your driver ed/training teacher. As most homeschool parents understand Education Code §44237, parents teaching their own children exclusively are exempt from the criminal record summary requirement, and could check the criminal record summary box in section 7, without needing to have the record check done. However, it is each family's responsibility to read the Education Code and make its own decision as to how to fill out section 7 of the requisition form.

Who Can Enroll in Your Private School's Driver Education and Training Classes?

The DMV is very concerned that students are taught driver education/training classes at their secondary schools of full-time enrollment or at professional driving schools only. According to DMV, the only students who should be taking driver ed/training classes from a private secondary school are the full-time enrolled students of that school. (Not public school students whose school does not offer driver ed any more and who hope that you will teach them instead, or students from another private school that has not acquired materials from DMV, etc.) The DMV cross-references all certificates of completion to the school that issues them and to the students who receive them. To avoid difficulties with DMV, we recommend that you offer driver ed/training classes only to the students for whom you provide exemption to public school attendance as described in Education Code §48222 and who are accounted for on your private school affidavit.

This does not mean, however, that your school and other small schools cannot pool your efforts when providing the course, speakers, field trips, etc. to your students. The teens in our local support group had a great time taking driver education as a group. Each individual school should just be certain to issue certificates of completion only to its own full-time students.

Course Planning

Students can either take both courses during the same semester, or can take driver education first and driver training later. If you plan to teach driver education only, or to teach driver education first and then driver training, the following sequence will serve your purposes:

- Enroll your student in driver education (classroom course) at your school
- When student passes the driver education course, issue the student a Certificate of Completion of Classroom Driver Education (DL387) and record the certificate information on the DMV Completion Certificate Log for driver education certificates
- When the student is 15 1/2 years old, the student applies for a provisional permit.

- After receiving a permit, the student enrolls in an approved driver training (behind-the-wheel) course
- After completion of the driver training course, the student's permit is valid
- If the student took and passed the driver training course at your school, issue the student a Certificate of Completion of Driver Training (DL 388A) and record the certificate information on the DMV Completion Certificate Log for driver training certificates
- Student practices driving for a minimum of 50 hours (10 at night) over the next 6 months
- When the student is 16 years old and has been driving with a permit for at least 6 months, the student applies for a provisional driver's license.

If you plan to teach the courses during the same semester, you will be teaching them "simultaneously" and the following series of steps applies:

- Enroll students who are at least 15 years old in driver education and driver training to be taken at the same time, or within the same semester
- Issue the student a Certificate of Simultaneous Enrollment in Driver Education/Driver Training (DL 391)
- Student's parents/guardians sign the Statement of Consent to Issue and Acceptance of Liability (DL 119) for the Student License
- Issue a Student License (DL 118) to be used during the driver training course
- The student applies at the DMV for a provisional instruction permit
- When student passes both the driver education and driver training courses, issue a Certificate of Completion of Both Driver Education and Driver Training (DL 388) and record the certificate information on the DMV Completion Certificate Log for certificates that cover both driver education and driver training
- Student practices driving for a minimum of 50 hours (10 at night) over the next 6 months
- When student is 16 years old and has been driving with a permit for at least 6 months, student applies for a provisional driver's license.

Why teach the courses during the same semester? The main plus to simultaneous enrollment is that the student can begin driving six months sooner, at age 15, and therefore practice longer before applying for a license. (The more practice, the better.)

Driver Education In the Classroom

A course that covers all the requirements set by the Education Code and Code of Regulations for public schools, and is a minimum of 30 hours in length, is considered an "approved" course, and includes the following as a minimum:

- Knowledge and understanding of the California Vehicle Code
- Rules of the road and other state laws, local motor vehicle laws and ordinances, and other laws of this state relating to the operation of motor vehicles
- A proper acceptance of personal responsibility as a driver
- A true appreciation of the causes, seriousness and consequences of traffic accidents
- Natural forces affecting driving; signs, signals, and highway markings, and highway design features which require understanding for safe operation of motor vehicles
- Differences in characteristics of urban and rural driving including safe use of modern expressways
- Pedestrian safety
- Critical vehicle systems and subsystems requiring preventive maintenance
- Effects of alcohol and drugs, and knowledge of the dangers involved in consuming alcohol or drugs in connection with the operation of a motor vehicle
- Education in the safe operation of motorcycles.

A standard driver education textbook and the driver handbook issued by DMV make it easy to cover all of these topics. In addition, there may be some topics you would like to add to this list based on your own experiences and locale.

Teaching the Class

Fun and informative things to add to the textbook portion of your driver education classes are visits by Mothers Against Drunk Drivers and the California Highway Patrol, field trips to your local traffic court and an auto wrecking yard (if you can get permission to go in the back, the crunched cars are memorable), and a First Aid/CPR class at your local American Red Cross. Also, getting together with other teachers and students for group discussions and activities adds a lot to the class. If several of the teens in your support group will be taking driver education at the same time, it's worth the effort to get the students together, particularly for presentations by guest speakers.

Driver Training Behind-the-Wheel

Course Content

The driver training course must consist of a minimum of 6 hours of on-the-street, behind-the-wheel training. The California Code of Regulations, Title 5, Section 10043 lists the skills to be covered in a driver training course. There is also a helpful list at the back of the *Parent-Teen Training Aide*, which your teens will receive along with their driver permits at DMV.

Teaching the Class

The driver training course may be taken after driver education is completed or at the same time as driver education. Before the student gets behind the wheel, the student's parents sign the liability release and the school issues the Student License, which is then held by the driver training instructor during each driver training session. (Instructions on how to issue student licenses are in the Secondary School DE/DT Handbook.) Upon successful completion of the six hours of behind-the-wheel instruction, the driver training completion certificate is issued to the student.

The teen driver may or may not have acquired a driver permit before the driver training course begins. If the student does have a driver permit from DMV, the permit is not valid until after the six-hour driver training course has begun. After the first driving lesson has been completed, the teacher of the driver training course signs and dates the student's Instruction Permit below the statement on the permit that says the permit is not valid until behind-the-wheel lessons have begun.

Though it is not required, we recommend that the student and/or instructor keep a log of each driver training session, noting the date, starting and ending time of the session, miles traveled during the session, road conditions, itinerary and comments. In addition, I've made up a checklist of skills to be covered that I carry with me during each training session. When the checklist is complete and each skill has been done satisfactorily, I sign it and keep it and the logs in the student's cumulative file for reference. I keep a photocopy of completion certificates issued in each student's file as well. [Editor's note: a ready-to-print driver log is in the California Homeschool Guide Companion CD.]

Resources

Most driver education textbooks cover all of the required topics quite well. Also, the curriculum for driver education/training is remarkably similar across the nation, which means that resources are fairly easy to find. A good first stop on the resource trail is the California State Automobile Association. Also helpful is a search on the Internet for "driver education" "driver training" and "driver safety." I found sources for free and low cost videos and some good "course of study" suggestions from various sites. Plan ahead and order early when ordering your materials. Many of the free loan or low cost videos take up to 8 weeks to arrive.

- California State Automobile Association, Traffic Safety Dept., PO Box 429186, San Francisco, CA 94142-9186. 415/565-2305. Ask for their Educational Materials and Video catalog. They offer many materials at no or low cost and have a free-loan video program. You can also purchase their textbook *Responsible Driving* through the catalog, though it's less expensive from used textbook suppliers.
- The Manocherian Foundation, Inc., 3 New York Plaza, New York, New York 10004. 212/837-4860. Free video, "The Aftermath" based on an accident that occurred in 1988 as a result of drinking and driving. The film

follows the arrest and conviction of the driver and also the families of the injured teens. It is a powerful film and comes with a discussion guide. Contact the foundation for ordering information.

- The Ultimate Driving Challenge Video, PO Box 8541, Dept. A, Prospect Heights, IL 60070. This video and teaching guide is available to teachers for $5.00. Problem driving situations and solutions are presented in question and answer format. Originally aired on CBS in 1993. Write for an order form.

- Insurance companies. Check with your insurance company to see what they have available to you—literature, videos, etc. My agent was willing to show a film to our group if we let him do a short "sales pitch" at the end, which was fine with us.

- California Highway Patrol. We were able to arrange a visit by a CHP officer to show videos and discuss traffic safety with our group. We learned a lot! The visual images and safety tips the officer gave us really stuck in our minds. Call your local CHP office and ask to speak with the Public Affairs Officer. Allow lots of lead time for planning the visit. These officers spend a lot of time giving presentations at schools and other organizations, and they do get booked up, but arranging a visit is worth the effort.

- Mothers Against Drunk Drivers (MADD). Our local chapter director came to speak with our group. This was an even more "up close and personal" version of what happens when people drink and drive than the videos and caught and held the attention of even the least attentive student in our class.

- Your local traffic court. We arranged a visit to our traffic court, and were sent to the wrong courtroom by mistake. Instead of seeing a succession of parking and speeding tickets being dealt with, we saw the short trial and conviction of a driver who had passed another driver at excessive speed and been reported to the CHP by that driver. Live and learn, as we homeschoolers say. Anyway, a trip to your local traffic court can be educational.

But if You Homeschool, You Can't Go to College!

"Based on...the experience of thousands of

homeschooling families, the picture for home

educated teenagers pursuing admissions

to colleges and universities is bright."

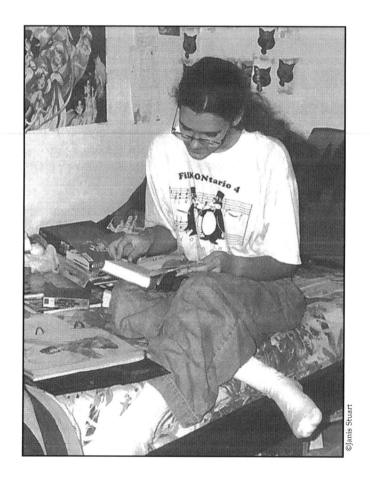

Homeschoolers in the Community Colleges

By Julie Castleberry Nunez

During the last few years a quiet change in student demographics has been taking place at your local community college. The number of young, homeschooled students registering to take full or part-time classes has been increasing steadily. While this is good news in the range of options for the family who is skeptical about their ability to tackle high school chemistry over the kitchen table, the trend is causing some changes among junior colleges as they adjust to this influx.

Consider this: a homeschooled student can essentially obtain his/her high school education at the local junior college, accumulating both high school and college credits, and graduate at 16 or 17 years of age with a two-year degree. Some families have used this option to dramatically lower the cost of a traditional four-year degree. By completing many lower-division, general education requirements at the junior college level, students can enter a four-year college with advanced standing as a sophomore or junior. Successful completion of junior college courses is also a way of providing a formal transcript of academic ability for homeschoolers.

The procedure for enrollment in junior colleges is relatively straightforward, varying somewhat from one college to the next. The most important factor is whether the student is enrolling as a regular or a "special status" student. Each of these approaches has pros and cons, and one approach does not preclude the other (you may start out as a special status student and later switch).

Briefly, enrolling as a special status student:

- limits the number of units the student can take (six) per quarter
- costs less at some junior colleges
- does not require high school graduation
- requires extra bureaucratic red tape (described below)

Enrolling as a regular status student:

- removes restrictions on the number of units taken
- requires full tuition for those units
- requires high school graduation (passing the California High School Proficiency Examination is the normal route for homeschoolers to meet this requirement—see pages 197-198)

Extra Hoops for Special Status

Parents seeking to enroll their child in the community college may do so by requesting a special student status contract from the college itself. This contract requires that the public or private school student is in good standing academically and has the written permission of: 1) parent/legal guardian; 2) high school counselor or principal; 3) the appropriate college official.

In the homeschooler's case, the parent, acting as principal of their own R-4 private school, signs the form giving permission as both parent and school official. A personal interview with the college counselor/dean is then usually necessary. Seeking the approval of the appropriate college official has always been the most challenging part of this process.

Today it is rare to find administrative personnel unfamiliar with the method for handling a request for enrollment from a homeschooled student. Indeed, homeschoolers on campus have become so commonplace that most counselors and instructors have personal familiarity with one or more of these students. Unfortunately, while our numbers have increased, so has the level of discomfort with our presence on campus. At some colleges, it is far more likely now that obtaining permission from the proper official will be a disquieting process in which both student and parent are required to jump through an ever-increasing number of hoops.

Homeschooling families interested in utilizing the community college can go a long way to facilitate the success of their student's petition for admission, while ensuring this option remains viable for future homeschoolers, by becoming more knowledgeable consumers. Here's how:

Know the Climate

If your student is interested in taking courses at your local junior college (JC), make a concerted effort to uncover whether or not the climate is homeschooler friendly before walking into the admissions office. Interview other homeschooling parents at park day or support group get-togethers. Put out a query on the homeschooling bulletin boards over the Internet. Just as admission requirements vary from junior college to junior college, so does the attitude of school officials; better to have some sense beforehand as to whether or not you are going to be met with open arms or vocal skepticism.

Track down a family who actually knows the ropes. Someone else's experience may save you both headache and discouragement in the long run. Homeschoolers who are already attending the JC can be helpful in recommending particular administrative staff or school counselors who are user friendly. Attempt to identify these people in advance so you will know who to ask for when making inquiries.

Know Your Rights

Check the written policy in regard to the admissions of "special status students" as outlined in the general college catalog for sale in the campus bookstore. You may likewise contact the admissions office and inquire about your JC's specific policy in regard to admissions of high school or K-8th grade students. The person answering the telephone may not necessarily be knowledgeable about "special status" admissions, and you should ask to speak with someone who is. Avoid using the word "homeschooler" in relationship to your inquiry. Keep in mind, if you have filed an R-4 affidavit with the Department of Education, your child is a private school student and has the right to attend a community college. California Educational Code §48800.5 states that any pupil "who is not enrolled in a public school" (that is, a private school student) "regardless of the pupil's age or class level," may directly petition the president of any community college to authorize the attendance of that pupil as a special part-time or full-time student on the ground that the pupil would benefit from advanced scholastic or vocational work. "Petitioning the president" may sound intimidating, but it simply means filling out a special application form that usually requires three signatures: one indicating a recommendation from the high school principal (you or your spouse), one indicating permission from the parent, and one from the student.

Be Prepared for a Few High Jumps

The increasing number of homeschoolers requesting to study at junior colleges has prompted school officials to make certain that college-level courses are filled with college-level students. The once optional college placement exam for special status students is rapidly becoming a mandatory prerequisite to being granted admission. The placement exam is a three-hour, multiple choice exam covering reading, writing, and math skills. Students specify the math exam they wish to take: Basic Math, Algebra, or Pre-Calculus. Test results are then used by school counselors as a guide to tracking students in regular or remedial classes. How pertinent is this exam in predicting the success of your 13-year-old budding linguist who would like to take French 1A? Not very, and parents should keep in mind that test scores are considered "advisory only" by most colleges.

Interviewing for Admission

After completion of the placement exam, the student will likely be required to submit his test scores and interview with either a college counselor or dean. At this point the parent/student should come prepared to make a strong case on behalf of the student's request for college admission. First impressions count, so dress accordingly. A portfolio of the student's recent academic work, standardized test scores showing above grade level performance, an outline of pertinent work experience, or letters of recommendation from a private tutor, may gain you the needed edge in this interview. Prepare your student for the unexpected; some homeschoolers have been asked to write a 15-minute sample essay as part of this interview. Students planning to transfer to a four-year college need to do some additional homework early in their junior college career. Do they want credit for their junior college units and advanced standing at the four-year college? Or do they want to enter as a freshman at the four-year college, using their junior college experience as the equivalent of their high school transcript? Universities have different admissions policies and in some cases a student's junior college credits could work against them. Researching policies ahead of time can prevent surprises later.

Community colleges offer great educational benefits to homeschooling families who wish to take advantage of them. Formal classroom experience, learning opportunities difficult to obtain elsewhere, low cost college credits, and preparation for more advanced degrees are all reasons to consider them.

> *Note: As we go to print on this second edition, CHN is hearing of potential problems for students who may want to be concurrently enrolled in college in the future, as thousands before them have. If changes occur, CHN will have the latest information placed on the website, www.CaliforniaHomeschool.net.*

Testing for the College-Bound Student
By Bj Darr

Standardized entrance tests are required by most colleges and universities as part of the application process. As the type and number of tests needed varies from school to school, applicants are advised to check the requirements early in their high school careers. Many students will want to sit for the entrance exams more than once to maximize their scores so test planning is essential. It is not too soon to begin gathering information by the beginning of the "freshman year." Home educated students should not expect to be exempted from the tests normally required of all applicants but should use such tests to further highlight their preparation for college-level work.

The ACT and SAT I

Most schools will ask prospective students to submit scores from either the ACT Assessment, commonly known as the ACT, or from the Scholastic Aptitude Test I, commonly known as the SAT I. Each college specifies which of the two tests is required; many will accept scores from either test. No college will require both. Applicants should be aware of each school's specific policy and plan accordingly.

The ACT examines four areas: English, Mathematics, Reading, and Science Reasoning. All questions are multiple-choice and provide four or five answers from which to choose the correct or best answer. The total testing time is 2 hours and 55 minutes. Certain calculators may be used for the Mathematics portion but they are not permitted for the Science Reasoning section. The ACT is given on pre-set dates throughout the academic year and it is usually not difficult to find an available test date. Early preregistration is required and homeschoolers do not need any special codes or permission to take the exam.

The SAT I: Reasoning Test is the other college entrance examination. Verbal and mathematical reasoning abilities are measured through test sections containing analogies, sentence completions, reading comprehension, quantitative comparisons, and other mathematical questions. Most of the questions are multiple-choice with the exception of one math section which requires students to record their answers on a grid. The total testing time is about 3 hours. Certain calculators are permitted but they are not required. The SAT I is given monthly from October to June. Early pre-registration is necessary. Homeschoolers do not need any special codes or permission to take the exam.

There are a multitude of test-preparation books and guides available in major bookstores and local libraries to acquaint the student with test format and content. Study books may also be ordered directly from the testing boards. In addition, there are useful and fun software programs available to help students prepare for both the ACT and the SAT I. Others may wish to take a preparatory course available at modest cost from a junior college, or a course offered by one of the major test preparatory services.

Both the ACT and the SAT I may be taken multiple times and many students find that their test scores do improve with subsequent sittings. Some colleges, however, frown upon excessive testing and view it as an indication that the student is placing unnecessary emphasis on one segment of the application process. Many college counselors recommend that applicants take the ACT or the SAT I no more than 2—3 times.

THE PSAT / NMSQT

The Preliminary SAT/National Merit Scholarship Qualifying Test is, as its name implies, both an introductory SAT exam and a determiner for a prestigious national award. Although this exam is only available once a year in public and private schools, many will permit homeschoolers to test with their regular students. Some private ISPs are also authorized to give the exam and will allow non-affiliated homeschoolers to test upon payment of an additional fee.

Like the SAT I, the PSAT contains both verbal and mathematical questions but also includes one additional section which tests writing skills. A high PSAT score will be noticed by colleges and honors programs and may give the student an edge in the application process. In addition, a high score may lead to identification as a National Merit semifinalist, finalist or scholarship recipient.

Given in October, many sophomores take the exam to gain experience, but only the juniors' scores are eligible for consideration for a National Merit Scholarship. It is important for homeschoolers in planning their "high school" years to be consistent in reporting their class rank. Count the four years prior to the semester in which you think you will begin college study as your "high school" years and take advantage of the practice PSAT year given to sophomores.

SAT II Subject Tests

The SAT II Subject Tests measure a student's knowledge and skills in specific subject areas. There are currently 24 Subject Tests offered in the general areas of foreign languages, sciences, mathematics, history, and English. All of the tests are one hour long with a multiple-choice format. The Writing Test also includes a short, student-produced, essay section. The Subject Tests are offered once a month between October and June, but not every test is offered every month. A candidate may take up to three SAT II tests on the same day but it is not possible to sit for the SAT I and any SAT II tests on the same day.

Due to rampant grade inflation and differing evaluative standards from one school to the next, more and more colleges are requiring SAT II tests of their applicants. The University of California system, for example, asks candidates to submit scores from the Writing Test, either the Math IC or Math IIC test, and a third test of the student's choosing. This statewide requirement is mandatory for application to any of the UC campuses. Many selective colleges have similar requirements and applicants should plan their testing schedule accordingly. Please note that the SAT II Subject II tests are not used to grant a student advanced college placement or credit.

A home educated student may wish to submit more than the required number of test scores if application is being made to a highly competitive college. In the absence of a traditional transcript, SAT II test scores may help to bolster the student's application.

The Advanced Placement Program

The Advanced Placement Program, a branch of the College Board, provides an opportunity for high school students to earn college credits and/or advanced standing through college-level courses offered during their high school years. Previously such courses have only been available through public or private schools, but it is now possible for anyone to order AP course descriptions and study independently. Exams are offered in 32 subject areas and are given in the spring.

Home educated students will need to make arrangements with a local high school in order to sit for these exams.

Unlike SAT II tests, AP test credits are not required for college application. They are favorably viewed, however, by most admissions committees as an indicator of a student's willingness to tackle challenging college-level studies. Applicants may also be granted up to a year's college credits, depending on their scores. Designed for the most highly able high school students, AP classes are generally seen as a more rigorous course of study than junior college classes.

College Admissions
By Cafi Cohen

We homeschooled two kids through high school. Both were accepted to their first-choice colleges and offered substantial scholarships. Our oldest gained admission to the very selective U.S. Air Force Academy, which accepts a scant 10% of applicants. Our youngest, decidedly not an academic and not a test-taker, won a hefty scholarship that made the private school that admitted her just as inexpensive as a state college.

That was back in the dark ages (early 90s), when many homeschooling families we knew gave up after grade eight and sent their kids to high school to assure college admissions.

How far we have come! Based on my research and the experience of thousands of homeschooling families, the picture for home educated teenagers pursuing admissions to colleges and universities is bright. The first half of this article fleshes out that bright picture. The second half makes some recommendations with respect to homeschoolers applying to college.

The Good News

Homeschoolers Readily Admitted to College

Homeschoolers have been admitted to most colleges and universities nationwide. Check out the Colleges For Homeschoolers web site *(http://learninfreedom.org/colleges_4_hmsc.html)* which currently lists more than 700 post secondary schools that have accepted homeschoolers. You will see names like Stanford, MIT, California Institute of Technology, University of California, and many ohers.

How do homeschoolers fare in the admissions process, compared to other groups? Kenneth Danford in a 1997 paper titled, *"College Acceptance Rates for Homeschooled Students,"* says that he could find no school that categorically rejects admission to homeschooled students.

Danford also found that homeschoolers win admission at roughly the same or higher rates as other students. Examples? Danford reports that in 1996, University of Illinois accepted 88% of their homeschooled applicants, 68% of their regular applicants; University of Maryland accepted 89% of their homeschooled applicants, and 62% of their regular applicants.

No Diploma Required

Despite a popular misconception, most colleges and universities, even very competitive schools like Harvard and Stanford, do not require a diploma for admission. The few schools that do require diplomas will almost always accept the results of the General Education Development Test (GED) or the California High School Proficiency Examination (CHSPE), both readily available to homeschoolers.

No Test Required

More good news. According to FairTest *(www.fairtest.org)*, an increasing number of colleges and universities—more than 10% nationwide—have made the SAT and ACT (college admissions tests) optional for admissions to bachelor's degree programs. Examples are Goddard College in Vermont, National University in California, and St. John's College in New Mexico.

Buyer's Market

Sean Callaway, a homeschooling father and college admissions counselor in New York City says that, "...in 1998 there are 3600+ institutions of higher learning. By the year 2015, there will probably be less than 2,000. We're looking at a huge shakeout and homeschoolers should be prepared to take advantage of the buyer's market."

That's right, contrary to the scary advertising, most colleges need us more than we need them. Go to college fairs in local high schools and malls and colleges. You will find admissions counselors eager to talk with you, eager to woo homeschoolers. Increasingly, we are seeing advertisements for homeschooled applicants in national homeschooling publications. A few colleges nationwide are even earmarking scholarships specifically for homeschooled applicants, among them Nyack College in New York and Bellhaven College in Mississippi.

De-Facto Open Admissions

A consequence of the market pressure is that it is easy for anyone to win admission to 80+% of colleges and universities nationwide. According to Barron's and other college guides, 80% of the roughly 2000 4-year colleges in the United States are either non-competitive (they admit nearly all applicants) or minimally competitive (they admit 90+% of applicants). They accept students regardless of SAT score or high school background.

Trailblazers

Fortunately for all homeschooling families, those homeschoolers attending college in the 1980s and early 1990s have left a good impression. We first experienced this positive fallout when our homeschooled son applied to a special college-credit-granting summer program for 16-17 year-olds at the University of Denver called "The Making of An Engineer."

That year, the program had 180 applicants for 60 slots. They gave the first 30 slots to sky-high SAT scorers, a group that did not include our son. Then they evaluated the other 150 applicants for the remaining 30 slots. Later the admissions officer told me that our son got one of these slots because he was a homeschooler. They had had good experience with homeschooled students in the past.

Diversity

At some schools, homeschoolers often have an edge in the admissions process because accepting them helps an admissions officer create "a well-rounded student body." Often, that's what they want, you know. Not necessarily a well-rounded student, but a well-rounded student body.

How do they create that student body? By accepting lots of kids with unusual backgrounds. Homeschoolers scream "unusual" on two fronts: by virtue of the homeschooling and by pursuing different activities than your traditional senior high honor student, class president, captain of the football team.

Policies

As I write this, in the spring of 1998, colleges and universities increasingly are discussing what to do about homeschooled applicants. Many are creating and writing policies to deal with the increasing number of homeschooled applicants they see each year.

These policies take different forms. Some are simply advisory letters sent to inquiring homeschooling families. Others are more detailed, providing recommended reading lists, courses of study, and more. Still others, mandated by state legislatures, specify minimum SAT scores and GPA's.

Most of the policies treat homeschoolers fairly. The policies were written merely to help homeschoolers negotiate the admissions process without the assistance of a high school counselor. A few of the policies (less than 2%) nationwide are, unfortunately, quite discriminatory. The most offensive ones, as of this writing, are the Georgia State Colleges, which require SAT II test results (these are Achievement Tests in specific subjects like Biology or American Literature) from homeschoolers, none from other students.

How Do Homeschoolers Apply?

Just like everyone else. Homeschoolers obtain applications directly from colleges, by telephoning or e-mailing or writing. They take standardized tests (either the SAT or the ACT, depending on what their first-choice school requires).

They submit transcripts or portfolios, ideally gearing the transcript or portfolio to the preference of the college.

Some homeschoolers write their own transcripts or compile their own portfolios. Others submit transcripts from independent-study schools, like American School in Illinois or Clonlara in Michigan. Both approaches have advantages and disadvantages, outlined in my book, *And What About College?*

Recommendations

Based on the current buyer's market and the homeschooling policies promulgated by colleges nationwide, I include the following recommendations in my workshops.

College Now?

First assess whether or not the student needs college to achieve his goals. I received an interesting e-mail from a former homeschooler about two years ago. He wrote that he expected college to include deep theological, political, and technical material to challenge his intellect. Instead, he said, he was subjected to the grown-up version of government elementary, middle, and high school.

Without completing college, he was hired as a civilian computer specialist by the US Military. Within two years—while working full-time—he became a Certified Novell Engineer (CNE), and a Microsoft Certified Product Specialist (MCPS) by taking night classes at a Drake-Sylvan Learning Center.

To decide if college now is appropriate, talk to people in the field of interest. Ask about their backgrounds, and—more importantly—ask about the backgrounds of people currently hired in the field. Consider also working for one to two years in the field to assess the working environment. Want to be a doctor? Train first as a paramedic or emergency medical technician.

Two titles particularly can help anyone assessing the value of college: *The Question Is College* by Herbert Kohl and *What Color Is Your Parachute?* by Richard Bolles.

College How?

Once teenagers have decided to attend college, familes need to look carefully at the burgeoning options. Does this student need traditional college? Or would college-at-home, part-time study, trade school, or apprenticeship be more appropriate?

Educational Philosophy

For those who will be applying to traditional four-year colleges, I would encourage the parents and teenagers to establish an educational philosophy and learn to articulate it. When our son applied to the US Air Force Academy and other competitive schools nationwide, he expected that college interviewers would query him about his flying lessons, or piano recitals, or diving team, or Civil Air Patrol.

But, largely, that did not happen. Instead, they asked about homeschooling. They wanted to know why we homeschooled and how we homeschooled. Our son, who at age 14 said that the only bad thing about homeschooling was having to explain it to everyone, was relatively unprepared to address how and why we homeschooled. Too busy learning to execute a perfect cut-away dive or pilot an airplane, it simply was not a subject to which he had devoted much time or thought.

Since then, I have interviewed numerous college admissions officers. Almost every one was very curious about why homeschoolers homeschooled. This is particularly true of very selective colleges.

To articulate an educational philosophy, we found it helpful to describe a day in our home, at our homeschool. Others describe how and why they began homeschooling. With either approach, you begin concrete (helpful to admissions officers who cannot quite picture anything non-traditional) and use the concrete example as an illustration of how and why you homeschool.

Recordkeeping

Develop or adopt a good recordkeeping system not later than grade nine, ideally earlier. Recordkeeping—for an eventual college application—is so critical that I tell homeschoolers it is more important to record what you have done than to plan what you are going to do.

The ideal recordkeeping system is free, efficient (takes less than 5 minutes each day), and includes everything, even activities that look non-academic.

SAT / ACT Practice

For those applying to colleges that still require the SAT or ACT, begin practice for these tests in grade nine. You can obtain free practice tests from any high school counseling office (just ask for the SAT registration materials). Any large bookstore sells SAT practice/study guides.

At very competitive colleges, performance on standardized tests is more important than it is for regular applicants. Many college admissions officers say that the standardized test score is one of few external assessments they have of a student's abilities. "External" in the last sentence is a code word for "unbiased" and therefore "trustworthy."

Ask Your Own Questions

Finally, do not rely on what I have written here or what any other homeschooler tells you about college admissions. Those policies mentioned earlier? Get this—they are changing not just every year, but from month to month.

Once you begin the college application process, you need current information. You obtain current information by calling colleges themselves, making your own inquiries. Here are some introductory questions to get the ball rolling:

- What percentage of applicants did you accept last year?
- How many homeschoolers applied last year, and how many were accepted?
- Do you have any special policies or literature relating to homeschooled applicants?
- How do you evaluate applicants from small private schools? (Many homeschoolers fit into this category.)
- Do you use a grade point average (GPA) and class rank to evaluate applicants? How do you handle situations where no GPA or class rank is computed?

For the Road

Homeschooling families need to do two things to maximize their teenager's chances for admissions to their first choice school. First, keep good records and thoroughly document all activities, not just academic ones. Second, communicate directly with the schools of interest and tailor applications to the college's requirements.

My web site, Homeschool-Teens-College *(http://homeschoolteenscollege.net/)*, has college application essays written by homeschoolers from all parts of the United States. Read these essays to learn how teenagers explain homeschooling to admissions officers and to see how they have handled high school. Please e-mail me if your teenager can contribute an essay. I use the material with permission; and the submitter retains the copyright.
©Cafi Cohen

CHN member, Cafi Cohen is a popular speaker at educational conferences nationwide. For more information about college, visit Cafi's website, http://homeschoolteenscollege.net/.

College: A Teen's Story
By Janelle Orsi

Can You Get Into College If You're Homeschooled?

Just the typical question appearing in the homeschooling skeptic's interrogatory sequence, usually falling somewhere in between "what about socialization?" and "do you have much homework in homeschooling?" Having been homeschooled for eight years, I got very used to answering all the usual questions, however the college question was always a little harder to answer. As we know, homeschoolers are unusual in comparison to the neatly packaged students who come out of public schools. To find the answer to this question, I had to experience the college admission process firsthand. Unscathed, undaunted, undismayed, and quite victorious, I, Janelle Orsi, age 18, have returned from my trip through college applications, ready to recount my adventure to all those who will follow me. I began my journey into the unknown expecting an uphill battle. I instead found that, in many ways, homeschooling has worked to my advantage.

Starting the Search

An important thing to remember about colleges is that they want you as much as you want them; it's incredible the amount of time, energy, and money colleges put into finding the brightest, most motivated students. Huge numbers of colleges have now discovered that homeschooling is a cache of bright possibilities. They recognize that homeschooled students are generally self-motivated and sincerely interested in learning. Some colleges have even declared that they "just love homeschoolers!"

Knowing this gave me a lot of assurance as I set out on my college search. Having selected a list of colleges that appealed to me, I made many visits and interviewed with college admissions officers who were very willing to work with me, and discuss what they expected from a homeschooler. As you read this, please consider the types of colleges to which I applied: competitive liberal arts schools such as Amherst, Pomona, and Wesleyan. None of these colleges has any more than 4,000 students; I expect that colleges like these are likely to spend more time examining and considering applications than a huge school such as Berkeley (30,000 students). So keep in mind that my experiences applying to these colleges may be somewhat different than applying to a huge university.

High School Transcripts

The first difference between a homeschooler and a high-schooler is that a homeschooler will not have the fancy transcript and convenient list of grades that most students will have. However, I've learned that this is easily compensated for. What all colleges have told me to do is make a list of all the areas that I've studied and describe how I obtained knowledge in those fields. This may include listing books from which I studied, classes or lectures that I attended, and related hobbies and activities. For instance my world history description looks like this:

World History: I've gained my knowledge of world history through reading numerous text books, historical novels, travel accounts, and other materials related to history, anthropology, and social science. I've taken two semesters of Western Civilization at Skyline Community College and have been studying current international issues, such as the Israeli/Palestinian conflict and issues in Cambodia, Guatemala, and Chiapas, Mexico. I've been particularly interested in Pre-Columbian Meso-American history and have read many books about it. During the summer of '96, I traveled to Belize and spent two weeks on a Post-Classic Mayan excavation with a group from Earthwatch. I am currently studying Asian history, art, and ideas.

With academic summaries in this format, I think that homeschoolers will have an advantage in the admissions process. The college will be able to get to know the student's motivation and creative approaches to learning. Don't you think a college admissions officer would find that description more interesting than this one:

World History .... A?

Grade and Test Scores

Many colleges have told me that they'd like to see some grades and/or test scores from me, along with my academic summary. They need concrete evidence that I really did do all of that studying and didn't spend four years watching sitcoms. That is where the SAT tests come in. There are two types of SATs, the SAT I reasoning test and the SAT II subject tests. The SAT I is the basic test with a math section and a verbal section. The SAT II subject tests are a variety of hour long tests on the various academic subjects; for instance, I took World History, Chemistry, Writing, Mathematics, and Spanish. Most colleges require that you take only three subject tests, though it was suggested that I take more than three to make up for the lack of grades in homeschooling.

Community College Classes

Some homeschooled students also choose to take community college classes; grades from these, assuming they're good grades, are also helpful in demonstrating the student's academic success as well as the ability to learn in a classroom environment. However, I did encounter an unexpected problem due to the community classes I've taken. After applying to Pomona College as a freshman, I received a phone call from a member of the admissions staff who said that, due to the large number of college credits I've obtained, they would not consider me as a freshman, and I would have to re-apply as a transfer. With small colleges such as Pomona, applying as a transfer is often very competitive, and this may have narrowed my chances of getting in. (Conversely, at large universities such as Berkeley, it is actually easier to get accepted as a transfer than it is as a freshman.) The other colleges to which I applied did not have any problem with my having taken many college classes; I asked that they view the classes merely as high school work. If you plan to take a large number of college classes while in "high school," be sure to find out the policies on this when you apply to a four-year college.

Letters of Recommendation

College applications usually require that students have at least two letters of recommendation. These are customarily obtained from high school teachers, but students can get a letter from a music teacher, coach, mentor, or boss as well. Parents, too, are perfectly acceptable for the letter of recommendation; however it might be good to look outside the home in order to show that the student is socially active. (And let's face it, moms and dads aren't always perfectly objective judges of their child's qualifications.) Frequently, college applications have a section that should be filled out by the high school counselor, but when I asked about this I was told that my parents should complete that part.

No Need to Fret

After sending my applications and waiting for what seemed like an eternity, I was ultimately accepted at Reed, Wesleyan, and Pomona, and put on the waiting list at Amherst. In my entire college search, I did not find anybody who was cold toward, or unwilling to work with homeschoolers. Every student will have a different experience in applying, based on academic background, but I doubt that homeschooling will be much of an impediment. I'm feeling very satisfied with my results, and I'm confident that homeschoolers are not only getting into colleges, but receiving enthusiastic welcomes as well.

Shouldn't Unique Learners
Be in School Where
They Can Get Professional Help?

"A caring parent can teach...with an effectiveness

that no classroom teacher can duplicate."

Toward Success for Every Child: Homeschooling Unique Learners

By Karen Rafferty

Parents with children labeled as "learning disabled" are increasingly turning to homeschooling. Many of these parents are uncomfortable, weary and defensive over the labeling that says their child is "deficient." They are resentful because they have been accused of being a part of, or the source of, their child's learning difficulties. They are also worried about their child's future, and discouraged that their child is falling behind academically.

Problems in School; No Problems at Home

The truth is, there may be nothing wrong at all with the child or family. There are many different reasons a child might have difficulty learning in a traditional classroom setting. The child may have a physical impediment such as a hearing or visual impairment or a chronic illness such as asthma or allergies. The child may have a different learning style that isn't being accommodated (see pages 111-112). The child's personality may cause friction because he is acutely shy, wildly gregarious or very independent. A child may also be developmentally delayed.

The predicament is that in an overcrowded classroom, the teacher needs a quick, pragmatic solution for the unruly, inattentive, or academically struggling child. By labeling the child, that child can be brushed off into special education classes and become someone else's "problem." The fact is that many of these diagnoses have no empirical basis. The label is applied because of the teacher's subjective observations. A teacher's classification of a child may differ dramatically from year to year, from class to class. Be careful not to accept an "expert's" label too quickly.

You are the Expert

Whether your child has a medically diagnosed problem, a behavioral label, a different learning style or is a late bloomer, homeschooling can be the answer. A caring parent can teach his child with an effectiveness that no classroom teacher can duplicate. No one knows your child better or cares for him/her more deeply than you do.

Homeschooling establishes a safe environment where a child escapes the ridicule of peers, the application of limiting labels and the censure of failure. Removing the child from a negative situation immediately reduces the stress felt by all family members. Now he can receive the one-on-one attention where education can be modified to meet his abilities, interests, learning style, and learning pace. The homeschool setting allows the flexibility needed so that the child can reach his/her potential. Plenty of slack time is available for climbing trees, playing with Legos, hugging the dog and daydreaming. The brain is not inactive during this slack time. While the body is relaxing, the brain is assimilating.

You may feel inadequate taking over when the professionals have failed. You may not be a professional, but you are the expert on your child. Be assured, moreover, there is no one best method for teaching reading, math, spelling or any other subject. All children are unique. The best method for your child is the one that works for your child. Plan on continuously modifying your approach as your child changes. Resources are provided in Chapter 15, pages 347-348, to help your family have a successful homeschooling venture.

Public School Resource

The federal government has passed two laws in an attempt to guarantee that educational services will be provided to students with special needs: The Individuals with Disabilities Education Act (IDEA) which has been funded, and the Rehabilitation Act of 1973, Section 504, which has not. These laws require that each state offer free special-needs educational services to qualified children. However, parents are free to refuse any service at any time. In other words, if your child has an Individualized Education Program (IEP) this does not prevent you from withdrawing him from school and/or refusing the suggested assistance.

Every student enrolled in a public school can request a full IEP or annual review from the local public school or school district. The federal law defines the failure of a school to provide these services as a criminal act on the part of the school personnel. The school has 50 days in which to provide an IEP screening from the day a formal request is made. IEP screening usually includes the public school principal, psychologist, parents, student and other school therapists and teachers representing the areas of the child's special needs. Once an IEP is completed, if a student's needs are assessed as sufficiently severe, some families who eventually decide to homeschool have continued to receive special assistance through the public school system in specific areas decided upon by the parents. Some districts are tightening this policy, however.

What You Should Know Before Pursuing Services from Your School District for Your Disabled Child
By Kate Jimenez

There are many reasons why a parent may want services from the school district. The biggest is that the family may not be able to afford to provide their child with the services that they can receive from the district at no charge. Some of the services a child may qualify for are special education, speech and language services, vocational education, psychological services, physical and occupational therapy and even respite care. But before taking this route, it is important to carefully consider whether it might be best to find alternatives to free services.

Why Shouldn't I Take Advantage of These Free Services?

Quality of Service. The quality of service a child receives varies from district to district and specialist to specialist. Given the fact that this system is a huge bureaucracy and bureaucracies are notoriously inefficient, it should come as no surprise to any parent if the level of service does not meet parental expectations. Parents seeking services from the government and local school district should be prepared to spend lots of time and energy pursuing this care. If you don't believe the school district is providing a quality education for children without disabilities, do you really expect they will be able to do a good job providing for your disabled child? The law states that disabled children are entitled to "free and appropriate education." Free and appropriate does not necessarily mean a "quality" education.

Diminished Privacy for Your Family. When you request an assessment for your child, you, your home and your entire family will come under scrutiny. You will not be dealing with just the school district. Interagency partnerships and computer tracking of your child have found their way into the 20th century. Family partnerships mean that the state "helps" you do an effective job parenting your disabled child. Regional centers that provide services to children and their families are operated by the state. Social Services, medical professionals and the

251

educrats will have their hands in your life. Make sure you are willing to accept this "partnership" to one degree or another before requesting help.

Explaining Homeschooling to the Professionals. You can homeschool and receive services from the district, but try sitting in a room with the school psychologist and other professionals who have just finished testing your child and explain to them your educational philosophy and homeschooling. If you're lucky, they will accept the fact that you are going to homeschool; if you aren't they can pressure you into putting your child into school. The law stipulates that you be an equal partner in determining what services your child needs. But the law cannot change the attitudes of providers of these services who may look at you as if you've lost your mind when you try explaining your child's learning style or your belief in child-led learning.

There are Professionals in This System Who Really Care. Yes, there are professionals who care. But sometimes the caring professionals are the ones you need to watch. They sincerely believe that they are doing what is best for your child. If they disagree with your decision to homeschool or your refusal of certain services that they feel are vital to your child's development, they can and will use whatever means are at their disposal to fight you.

But My Rights are Guaranteed Under the Law. You have several "rights" under the law. Some of these rights are the right to request a reevaluation, the right to your child's records, the right to be informed of any changes made in your child's placement or services. You even have the right to refuse to sign an IEP. But what happens if you refuse all or part of the IEP? Here is what the California Education Code says:

§56346: No pupil shall be required to participate in all or part of any special education program unless the parent is first informed, in writing, of the facts that make participation in the program necessary or desirable, and of the contents of the individualized education program, and after this notice, consents, in writing, to all or part of the individualized education program…If the district, special education local plan area, or county office determines that the part of the proposed special education program to which the parent does not consent is necessary to provide a free and appropriate public education to the pupil, a due process hearing shall be initiated… unless a prehearing mediation conference is held. During the pendency of the due process hearing, the district. . . may reconsider the proposed individualized education program, may choose to meet informally with the parent. . . or may hold a mediation conference. . . . As an alternative to holding a due process hearing, the parties may hold a prehearing mediation conference. . .to resolve any issue or dispute. If a due process hearing is held, the hearing decision shall be the final administrative determination and shall be binding upon the parties. While a prehearing mediation conference or due process hearing is pending, the pupil shall remain in his or her then-current placement unless the parent and the district, special education local plan area, or county office agree otherwise.

Remember that caring professional? In a worst case scenario that same caring professional will be the one standing before a judge explaining why the recommendation they gave is necessary and in the best interests of your child.

According to Tom and Sherry Bushnell in their article "8 Ways to Avoid Trouble with Medical and Educational Professionals" (*NATHHAN News*, Fall 1997), "If parents do not agree with the decision made by the social worker, they can request a mediation. The social services mediation meeting generally goes something like this: The agency worker tells the parent just what they told them before. The parent objects and the state worker responds, 'Fine, we'll see you in court.' At the court hearing, the administrator usually puts much weight on the findings of the psychologist who did the testing as well as the guardian ad lidum (the social worker who was asked to tell what the government is going to do to 'help' the family). If it sounds like we are trying to discourage you from going to the state for help, you are right!"

Seeking Help Outside of Social Service Agencies

First, you must educate yourself about your child's disability. Regardless of where you receive services for your child, you need to make intelligent and informed decisions and learn to advocate for your child.

Join a local support group for parents who have children with special needs. If there isn't one, start one by placing ads in the paper and hosting a meeting at your home. Do not isolate yourself.

Seek out "homeschool friendly" professionals who can help you with testing and evaluating your child's needs.

If you live in a small community where no support group exists, getting online to get the support you need will be extraordinarily beneficial. There are many good chat rooms and helpful web sites for parents that can help enormously. Information on laws, treatments available, and support will be available to you immediately.

Involve your church community. Many churches will offer respite care to families in need. Speak to your pastor and see if there is help available, or volunteer to start a group for your church.

Involve your homeschool local support group. Let them know of your difficulties. Ask for references to reliable babysitters so you and your husband can have an evening out.

And last, but not least, ask your family for help. They may be able to help financially or at the very least just be available to listen to what you and your family are going through.

Know the Law

California Education Code §56300 says, "Each district, special education local plan area, or county office shall actively and systematically seek out all individuals with exceptional needs, ages 0 through 21 years, including children not enrolled in public school programs, who reside in the district or are under the jurisdiction of a special education local plan area or a county office." §56302 says in part, "Identification procedures shall include systematic methods of utilizing referrals of pupils from teachers, parents, agencies, appropriate professional persons, and from other members of the public."

What this means is that anyone from your doctor to your next door neighbor can refer your child to the school for possible services. Parental notification and consent are required before assessment from the school district can take place, however it is important that parents receiving private medical and rehabilitative services carefully document these services in the event they have to "prove" to the district that they do not need their help.

If you are receiving state services and wish to discontinue services you are not happy with, it is best, according to Tom and Sherry Bushnell that you "[a]lways be calm, confident, and, with a smile on your face, be thankful. State simply, that you have found a private program that suits your child to a T and you are very happy with the progress you are seeing. Thank them for their input and help thus far. Do not belittle them, anyone on staff, or their program in any way. Do not express frustration at them, even though you feel they deserve a piece of your mind! It is better to leave on good terms. *Just let go and generally they will let go, too!"*

Special Education and the Law
By Luana Holzer

California Education Code §8250-8252 states that the Superintendent of Public Instruction shall ensure that eligible children with exceptional needs are given equal access to all child care and development programs. The Superintendent shall establish alternate appropriate placements, such as self-contained programs and innovative programs using the least restrictive environment. It includes plans or programs, or both for the care of the children when they are sick. It also covers the procedures for referring a child in need of care as part of the provision of protective services.

Individuals with Disabilities Education ACT (IDEA) was formerly called the Education for all Handicapped Children Act or EL. 94-142; its name changed in 1990. This federal legislation mandates a free, appropriate public education for all children with disabilities. Part B of the act refers to special education services for children age three through twenty-one. Part H refers to the early intervention program for infants and toddlers with disabilities from birth through age two and their families.

Defining Terms of the law

Due Process
> A system of procedures ensuring that an individual will be notified of, and have opportunity to contest, decisions made about him. As it pertains to early intervention (Part H) and special education (Part B) of IDEA, due process refers to the legal right to appeal any decision regarding any portion of the process (evaluation, eligibility, IEP or IFSP, placement, etc.).

Free Appropriate Public Education (FAPE)
> The words used in the IDEA to describe a student's right to a special education program that will meet his or her individual special learning needs, at no cost to the family.

Individualized Education Program (IEP)

A written plan for each student in special education describing the student's present levels of performance, annual goals including short term objectives, specific special education and related services, dates for beginning and duration of services, and how the IEP will be evaluated.

Individualized Family Service Plan (IFSP)

A written statement for each infant or toddler receiving early intervention services that includes goals and outcomes for the child and family. It also includes a plan for making the transition to services for children over age two.

Least Restrictive Environment (LRE)

Placement of a student with disabilities in a setting that allows maximum contact with students who do not have disabilities, while appropriately meeting the student's special education needs.

Handicapped Children's Protection Act

The law providing for the reimbursement of reasonable attorney's fees to parents who win their cases in administrative proceedings under IDEA.

Inclusion

Ensuring that necessary supports and services are provided so that children with disabilities can participate with children who do not have disabilities in school, community, and recreation activities.

Americans with Disabilities Act (ADA)

An anti-discrimination law giving individuals with disabilities civil rights protection similar to those rights given to all people on the basis of race, sex, national origin or religion.

Rehabilitation Act of 1973 (Section 504)

A nondiscrimination statute. Section 504 of the Act stipulates that individuals with disabilities may not be excluded from participating in programs and services receiving federal funds. It also prohibits job discrimination against people with disabilities in any program receiving federal money.

Individualized Determination Plan

A written plan for each student who receives services, modifications, and accommodations under Section 504 of the Rehabilitation Act of 1973. Some schools referred to as a "504 Plan."

Rehabilitation Act Amendments of 1992

Federal legislation that requires state vocational rehabilitation agencies to work cooperatively with local agencies, including schools, to create a unified system to serve the disabled.

Buckley Amendment

More commonly known for the Family Educational Rights and Privacy Act of 1974. The law gives parents and students (over age 18) the right to see, correct, and control access to school records.

Carl D. Perkins Vocational and Applied Technology Education Act (1990)

A federal law stipulating that students with disabilities be guaranteed the opportunity to participate in federally funded vocational programs that are equal to those afforded to the general student population.

Is My Child Eligible for Special Education?

By Luana Holzer

Children (from birth to age 21) who are eligible for special assistance may be deaf, blind, motor-impaired, retarded, emotionally disturbed (this could mean disruptive, withdrawn, or psychotic), or learning-disabled. Learning-disabled children are defined as follows:

> Children with special learning disabilities exhibit a disorder in one or more of the basic psychological processes involved in understanding or in using spoken or written language. These may be manifested in disorders of listening, thinking, talking, reading, writing, spelling, or arithmetic. They include conditions, which have been referred to as perceptual handicaps, brain injury, minimal brain dysfunction, dyslexia, developmental aphasia, etc. They do not include learning problems which are due primarily to visual, hearing or motor handicaps, to mental retardation, emotional disturbance or to environmental disadvantage.

The Individuals with Disabilities Education Act (IDEA) leaves the specific procedures for classifying learning-disabled children up to individual school districts. The classification process is exclusionary: to be categorized as learning-disabled, the child must not fit into any of the other handicapped categories. IQ must be above 70; the child must not be deaf, blind, emotionally disturbed, or economically deprived. (If a child's primary disability is deafness, then funds for that child's special educational needs are to come from the budget for deaf children, etc.)

Is There Anything I Need to Know Before I Request Special Education for My Child?

Yes, it's always best to be informed. Contact your district and ask for a copy of your local school system's procedures and regulations for special education. These are available to all citizens.

Next, write to your state director of special education (See Chapter 15, page 347) and ask for a copy of the state regulations governing special education (these are public documents). Also request a handbook describing the special education process. To be an equal partner in this process, and the best advocate for your child, it is wise to be prepared. Make a list of your child's strengths and weaknesses (if possible use the six general areas of child development: movement, communications, social relationships, self-concept/independence, thinking skills, and senses/perception) and list the questions you would like answered.

What is the Procedure for Requesting Special Education for My Child?

Referral
Write to the principal of your local school to request special education for your child. Schools have referral forms that you can request, but a letter is sufficient.

Evaluation
The next step is for the principal to convene a committee to consider the referral. The committee must be composed of at least the following: school administrator, student's teacher/tutor, parent/legal guardian or surrogate parent, student, usually other specialists attend who have particular knowledge of the problems the child seems to be experiencing. The committee's major purpose is to determine whether the child's learning and developmental problems are severe enough to require a formal evaluation by other specialists. If the committee believes a full evaluation is required, they send a written recommendation to the school's special education administrator. If the screening committee does not recommend that your child be referred to the special education director for formal evaluation, you can dispute the

decision through a formal procedure called a due process hearing. IDEA requires that the evaluation be conducted by a "multidisciplinary team," a group of professionals with expertise in different areas. You give permission or refusal to evaluate, including the tests used.

The Evaluation Conference

This meeting will explain the results of the testing. If the person in charge of your child's evaluation does not suggest this meeting, you should request one. Make sure that you understand the conclusions of the evaluation process and that you request a copy of the reports in writing.

Eligibility

This is the part of the special education process where a multidisciplinary Assessment Team Committee (known by different names) determines whether your child's disability affects his learning to the extent that he will need special education. You will want to be involved in this meeting. The job of the eligibility committee is to compare the results and conclusions of the evaluation against the definitions of the disabilities that qualify for special education services. If the results correspond with one or more of the definitions, your child will be eligible for special education services. If the committee decides that the results of the evaluation don't meet the eligibility criteria, your child will be found ineligible for special education. In either case, you will be notified in writing, and you may appeal the decision through due process procedures. If your child is found ineligible for services under the criteria for special education under IDEA, he/she may still be able to receive some services under Section 504 of the Rehabilitation Act or the Americans with Disabilities Act.

What is an Individual Education Program?

An Individualized Education Program (IEP) describes the education and related services specifically designed to meet the needs of a child with disabilities. The IEP is developed jointly by parents, educators and, often, the child. The goals and objectives are based on the child's current levels of functioning and are outlined by everyone involved in planning and providing services. The IEP specifies the educational placement, or setting, and the related services necessary to reach the goals and objectives. The IEP also includes the date the services will begin, how long they will last, and the way in which your child's progress will be measured. In addition to the goals and objectives for your child's special education program, the IEP describes related services to be provided, at no cost to you. They must be designed to assist the child with a disability to benefit from special education in the least restrictive environment (as outlined in IDEA).

The IEP is the heart and soul of the IDEA. The law works as long as the IEP is appropriately serving the child and is satisfactory to the parents. It is important to be a full and equal partner in the above procedures. You know your child best. While teaching, I served on the Assessment Team Committee, and I'll never forget the mother who brought a picture of her son to keep us focused on the meaning of our meeting. I strongly suggest that both parents attend the meeting, in addition to anyone who knows/works with your child. As homeschooling parents, we know how important it is to be informed of the laws that allow us the freedom to choose homeschooling as a means of educating our children. This same truth holds if you choose to receive special education through the public school—know the law and your rights.

Editor's note: The following special ed homeschooling success story is well known to many CHN members. Joe is now successfully on his way to young adulthood, and continues to make his parents grateful that they made the decision to homeschool. As his mom says, it was the "best decision" she ever made.

The Best Decision I Ever Made
By Marie Rodriguez

The silence in the room that day broke my heart. That was the day it hit me that public school was damaging my son. Joe is an average thirteen-year-old in most ways. He loves video games, baseball, and Star Wars. He wants to be a paramedic, fireman, or an actor, depending on what day it is. He is helpful, funny, and sensitive and caring towards children and animals that are small or weak. To me he has been "the son every mother wants."

In public school it was a different story. Joe was not an average student. It started in the second semester of first grade when he fell behind the rest of the class in reading. What followed was a school career of learning disabled labels, counselors, special tests in competency, speech therapy, parent/teacher meetings, ARD meetings, special education classes, low grades, and low self-esteem.

Joe endured it all pretty well. For several grades, his best friend (who was a straight-A student) and he were in the same school. Once they were in the same class. Joe enjoyed the social aspects of school, and he did enjoy learning.

The child was no fool. He knew he was in the "dumb" class. He sat through award ceremonies in which everyone, but a handful, won ribbons. Usually he didn't get any ribbons, but he kept on trying, and was proud of the B's he occasionally received. After "passing" from kindergarten to first grade, he never "passed" again; he was "placed."

He finally reached Middle School. A career opportunity moved our family from Texas to California at the beginning of the school year. Joe's public school career ended within five months of the move.

His grades dropped by about ten points. B's became C's, and he began to get F's which he had worked very hard to avoid. He started to become ill at school; I would pick him up and he would be clammy and pale. He would complain of headaches and would refuse to get up in the morning. I tried (for the second time) to make an appointment to see his teachers, and the earliest date I could get was four weeks later.

Something was very wrong. During all this time, I would try to talk with him and try to help him with his work. He was becoming angry and withdrawn. I finally went to the school board. They were able to move the appointment up two weeks. That meeting was the moment when I realized I could no longer leave my son in public school.

I am sure my experience has been repeated many times over. I am sure that this meeting has been mirrored in other classrooms. My husband, son, and I met with Joe's teachers, the special education teacher, a representative from the school board, and a counselor. My intentions going into the meeting were to address the difficulties my son was having, discover if all his teachers were aware of them, and try to find a way of making his school environment more learnable for him. I knew it would take effort both on his part and on theirs. I knew the responsibility was not solely theirs, but his, too. I just wanted Joe to see that they understood his difficulties, and that if he tried, they would be supportive of him and help him.

Instead what followed was a "Joe bashing" I could not believe. One by one, the teachers told us how: "Joe isn't turning in work . . ." "If Joe would only get organized . . ." "Joe doesn't pay attention . . ." "If only Joe would stay on task . . ." "Joe isn't motivated . . ." "Joe doesn't complete work assignments . . ." "Joe needs to pay attention and write down his assignments . . ."

One teacher wasn't even aware that Joe was in special ed. I was shell-shocked. Our family already knew what they were telling us. This meeting was our "cry for help" for Joe. They were making this his problem, and he was the one they expected to come up with the solution. I became very angry. Then I asked one very important question—the question that made me realize public school was damaging my son. I asked, "Can't you tell me about Joe's strengths, what his qualities are, something he is good at?" I got silence back.

Both my husband and I work full time. We cannot afford to live even modestly on one income, but I decided then and there that homeschooling would be the solution. I would make it work.

It has worked. It takes careful cooperation with my husband, and it takes time, but in the one year we have been homeschooling, Joe has improved 100%. He is excited about learning new things, his self-esteem has been rebuilt, and he has taken on a special project in which he has been a great success. He is raising a Guide Dog puppy for the blind. Joe and the puppy recently went to a field day and competed in an obstacle course. They won a blue ribbon and a medal. I wrote a story about the work Joe is doing and it was published in the *San Jose Mercury*.

Joe has signed up with a casting agency and taken acting classes at the local community center. I took him on a field trip to the airport fire station, and then another "field trip" to Boston. He visited the Paul Revere house, the USS Constitution, and Boston Commons. We also took a drive up to Maine. He has discovered horseback riding. He joined 4-H. He has done a public Bible reading. He witnessed a fire in a high-rise building, and took excellent photos of it. (He has a real instinct for "framing" a picture.) He loves to learn.

Joe has great talents and abilities, and now he sees them for himself.

Isn't Homeschooling Expensive?

Pennywise Homeschooling

"...much of what you can do for free

will promote the best possible learning."

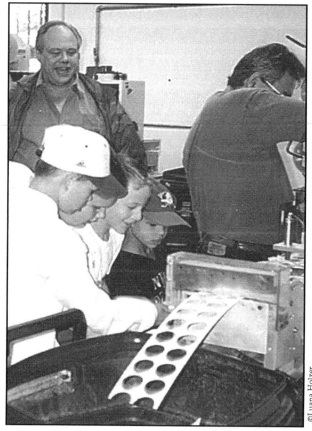

©Luana Holzer

Pennywise Homeschooling

By Karen Rafferty and Karen Taylor

A decade ago everyone homeschooled for less. There were very few publications, curricula or conferences serving homeschoolers. As our number increased, a budding market was recognized, and more and more products and services were developed to target our growing community. The explosion of products has not necessarily made homeschooling better. Homeschooling is not about the slickest textbooks, the best-packaged curriculum, or the latest innovation in interactive learning. Commodities will not make your homeschool successful. Homeschooling is about actively participating in the lives and interests of your children. Homeschooling is not the state of the art; it is the state of the heart. It is about families loving and learning with and from one another.

Are You Afraid You Can't Afford to Homeschool?

Let's turn that question around. Can you afford not to homeschool? If you've come this far, and now believe that homeschooling is the best option for your children, then you need to find a way to do it, and we are here to emphatically tell you that *yes* you can afford to homeschool! It's possible to spend thousands of dollars if you use the catalogs to compile an unrealistic "wish list", and go on a spending spree. It's also possible to spend less than you are currently spending to send your children to a public school.

The good news is that homeschooling can be an inexpensive part of raising children. The best rule of thumb is the same one that applies to all aspects of your life: if you don't have it, don't spend it. Live within your means. If you see something you like and you can afford it, well, go ahead. But, if you don't have the cash, don't succumb to advertising designed to make us think there's only one really good way to homeschool. Money should not be your determining factor in deciding to homeschool. Find alternatives. Just as home cooking tastes better than store-bought, some of your free or home designed materials may be superior, and you may end up with a more thoughtfully planned homeschool program.

Needs Versus Wants

Start with a realistic list of what you really need, and review it regularly. It's just as easy to slip some wants into the needs column in homeschooling as it is in every other aspect of life, so beware. In homeschooling, we have the additional pressure of wanting to do a good job educating our children. Those wonderful catalogs are there, tempting us with goodies, and also preying on the insecurities that lead us to think that without elaborate and costly programs, our child may never learn to read or understand math, or be appropriately enriched! In actuality, our children don't need any of it.

We want, want, want, because we care so much, and the bells and whistles programs are such a lure. Now, don't get us wrong—we adore catalogs too! They are inspiring and we learn much from them, and most of us buy from them too. Catalogs are more than places that accept credit cards; they are also terrific resources with great teaching ideas. Within them, you'll find some good book lists to take to the library, and ideas for things that you can make at home for free. Sometimes, it's worth the extra expense to purchase something, because it is so convenient, or extraordinarily good and not easily reproducible. If it's a book, game, a building kit or a science kit, it will be much appreciated at a gift giving time. You'll find some quality, enduring gifts by shopping at an education store or catalog.

A special caution to new homeschoolers: Hold off making many immediate purchases. The euphoria of deciding to homeschool has caused many a new homeschooler to overspend initially, and much of it is never used because too much was purchased, or it doesn't really suit their child. Newbies are like the proverbial kid in a candy shop. We've all been there, so if you can possibly restrain for just a little while, you'll be glad you did. Ask any experienced homeschooler about this, and you'll probably get a sheepish confession, and a suggestion to perhaps spend your first few weeks reading books from the library out loud, while snuggling on the couch munching those chocolate chip cookies you just made together, followed by a trip to the park to enjoy the outdoors.

Why Read a Catalog if You Can't Afford Anything in It?

- You'll learn of good books and tapes that can be borrowed from the library. Some you may eventually want to own, but many are read once, so borrowing from the library is quite practical and money saving.
- You'll become aware of excellent educational games and books and be the only one in the crowd who recognizes their value when you see them for next to nothing at a yard sale or thrift shop.
- You'll get good ideas and find ways to design a similar program at home.
- You'll use the catalog for your shop-at-home gift purchases, saving gas and wear-and-tear on yourself, while getting high quality gifts.
- You might decide to buy something jointly with some homeschool friends.

Homeschooling Can Be Your Cheapest Option

People automatically assume that public school is the cheapest form of educating available because taxpayers have picked up the tab. If you are contemplating keeping your child in school solely to take advantage of this supposed savings, consider some of the hidden costs of public school:

- How much do you pay for back-to-school clothes each year because your child needs just the right look to avoid ridicule? Are there clothes in the closet that still fit? Do the clothes have to be brand new to avoid stigma at school?
- How much extra do you pay for the latest in hairstyles, also because your child will feel left out and shunned at school without it?
- How much does that new backpack cost? It has to be new since no self-respecting school child wants to go to school with last year's bag! Horror of horrors if you dared suggest such a thing. Ditto for binders, pencils and you name it. Everything used last year is obsolete for the schooled child.
- What will the school ask you to help pay this year? What supplies have you been asked to bring because the school doesn't have the money to provide it? In addition to paper and pencils, it might even be toilet paper and soap!
- Do you drive your child to school because the bus is so slow or

downright dangerous due to the unsupervised threatening behavior of other children? Gas isn't cheap.

- What fundraiser is the school having this year? Are you a vegetarian finding yourself buying beef jerky? Are you buying overpriced candy that you don't want? Are you buying the entire box to spare your child the time spent bugging the neighbors so that his/her homework can get finished?

- How much will you spend at the school carnival so your child's class wins first place and gets a "free" pizza party?

- How much do you pay for a year of school lunches?

- How much extra do you pay for doctor bills because your child catches something at school and brings it home to the family? Some schools put so much pressure on attendance that they encourage children with so-called minor illnesses not to miss school. This, combined with working parents not wanting to miss work, means it's not uncommon to have contagious children at school, infecting others.

Just how much does it cost to get a "free" public education? If your child is home with you, you save much of the above. You can also educate your child for free, if you choose (or need to), and spend only when you want to. Homeschooling is starting to sound like a pretty terrific bargain from a financial point of view! Read on to learn how to implement your pennywise homeschooling plan.

Educator Discounts

Some stores are known to give educator discounts, and here's a website that lists some: *http://www.geocities.com/Athens/8259/discount.html/*. Most require some kind of educator proof, which is why CHN sends its members a membership card. Other people make their own ID, or even bring in a copy of their R-4. Some stores will only offer the discount on items they deem to be educational, and others are liberal in their interpretation. If you don't have internet access, some of the businesses listed at this site are: B. Dalton Books (20%), Barnes & Noble (20%), The Book Market (2 stores in San Diego area—15%), Book Warehouse (15%), Borders (20%), Foozles (15%), Hollywood Video (free educational videos), Imaginarium, Jo-Ann Fabrics, Little Professor Book Center (20%),

Mediaplay, Natural Wonders (10%), Walden Books, and Zany Brainy (10%). Michael's is not on the list, but we've heard homeschoolers get discounts there. If a store isn't listed here, perhaps they haven't been asked yet. Try asking any store if they offer an educator's discount. They may just say yes!

Thrifty Ideas

You'll find thrifty ideas and resources in the library, and on the internet. The three *Tightwad Gazette* volumes by Amy Dacyczyn are very popular. Look also for *Raising Kids with Just a Little Cash*, by Lisa Reid, *Free Family Fun*, by Cynthia MacGregor, *The Penny Pincher's Almanac: Handbook for Modern Frugality*, by Dean King, *The Best of Living Cheap News* by Larry Roth, books by Don Aslett, and many, many others. These are just suggestions—see what is available for free in your library.

The internet has more to offer than you'll have time to use. Some sites specialize in information on a particular subject, and others offer general lists of free resources, or thrifty living suggestions:

- Homeschooling on the cheap *http://www.bcpl.net/~owl/homeschool/ HomeschoolingOnTheCheap.html*
- About.com freebies *http://freebies.miningco.com/shopping/freebies*
- Games for learning *www.angelfire.com/wi2/GamesForLearning/*
- The Dollar Stretcher *www.stretcher.com/menu/subscrib.cfm*
- Homeschool Freebies and Cost Cutting Ideas *www.geocities.com/Athens/ 8259/savers.html*
- All-4-Free: *www.all-4-free.com/educational.html*

Other favorite thrifty resources that homeschoolers use to the fullest are: real life experience, the library, sharing with other homeschoolers and taking advantage of used curriculum sales, freebies from the government and businesses, thrift stores and yard sales, discarded books, and the internet (for a list of selected educational websites, see Chapter 14, pages 313-315).

Real Life: A Great Curriculum!

Homeschooling allows children to learn from everyday experience. This is a big money saver, because you don't have to purchase materials to create an artificial learning environment. Here are some ideas to get you started in looking at your daily life from an educational perspective:

Cooking. You don't need to purchase expensive manipulatives to teach math when there are dried beans handy. Use the measuring cups in your kitchen, divide a pizza for fractions, divide one recipe in half, and double another to sharpen math skills. Your mathematicians can even make a tasty dessert while they learn.

Gardening. Become a botanist and reduce the family grocery bill by growing your own delicious fruits and vegetables. While outside, your child may expand his interests to include science when he discovers an interesting insect or bird nest in the garden, and wants to learn more. Or he may be inspired to draw what he's seen outside.

Grocery Shopping. Forget paper money, plastic cash registers and fake food. Just take your children grocery shopping. They will learn estimation, cost comparison, addition, subtraction, making change, nutrition, and consumerism. Let them weigh the vegetables and figure out the best buys. Let them clip and organize coupons. They can also learn to stand in line, thus allaying the fears of the homeschooling opponents who are so certain that the only place a child can learn to stand in line is in school!

Laundry. Let them sort, match, learn about fabric care, and eventually do it all. Matching is a math skill for a young child, and for the older children, it's home economics.

Allowance. Give them an allowance and they'll soon be able to figure out to the penny how much they can buy, tax included. When they get older involve them in family budgeting and let them take over writing out the checks for the bills. You can take them to the bank to open their own savings account, and let them fill out the application, and speak to the teller.

Plan a Party. Give them a budget and let them plan the food, decorations and invitations. They'll develop many necessary math, writing, thinking and social skills.

Play Games. Monopoly, Scrabble, Rummikub, puzzles and many, many other games develop basic academic and thinking skills while having fun.

Do-it-Yourself Projects. Build a treehouse, a deck or a toolbox. Make your own pottery. Fix an appliance, or at least take it apart and check out all those pieces before discarding it. Hands-on craft projects increase spatial intelligence and many of them require math skills, such as measuring.

Plan a Trip. Math, reading, writing and map-reading skills will surely be a by-product, along with geography at its finest.

Visit Businesses. Many businesses offer tours and/or written materials about their products and services. Children can learn about careers, advertising, economic principles and much more as they get out into their communities.

We've barely scratched the surface with this list, but it's a start. What else can you think of that's available in your home or your community? Opportunities to learn are everywhere, and it doesn't have to be in a classroom to be valuable, nor from a purchased textbook. In fact, much of what you can do for free will promote the best possible learning. Now that's a good deal!

The Library

As homeschoolers, we simply can't say enough good things about a library. It's truly a homeschooler's most important resource. Books on every imaginable subject are just waiting to be checked out at no charge. In addition, many libraries carry reference books, children's magazines, books on tape (great in the car), CDs, instructional videos, and increasingly, computers with internet access. If they don't have the book you want, many libraries will request it from another library (interlibrary loan) for free or a very small charge—usually the cost of postage to notify you. You may also find that they have library programs that will be of interest to your family. Preschool story hours are common, but some libraries also offer programs for older children and adults as well. If your community has more than one library, or a college library, visit them all, since each library will have a different collection.

Generally, we've found that homeschoolers are very welcome in the library. Librarians are thrilled to see children who are being exposed to so many books. If you need help, just ask; they'll be happy to assist you, especially if you're able to visit during their less crowded hours while regular school is in session. If you need direction in selecting books, there are books on this subject at the library, many booklists on the internet, and also the recommended books in homeschool catalogs. Take some of these lists with you, and your library visit will be even more successful. Another good place to start is with a list of the Newbery winners, available on the internet and also in *The California Homeschool Guide Companion CD*.

We know a few homeschoolers who have avoided their library for years because an old fine has grown to overwhelming proportions and they are unable to pay it. If this describes you, then it's time to take action. Consider going to the librarian to request a second chance. If that old 50 cent fine has grown to $50, talk about it. What alternatives are there? Could you work off that fine? Every library needs help. Explain your situation, along with a sincere desire to make amends so that you can once again become an exemplary library patron. There is no guarantee your offer will be accepted, but you have nothing to lose, and this is one of those times when the right attitude might make a big difference. Offer to wash the books for them (you know how grungy those plastic covers can get), or mend the books, or help shelve books for a month, straighten the children's section, or whatever they need.

Librarians care about their patrons, and really want you to be able to take advantage of what they have to offer. Once you have a clean slate, keep it that way! Write the due dates on your calendar, and keep the list of books in one place and check off each and every book when returning so you know you haven't forgotten one. Have you considered returning each book in better condition than it was when you checked it out? What a great ongoing community service project! You will be teaching your children by example how to take special care of your borrowed books because as a taxpayer, they really do belong to you. You can wipe the cover with a damp rag if needed, or fix a small tear with tape, erase pencil marks, and bring anything else to the attention of the librarian when you return it. Consider keeping the books on your own "library" shelf or box so you don't forget or lose them ever again. And, if you can't return a book on time, ask to renew it by phone.

The Homeschool Support Group

Some homeschool groups have their own lending library, others hold an annual used curriculum sale/exchange, and both are great ways to supplement your resources. Sometimes you can borrow a book privately from someone in the group, either to use it or just to see if you want to purchase it. You'll also get some honest feedback on just how good a resource it is. Another advantage to groups is that they usually get discounted or even free admission to just about any activity.

Frequently you will hear about quality, inexpensive resources from other homeschoolers, and helpful hints. For example, one thrifty tip that is often shared amongst homeschoolers is to make your own dry erase white board from a piece of laminated shower board from a hardware store.

Freebies from the Government and Businesses

Some government agencies and also businesses offer excellent educational materials for free or low cost. Below are just a few resources available. If you are interested in a particular subject, search the internet, or ask an agency or company if they have educational materials:

- Free Federal Resources for Educational Excellence (huge site) *www.ed.gov/free/*

- Federal Consumer Information Center offers free and low cost publications. Order their free catalog by calling 888/878-3256 or online at *www.pueblo.gsa.gov/*

- USGS National Mapping Information Educational Resources *http://mapping.usgs.gov/www/html/1educate.html/*

- Interesting and useful teaching packets and resources are available through the Earth Science Information Center at 1-888-ASK-USGS (275-8747)

- Environmental Protection Agency, 1200 Pennsylvania Avenue, N.W. Washington, DC 20460 202/260-2090 *www.epa.gov/enviroed/*

- Federal Reserve Bank of Atlanta Public Affairs Department, 104 Marietta St. NW, Atlanta, GA 30303. This is an outstanding resource, with many free educational materials from comic books to videos available. *http:// www.frbatlanta.org/about.cfm* is the home site. A direct link to the teaching aid ordering site is: *http://app.ny.frb.org/cfpicnic/frame1.cfm*.

- National Park Service 1849 C Street, Rm 3317, Washington DC 20013. *www.nps.gov/index.html/*. This web site leads to numerous educational resources.

- NASA Education Program. NASA Headquarters, Washington DC 20546. 202/358-0000. *www.hq.nasa.gov/office/codef/education/* Extensive educational resources and opportunities are available.

- US Department of Agriculture County Extension Agents. For local offices look in your phone book under U.S. (or Federal) Government, U.S. Department of Agriculture. This is a good resource for advice on gardening and other homemaking skills.

Thrift Stores and Garage Sales

Thrift stores and garage sales are highly valued by in-the-know homeschoolers who have located terrific "finds" using this fun resource. Whether shopping for clothes, games, or books, buy on the spot when you find a bargain you like, even if it won't be used for several years. Whether you shop in thrift stores or at garage sales might depend on your community. Some garage sales have better prices, but they aren't consistent, and a lot of time can be spent driving to them in spread-out communities. They are unbeatable for baby items, but when children grow older, sometimes it's easier to drive to a few select thrift stores where the selection is greater. Most thrift stores have bargain days or hours, so planning ahead may save an additional 50%.

What bargain is waiting for you? Sometimes it will be a book or an expensive educational game. What might seem like a dull item to a typical shopper might be identified by a homeschooler as the quality item that it is. It's truly a thrill to locate an out-of-print children's book that may no longer be available even at the library. Many homeschoolers seek these older books because the reading level is higher than today's "dumbed down" books. With a little luck, a good eye, and a willingness to spend some time browsing, great bargains will be found. Sometimes, parts of games are found, and become almost giveaways, but some pieces might have a use. It might be the questions of a trivia game, a few missing parts to a construction set you already own, some small toys or blocks to make your own math manipulatives, or a math or handwriting workbook. Puzzles for young children are a good buy, and it's possible to count the few pieces and have a good idea if anything will be missing. You might even stumble across a partial or even complete homeschool curriculum at a fraction of the original cost.

And, finally, once all those academic needs are met, turn to the used clothing and snatch up the great bargains. You can pay full price for a new pair of jeans and let your child run out to play and make the first hole in the knee, or you can pick up a used pair for much less and patch the hole made by the previous owner. Or, cut off the legs of really worn almost-free jeans and make shorts. Or, for just a little more, you might get something very new looking. What a lesson in economics for our children, as well as instilling a good value system that will serve them for life. They will learn about reusing and not wasting, two important environmental lessons, and also learn about how to make the budget go further. It has nothing to do with your financial situation, but rather how you choose to spend the dollars that you have, whether abundant or limited.

Discarded Books

Local school districts regularly give away textbooks, and other books, some of them brand new. Their logic is that if the standardized tests show the kids aren't learning enough, perhaps it's the books, so they replace them, even if they have never been used. It's the grass-is-always-greener mentality, along with some pressure, one can only imagine, from textbook companies who want to sell new books. Using the band-aid approach to education, they "fix" the problem with something new, even if what they had before was just fine. Or, it might be slightly outdated, or suddenly not politically correct enough to be used, but will be fine for your purposes.

Some school districts give their books away at the local district office, and some through the county. Call and ask if they have used books to give away. They usually don't care who gets the books. It might be an annual clearout, or ongoing. Some books will be better than others, naturally, and it will depend on how you feel about textbooks. A math book might be great, but perhaps you'll be terribly bored with a health book, or a social studies text, and vow not to bore your child with it, even if it's free. Or, it might be just what you've been looking for. Use your own good judgement and don't use it just because it came from a school.

If you're lucky, you might even stumble across a school library giveaway, and be the lucky recipient of a few boxes of perfectly good fiction that only needs a little washing and mending. The school may have decided that new paperbacks would be more popular with their students, or they may be looking for current books that are easier to read.

Depending on where your free books are being stored, there are a few supplies you'll need when you go on your book collecting mission. If it's a dark warehouse, bring a flashlight. A hand truck/dolly is very convenient, as is your own supply of sturdy boxes. Moving books is hard work, so bring a drink and also something to clean your hands (baby wipes, perhaps) because once you are done, you'll notice your hands are really dirty. Bring a friend, and it will be twice the fun as you help each other out!

Public libraries also sell discarded books along with donations that they aren't adding to their collection. Some have ongoing sales, and others plan a major event once or twice a year. Learning about these sales is a good way to find special books at a good price. Volunteer to help, and you'll probably get to purchase your selections before the sale opens to the public.

Low-Cost Resources for Materials and Activities

Look around your community for things that are low cost or free that will help you with your homeschooling:

- Museums often have free days, some as often as once a month. Ask them. A family membership can also be a good buy so that you may visit often during the year. If your museum is a passport member of ASTC (see www.ASTC.org/) your membership will be an even greater value since you will often have free admission just by showing your family membership card in one of the many museums around the country that are part of this association.

- Art/craft/sewing classes may be offered inexpensively by local businesses. If you have a group willing to sign up at the same time, some businesses might agree to offer a special school rate. It's worth asking.

- Free newspapers. Many communities have free parenting publications with local information for families that are often available at the library. Nationally, *The Link* (*http://www.homeschoolnewslink.com/*) and *Homeschooling Parent* (*www.homeschoolingparent.com*) are free.

- Local Community Activities. Check the parks and recreation publications, and also look for music concerts, holiday activities, fairs, parades, cultural events and much more that are sponsored by many cities.

- Youth Organizations such as Girl Scouts, Boy Scouts, 4-H and Campfire (which now includes boys in their membership) may have low-cost publications full of ideas for activities and projects. You might find homeschool clubs sponsored by any of these organizations.

- Friends, relatives and homeschool support groups have endless skills to tap. Real scientists, engineers, manufacturers, computer programmers and other professionals often welcome the opportunity to share their passion and expertise with interested youngsters.

- Small printing businesses will sometimes save odd sized pieces or left-overs. Ask them if they'll give you their throw-aways.

- Newspapers used to give away end rolls of newsprint. All you can do is ask and find out, although it's likely these are spoken for. Large warehouse stores such as Costco or Sam's, or restaurant supply stores are another paper source—buy a roll of butcher paper and have a lifetime of quality art paper for those big art projects or painting adventures.

- Teacher or craft magazines. Libraries often have back issues, and you'll find useful ideas and reproducible games.

- An outdated art calendar is worthless to everyone but a homeschooler, who can cut the pictures out and rotate a display of art for the child's enjoyment and learning. At some point, someday, he'll see that picture somewhere else and recognize it with delight. Art appreciation has begun!

The outstanding education that you desire for your children does not have to be expensive! The pennywise tips in this chapter are just the beginning, and we encourage you to think of more ways to save. The question may soon be not whether you can afford homeschooling, but what will you do with the money you save.

13

Am I the Only Homeschooler in Town?
How Do I Meet Others?

"A homeschool group is sometimes

able to take advantage of

cultural and educational opportunities

usually reserved for school groups."

©Luana Holzer

The Importance of Homeschool Support Groups
By Luana Holzer

Support groups are often one of the first contacts that new homeschooling families have with the homeschooling community. Groups reassure these families that they are not alone in their choice of an alternative method of education. Newcomers find that there are as many reasons and methods for homeschooling as there are members in the group. Group gatherings become a smorgasbord of information, methods, ideology, and cultures. No matter how long a person has been attending the group, new information is constantly being shared. Needs change as children grow older and educational requisites become more complicated, so a homeschooling family seldom outgrows the need for support.

Generally, the reason people come together in groups is for the strength and support for their choices that they might not be receiving from their relatives, neighbors, or co-workers. They are relieved to find they aren't alone. It's comforting for them to know that others have taken this alternative route successfully, and their children are the living proof! The discussions new homeschooling families have with the non-homeschooling world often present many questions that are difficult to answer. These concerns may be brought to the group where many varied opinions are shared, providing the newcomer with solid information to impart to those concerned friends and relatives who are not sure about homeschooling.

Newcomers soon discover that there are many options in homeschooling and that there is no "right way" to educate children. Within the diversity of a group, a person will find structured homeschoolers, unstructured homeschoolers, and all those home educators in between. Each is encouraged to explore and find what works best for his or her own family. The inevitable conflicts and misunderstandings inherent in diversity can be beneficial for learning peaceful ways to resolve conflicts.

Support groups offer an exchange of ideas and networking of educational resources, including methods of presenting basic and complex concepts, local points of interest, sources for supplies, and referral to people willing to tutor. When a challenge presents itself to a homeschooling parent, often that same challenge has arisen and been met by others in the group who are usually very willing to share their experience. Although a particular method may not work for someone else, it may open up the creative channels and resources of other members of the group who can help discover a solution that will work.

Exchange of materials is another aspect of support groups. Books, curricula, textbooks, workbooks, and other traditional methods of education are traded and sold. Catalogs for educational materials, book discount houses, and library resources are passed around. Some groups develop lending libraries.

A homeschooling group is sometimes able to take advantage of cultural and educational opportunities usually reserved for school groups. Some museums, theaters, and institutions have special programs for groups that are not available to individuals, and most of these institutions will recognize a homeschooling group as a school. For example, the National Geographic Society allows homeschoolers in a support group to participate in the National Geography Bee. Most homeschool groups plan field trips to take advantage of these special programs.

The socialization that takes place within a support group is invaluable because it crosses the arbitrary age barriers that exist in traditional educational settings. Children present at meetings, park trips, and field trips develop relationships with everyone: adults, babies, and all those in-between. Older kids may organize games that include all ages and skill levels. Adults often draw a gathering of children to them when they share craft, art or academic skills. Children who frequent homeschooling support group activities learn to interact with people of all ages.

Connecting with other homeschoolers can also provide visible evidence to the community that there is an alternative to school. When a homeschooling group visits museums, theaters, arboretums, aquariums, libraries, and fire stations, many people in the general public become aware of homeschooling for the first time. People who come in contact with a homeschooling support group see that homeschooling is not an isolated incident but an entire community, and a healthy and vigorous one, at that!

The basic local homeschooling support group is the foundation of an ever-growing support system that now reaches across the nation and around the world. Support groups are vital in sustaining the home educating family's spirit of dedication to this alternative lifestyle.

Finding a Support Group for Your Family

There are two important steps which you may take simultaneously or one at a time: (1) think long and hard about needs that your family hopes to meet in a support group, and (2) *network, network, network*.

Think about your needs and hopes. Consider your personality, your lifestyle and schedule, your homeschool style, your community, and particularly your children's ages and personalities as you answer these questions:

- Do you want a support group that will provide planned activities for children and/or parents at least some of the time, or do unstructured park days appeal to you more?
- Do you want to meet once a month, once a week, or something in between?
- Ideally, what size of support group would you like to belong to?
- Do you want field trips? Academic-based activities like science fairs and math circuses? Holiday parties (such as Halloween or Valentine)? Sports activities? Unstructured play days? Planned sharing between parents and/or kids (such as Book Talks, Resource Day)? Group activities (such as a choir, a play, an orchestra, or group science lessons)?
- Would you feel more comfortable in a specialized group—one with only younger children, for example, or a group for people of a particular faith? Or would you like an inclusive group with a range of ages and lifestyles?

Once you know what you want, networking will help you find a group:
- Start with your Local Contact. He or she is an experienced homeschooler in your community who has volunteered to answer homeschooling questions and direct homeschoolers to homeschool groups in the community. Local Contact listings are in each issue of CHN's newsletter, the CHN website *www.CaliforniaHomeschool.net* or by calling 800/327-5399.
- Directories of homeschool state groups may be found in *Home Education Magazine*, NHEN, *The Link*, CHN's website, and some homeschooling books.
- Some correspondence schools and public or private ISPs sponsor or keep lists of support groups.
- Post a notice in your local library, "Looking for Homeschoolers to Network With." Ask all of your relatives, friends and acquaintances in playgroups, at libraries, in stores or at church if they know of any other homeschoolers. When you follow up on leads, ask these homeschoolers in turn what groups and individuals they know.
- Check local newspapers, especially parent newsletters.
- Print a notice in the local papers in the public service section.
- Attend a homeschooling conference and network with people there.
- Join a free homeschooling e-mail group, such as CaliforniaHS

(http://groups.yahoo.com/group/CaliforniaHS). After you sign up, try asking if anyone lives near you—with hundreds of other California homeschoolers on this list, you may be pleasantly surprised to find there might be someone who lives near you!

Start a Support Group

The same steps that might help you to find a support group that meets your family's needs will also help you to start a group, if you cannot find one.

- First of all you need a few families (or just one) interested in getting a group started. Start networking!
- Use all the networking techniques suggested above to find other homeschooling families in your area. Then call or write them to ask if they would like to get together to discuss their support group needs.
- Set a date for a meeting about starting a homeschooling support group, and send notices to local newspapers (public service section), local and state homeschooling newsletters; post fliers in libraries, pediatrician offices, book stores, teacher supply stores, health food stores, and other community centers.
- Many support groups are experiencing tremendous growth pains with the increasing number of people flocking to homeschooling; while some are changing their group dynamics to accommodate this growth, others are opting to close their membership to keep a manageable size. These "closed" groups would most likely welcome your interest in starting a new group and could refer their inquirers to you.
- Homeschoolers are known to drive far and wide for meetings and field trips, so don't limit your efforts to a small geographical area.

The Initial Meetings

As you try to meet other homeschoolers in your area, it may be appropriate to express what sort of a group you would like to belong to, if you know. This might save you time and eliminate the problem of people working at cross-purposes. On the other hand, it may eliminate certain possibilities you haven't thought of, or it might turn off people who would be valuable support group members.

At the initial meeting, discuss the needs of the people involved and get everyone thinking about the group's formation. Creating a questionnaire can help define the group's intent and direction.

At the next meeting, you can finalize the group's intent and purpose or philosophy. This can be as simple as, "to provide a support group to homeschooling families by having a monthly meeting for parents and a monthly parkday/field trip for everyone." If you want families of the same religious background or other special focus, include that in your statement.

Next you will need a name for your group; the name helps to make the group sound "official" when soliciting members through public fliers and newspapers, and also when signing up for field trips. Many groups use the name of the town or area they live in as part of their name.

How organized does your group want to be? Do you want regular meetings? Where and when will they be? Do you want a newsletter? What degree of organization do you want? Most groups function better if the workload is evenly distributed, with everyone lending a hand. The degree of organization everyone wants will determine how many jobs there will be. Some potential jobs are newsletter editor, group directory publisher, meeting planner (this can rotate), field trip coordinator (this can be shared by all), a "welcome person" for new members, phone tree coordinator, and special events coordinator. In the beginning you may want to have a requirement about member activity, such as everyone has to plan one event, or that everyone commits to one job for six months.

What Makes a Support Group Successful?

One of the keys to success is how well the support group addresses the needs of its members. A key ingredient is some form of regular contact and communication. This can be through a newsletter (which can be as simple as an activity calendar), a contact person, or regular meetings. In many groups this takes place at periodic planning meetings, monthly parent meetings, an informal Mom's Night Out, or at park day. No matter what the organizational structure of the support group, families need to have a voice.

And of course, the people themselves make a group successful. Contact leads to closeness. If families try to make it to all of the planned activities of the group, then there will be more cohesiveness. Once people make friends, share interests and ideas, they will be motivated to go to more events to be with each other.

Having a membership which lives in close proximity makes it easier to get together, especially in the early formation of a support group. But you will find that long-established support groups have members driving across many counties to join in on the activities.

Maintaining the Successful Group

Each support group will have an evolutionary process of its own. Many grow and become long lasting and successful, others stay small by choice, and are tight-knit. Some lose members and enthusiasm until they dissolve. Some become conflict-ridden and disintegrate. People change, and their needs change. If your group is to have a long life, it will need to stay open to change. Families need to have a voice and a sense that their needs do count.

Over time, members will leave and new ones will take their place. It is important to include these new members into the heartbeat of the group by allowing them to be contributors. Many successful groups share the "burden of the load" and elicit help from everyone, thus the responsibility for the group is on the many, and not the few. Distributed responsibility empowers members to change things that are not working and to take delight in the things that do work.

Support groups can be anything the group wants them to be. The more the members are involved, the more they will get out of the group. Each member is an asset, with unique talents and ideas to bring to the group. There is no one right way to homeschool, or to form a support group, so how can you go wrong?

Survival Guide for the Newcomer to a Homeschool Group: A 12-Step Plan

By Ofra Obejas

Author's Note: This 12-step guide has 14 steps, which goes to emphasize the point that you should be prepared for things not to go exactly as you expected.

Although it's possible to homeschool without ever attending a support group, the substantial benefits of a group compel most homeschoolers to join one. As a result, group dynamics become a homeschool issue. Here's a quick 12-step guide to assist the newcomer:

First, develop a thick skin. You didn't become a homeschooler by piercing your left ear twice just because Jenny Kwaitowski did it. Neither did anyone else in the group. Some of the people might come off just a tad opinionated. You won't last long if you take someone's firm view of how many minutes a day a fifth-grader should spend reading as a criticism of your parenting.

Throw that chip off your shoulder. Even if you have been done wrong, it's not the people in the group who've done it. They don't want to spend the whole afternoon listening to how that second-grade teacher used her cell phone to call your home—in the middle of class!— and left a message on your answering machine about your daughter's inadequate book report. Nor do they want to hear about the years of therapy that resulted from that incident.

Don't expect all your homeschooling questions to be answered on your first visit. Or ever. The people in the group haven't figured it all out themselves. If they had, they'd be on the homeschool lecture circuit, or they'd talk to you, but they'd ask to be paid as consultants.

Don't monopolize one person's time. Even if she wants to be helpful, it is this mother's time off. She came to the park to relax and see her friends, not to serve as a one-person hospitality committee.

Don't expect to make friends instantly. The group probably has new people popping in every other week, and most of them are never seen or heard from again. Don't make promises about becoming a pillar of the group (as did everyone who was never seen or heard from again). Show up fairly regularly. When they see you are serious, they'll warm up to you.

Contain your enthusiasm. Even if you have brilliant ideas on how to improve everything in the group, shelve it for at least 6 months. The group has been around long before you showed up. There are reasons why things are the way they are, which you will find out in good time. Before you try to change anything, find out those reasons. However, if the group ignores your questions and you are not happy with the way things are, this might not necessarily be your fault. It might not be the right group for you, or it might be a plain awful group. Don't spend time blaming yourself or trying to change it. Find another group or start your own (that's how 90% of groups get established). When you're in charge and the group is still bad, THEN you can blame yourself.

Find out, in advance, if there's a common philosophy. That way, you won't show up at the park and proceed to hand out sandwiches to your kids, when the entire group is observing the Fast of Ramadan. (This isn't a hypothetical example.)

Assume nothing. Just because everyone in the group is homeschooling, doesn't mean you have anything else in common. Don't presume that everyone shares your ideas about education, breastfeeding, or politics. There's nothing like making a Bush joke and finding out you're the only Democrat.

Assume nothing. This point was already made, but it bears repeating. Everyone has a public face and a private face. You don't know that another mother isn't going home, opening her kid's closet, and screaming, "NO WIRE HANGERS!"

Lurk for a while. If the group uses e-mail to communicate about upcoming events and general ideas, don't jump in. This is a good idea for a newcomer to any e-group, but in this case, the people in the loop have actually met face to face. You don't want half the people to say, "Who IS this Peggy person, and why should I care what SHE thinks about how to run sports day?"

Resolve your childhood issues. Or, in the very least, don't bring them to the group. The sight of grown women sobbing at a park table gives homeschoolers everywhere a bad name.

Preaching is for church. People don't come to the group to be lectured to about effective discipline, proper nutrition, or the only right way to teach math.

Show that you can give before you ask to receive. Demanding, on your first visit, that the meeting time be changed to a day that's better for you pretty much guarantees that everyone will hate you. Maybe they were thinking of changing the day, but now they are not going to, just to spite you.

Last, but not least, remember that this is a network of people who at one time were exactly where you are. These are not licensed education consultants or child-development experts, but ordinary parents just like you. They are all looking to receive support as much as to give it. They are not all there to serve you. Be patient and persevere. You might make new friends, and you might get some nifty ideas about how to do this home-study thing. Before you know it, you'll be the one welcoming a rookie who shows up at the park and doesn't know what to expect.

Meet Five Established Support Groups

We invited some homeschoolers from around the state to tell us more about their groups. Support groups are always changing, and if you visit these groups someday, you'll probably find they are doing new things, have new policies, and perhaps new members with new interests. Even so, the value of what our writers have shared remains very helpful, and we think they offer many good ideas for new support groups to consider.

Humboldt Homeschoolers
By Paige Smith

We are an informal and friendly group, whose members are actively homeschooling (or are thinking about it) and want to educate themselves about homeschooling as a positive, rewarding alternative to schools. We also enjoy getting together for fun. Everyone is welcome regardless of age, gender, ethnic background, homeschooling style or spiritual beliefs. We all learn much from each other as we share our wealth of knowledge and experience.

Our support group is very informal. We do not have directors, membership dues or requirements, and we are not affiliated with any other religious group, support group or independent study program.

We do have a "leader." Some years back, friends asked me to start a support group, and I did. So far, nobody has wanted my job, although it is available should someone want to do it, and I don't regard being the leader as any big deal. As done by me, the job consists of: setting up the phone tree, maintaining newsletter subscription lists, organizing our "Introduction to Homeschooling" nights for the public, motivating people to set up and participate in classes, field trips, etc., and talking to new or prospective homeschoolers. For the rest of my job, I have lots of help. Our group wouldn't function otherwise.

We offer a newsletter, phone tree, field trips, gym days, beach days, classes, a resource library, and other events. All of these things are organized by volunteers. Our phone tree is used mainly for field trips or other free or low-cost events that might be of interest and didn't make it into the newsletter, and for legislative-alert calls. We have one person who puts messages on the tree. That person calls three or four people. The next people call one or two people. Newcomers and people taking a break from the "front" of the tree rotate out to the tips of the branches. We try not to burden anyone, and our tree works pretty well. Our policy on legislative notices is that we ask everyone to please pass on the message. We don't recommend a course of action, feeling that each individual needs to make up his or her mind as to whether to call legislators, write letters, etc. The important thing to us is to get the word out, not to tell people what to do.

Field trips are set up by people who want to go on them and by two kind volunteers who set them up when things are sparse. We announce field trips in the newsletter, and people call the organizer to sign up. Lately, we've been giving sign-up priority to subscribers, but anyone is welcome to come to any of our field trips or other events.

We try to have a gym or beach day once a month. The gym is reserved by a member of the church where it is located. They offer it to us for free, but we try to collect a small donation for the church each time. The beach days are set up in likely months by our editor. She looks out the window and at her calendar and says, "Let's try this date." Occasionally, we go to the beach in the rain.

Classes are set up by a family that is interested. We don't have a lot of classes, but swimming lessons and art classes happen fairly regularly. I set up art classes about three times a year. A local art teacher who works well with kids and has a studio in her home is our teacher. She and I decide on a time and subject, I put it in the newsletter and take sign-ups. Another mom arranges swimming lessons for the group through a local public pool.

It may be that as more of our homeschoolers get into high school there may be more call for academic classes, but so far, arrangements for tutoring have been made instead. For instance, we trade Spanish lessons for my oldest son and myself for computer time for our teacher's sons.

Our resource library got its start when a retired schoolteacher, our local support groups, and a church got together. What started as one wall in a Sunday school classroom with some textbooks and unit study boxes on its shelves has grown through donations by homeschool families, schools and more retired teachers to fill the entire classroom with curriculum materials—readers with the stories cross-indexed by topic and grade level to go with over 40 unit study boxes on topics in World History, American History, Life and Physical Sciences, Character Building, Home Economics and more; curriculum planning information; homeschooling books and magazines; parenting books . . . the list goes on and on. So far, we're open two days a month (volunteers again), which isn't a lot but it seems to work. Textbooks and readers can be checked out for the full school year. Everything else can be checked out for a month, although if a family is in the middle of a unit study and doesn't want to stop, we ask that they bring back the box and just keep out the materials they will be using, so the next family can get started.

Once a year we offer an "Introduction to Homeschooling" evening event to the public. We advertise in newspapers, put fliers up in likely places and announce it in newsletters. We have various homeschooling books on hand for people to buy and/or look through and lots of experienced homeschoolers there to answer questions. We serve cookies, juice and coffee. It's a casual affair.

All Ways Learning
By Monica Cardiff

All Ways Learning is an inclusive group of homeschooling families, which accepts and respects each member. The purpose of the group is to empower its members to seek out, organize or create all the resources desired to homeschool, and to support its members in every facet of homeschooling. All Ways Learning believes it is the right of the parents to educate their children without government control or interference. All Ways Learning welcomes anyone who honors the following guidelines:

Responsibilities. Families arrange and develop activities that enrich the learning atmosphere of the group. Each member promotes a safe environment for all individuals to participate physically, mentally, emotionally, and spiritually. Each member represents All Ways Learning by behaving in an appropriate manner while participating in group activities. Each member is willing to resolve conflict as it arises.

Communication. Sharing of ideas and information is facilitated by the newsletter, announcements at park day, a buddy system for newcomers, meetings, phone tree, conversation, the field trip/event binder, and portable mailbox. The mailbox is a file box containing a folder for each family; messages can be "sent" by leaving them in a family's folder.

Park Day. Our park day is a time for the whole group to meet together, so no formal programs are arranged for park day, except for sharing time for those interested at the first park day of the month. In order to create a safe environment for all, each parent is responsible for his or her own child(ren) unless other arrangements have been made. Children need to remain within designated physical boundaries, and each child needs to let his or her parent know if (s)he plans to leave the area. Children are expected to resolve conflicts with each other (with parental assistance as needed). Parental supervision of the various play areas is also important, and this supervision can be rotated to allow different parents time to visit with other parents and check the field trip/event binder.

Field Trips and Group Events. All decisions regarding an event are made by the sponsoring individuals. Sign-up sheets are in the field trip binder. RSVP dates need to be respected. Parents pay with a check, or get a receipt for a cash payment. Commitments impact others, so members are requested to inform the field trip or event coordinator of a cancellation.

Buddy System for Newcomers. Each new family is paired with an All Ways Learning family to acquaint the newcomers with the group, i.e., give guidelines, introduce parents and children, explain physical boundaries, accompany on supervision, explain mailbox, field trip/event binder and park day format. Rosters will be given out only after a family joins the group.

Meetings. Resource meetings, Moms'/Dads' Nights Out are arranged when desired. Short business meetings are held at quarterly family potlucks.

Contact Person(s). A contact person receives and disseminates information, acts as mediator, and sees that All Ways Learning responsibilities and practices are carried out.

Dues. Annual membership dues are $10/year and cover the newsletter expenses, photocopies, and miscellaneous group events.

Lompoc Valley Home Educators
By Christine Tykeson

We welcome anyone interested in home education. We are a support group for kids and their parents who are taking responsibility for their own learning, who know they have many options and choices about where to find knowledge, and who are home educating for many reasons and in many ways. We have no leaders, but provide support and resources to each other by voluntary participation with each other; offering what skills, ideas, knowledge and enthusiasm we each wish to share and accepting from each other whatever meets our needs.

Lompoc Valley Home Educators is fairly informal in organization. Activities are set up by members and participation in all activities is voluntary. Activities which aren't successful usually die away through lack of participation or are improved by members who care about them, while successful efforts thrive. We have a general policy sheet for field trips, but otherwise policies are established by the member initiating the event.

We hold monthly meetings at a local park on the first Thursday of every month. The meetings are distinct from the other activities in that no one member organizes them for the rest. They tend to be consensus affairs. Because the monthly meetings are for all the members, we avoid offering narrow agendas, programs or presentations at these gatherings. Special agendas can best be handled by offering a separate activity in the newsletter calendar.

In the past our routine has been to set out materials in our lending library (donated homeschooling and education books in a box) on a table or blanket on the grass. Now our librarian catalogs the books, gets a list to each of the members and brings along the books members have requested. It saves the effort of carting a library around, especially as it's getting bigger and expanding into educational materials. Members still do bring books and materials to share and these are usually laid out in the middle of our gathering spot, customarily a circle of blankets on the grass.

At first our meetings were extremely informal; we would simply discuss any interests we had while the children played. As our group grew, however, the atmosphere at the meetings became incredibly hectic as members clamored over each other to make announcements, bring up concerns and share information. We responded by initiating just enough form to handle the situation. We now have rotating leaders for the meetings; a volunteer from the previous meeting handles the responsibility for keeping things running smoothly. We also set aside time at the beginning of each meeting for the children to share or "show and tell" something they've done or made or learned. This is an "if you want to" activity for the kids. We put this activity at the beginning of the meeting because we found that once the kids started playing they didn't want to be interrupted to come back to the meeting later.

After the children share, the parents take turns making announcements or bringing up items for discussion. We found that once the members knew they would each have a chance to share and be listened to, the meetings took less time and were more pleasant to attend.

As our group grows, I wonder how informal we'll be able to keep it. Occasionally I hear a member remark how much they liked it when we did less and had more time to just sit and talk while the kids played. One summer a mother set up a separate park day just to take care of this need. She expressly stated that her event would definitely not be for the purpose of conducting any homeschool business.

Some of the services our members offer are:

- A field trip coordinator to make sure that at least one or two field trips happen every month. Anyone is allowed to set up a field trip, but we ask that they coordinate the date with the person in charge of field trips to avoid conflicts.
- A coordinator to organize weekly swims at the Municipal Pool.
- Classes. Anyone can offer a class that they are interested in teaching. We've had a lot of art classes because one of our members is an artist who loves sharing her skills and knowledge with the kids.
- Scholastic book order contact.
- A newsletter editor and publisher. This is the most demanding job of all, but it's too important to the cohesiveness of the group not to have it done. Our first newsletters were handled by one editor, but since then it's become common for two people to share the work, dividing it up as it works best for them. We could easily have three volunteers for this project. I think that we do a good job; it's a relentless one, though. The newsletter editor sets the subscription price and handles all the other

newsletter decisions. And, of course, she gets to listen to lots of complaints if things aren't just right and lots of praise if they are.

- A phone tree. We use the phone tree for legislative alerts and to let members know about events or other opportunities that come up on short-notice. We had a phone chain for a very short time. It proved unsatisfactory from the beginning—too many weak links. But the phone tree is working just great. To initiate a phone tree message, any member calls just one person, the phone tree contact. She relays the message to four phone tree captains, who in turn pass on the information to the rest of the members. The phone tree is updated every year and sent out to all the members in the September newsletter.
- Whatever anyone wants to volunteer to do. We've had campouts, discount group theater tickets purchased, beach days, and more.

We have no charge for membership. Fees for activities, classes or other events are set by whoever organizes them. We don't have a board or central leadership deciding what the group does. Ideas, activities, suggestions bubble up from the membership and constantly create and recreate the group's structure. For a support group about our size (20 - 30 families), this set-up seems to be workable. As we grow, managing bigger numbers may force us toward more formality.

Coastside HomeScholars
By Jackie Orsi

Coastside HomeScholars has no philosophy, no rules, no officers, no elections. No fooling. We do have an unofficial motto: "Take nothing too seriously." Attempts to "get serious" are suggested every September and fall flat by October. Sometimes we surprise ourselves, though, and then we do remarkable things in spite of our haphazard organization.

The group is so loosely formed that it changes character noticeably each year as new members come in and others move on. Membership hovers around 45 families. Some years we're very ambitious and productive, and other years we muddle along. Without designated leaders, the job of keeping everyone straightened out usually falls to the newsletter editor, who becomes the unofficial "Queen" by dint of being the only one who really knows what's going on. (Knowledge is power.)

Parents' meetings are formless and even sometimes pointless affairs, yet people often stand around still gabbing and laughing late into the evening. Gabbing and laughing, we therefore conclude, must be the point of the meeting. We also share ideas, resources, and concerns, and try to get organized, which happens more often than not.

We keep a treasury, usually $300 to $500 per year, which we raise by selling fruit drinks at a community fair, at a yard sale, and through other opportunities as they arise. Insofar as possible, we try to avoid fund raising, in favor of fun raising. Whenever it becomes a chore, we stop doing it. Whosoever is present at the moment someone suggests how to spend some of our money gets to vote. Typically we have spent our funds on charitable donations to community causes, thank-you gifts, facility rentals and food for events, our arts and crafts program, a leather-craft kit (which is owned in common), guest speakers, donations of homeschooling books and literature to local libraries, memorial gifts, and other purposes. Our "Treasurer" keeps the money in a cigar box and reports to us in round figures, i.e., "We have about $260, more or less."

At this writing, Coastside HomeScholars has a fabulous newsletter because it is completely in the hands of the students. Our columnists range in age from 10 to 16, with lots of contributions from the younger set. We also have a drama program, an orchestra (completely organized by and for the kids), an art class whose work was routinely displayed at a Post Office which "adopted" Coastside HomeScholars as its "school." We go bowling and ice skating once a month. Field trips, holiday observances, etc., also happen when someone organizes them. We try to have at least one big campout or trip yearly. Twice we've gone to the Mother Lode to make our fortunes in gold; once we went to Sacramento and soaked up history and politics there. Other trips have taken us to Pinnacles National Monument and Big Sur. Our campout sing-alongs are the stuff of legend.

Inland Empire Area Homelearners
By Roberta Jackson

IEAH started with five moms who all shared the same dream: to have an inclusive support group with planned activities and field trips. Since we all had teens, we wanted to focus on their particular needs too, so Southern California Area Teens, "SCAT", was also formed. We meet weekly, and offer many services such as a preschooler's group, teen group, holiday parties, yearbook, an educational co-op, tennis lessons, basketball, along with park day activities, events, and a 22-page newsletter. All of these services are offered at little or no cost. There is no membership fee to participate in the group, but we rely strongly on parent skills, talent, and participation.

The group has a good working relationship within the community, and we consider outreach to be important. Monthly Barnes & Noble Homeschooler's Nights in Rancho Cucamonga are organized. This gives our own members the opportunity to hear well-known speakers, and it's also a way for prospective homeschoolers in the community to learn about homeschooling. Other businesses such as Home Depot also welcome our group on an ongoing basis. IEAH also sponsors a few annual events such as our "Thanksgiving Reenactment Day", where the group invites homeschoolers from all over to participate. A "Preschooler's Open House", is held the first week of April and is the group's way of doing community outreach to mothers with young children who wish to obtain information on homeschooling for their preschool or school-age children. This event usually consists of a clown, face painting, crafts and the neighborhood fire truck. The teen group sponsors a Teen Christmas Dinner and an "End Of The Year Teen Party" for all homeschooling teens that allows an opportunity to recognize teens who are graduating.

Conflict Resolution

Breaking Up Is Hard to Do
By Karen Taylor

No one knows why it happens, but homeschool support groups do break up, and it usually is not a quiet, amiable parting of the ways. More likely, it becomes a painfully vocal and ugly divorce. After becoming close to other families, and feeling that you've found lifelong friends, something triggers a reaction and the conflict takes on a life of its own. Sometimes with no warning, a cohesive group is at odds, and everyone is taking sides. Accusations abound, and in the saddest cases, sometimes children are even involved in the adult argument.

What causes this phenomenon? Many support group leaders have pondered this. Frankly, we don't know the reason, or why it becomes so emotional, but it happens all too often, and sometimes when least expected. With many groups communicating via e-mail these days, the opportunity to speed up the conflict exists since the people at odds aren't resolving their problems in person, and instead are letting the e-mails fly. Hurtful things get said that can be read and reread, and they can't be taken back. Sometimes the group is able to resolve the problem, but sometimes friends go their separate ways, never to speak to each other again.

A major support group conflict is very sad to observe, and it's downright painful to be a participant. There are no winners. Some groups take steps to lessen their chances of having a major split by dealing with conflict resolution beforehand. Sometimes that is not enough, however, and a group of dear friends who share a love of children and homeschooling do indeed split. If it must happen, we offer the following as you pick up the pieces:

- If you disagree with a group, leave quietly, so that those who remain can live in peace. Going out in a blaze of glory won't be appreciated.
- Remember why you got involved—it was for your children, right? If you disagree with the group, start a new one, and strive to remain civil with the old group! There's room for many groups with many different philosophies. What a great lesson for your children.
- Remember why you are homeschooling, and why you got involved in a group—yes, it's the children, again! If you persist in remaining involved in a major conflict, your happy home will be filled with a tension that your children will feel. It's not worth it!
- Consider swallowing the pain—again for your children, and set an example of dignity by moving on without trying to destroy the people you disagreed with. That hurt can come back to harm you and your family in many ways.
- If your children aren't a good enough reason, then think of the new homeschoolers who have yet to learn about your new (or old) group. They are not interested in your conflict, and will back away if they detect trouble, even if it's old news. You'll gain more by having something nice to say about former group members or saying nothing at all.

In the meantime, while all is going well, we invite you to read what some experienced groups have to say about their conflict resolution preparation.

Lompoc Valley Home Educators
By Christine Tykeson

Our main means of conflict resolution (conflict avoidance) is built into Lompoc Valley Home Educators (LVHE) through our flexible structure which allows us to accommodate a diverse membership. We don't have to fight over what our group does or doesn't do. Anyone is free to try out an idea or attempt to meet a need as long as they don't impose on others. This arrangement allows for maximum independence for each member, minimal favoritism and provides plenty of leeway for the group to grow and change. For the most part, our structure has served us well, but problems still do arise.

Our usual method of meeting conflict is for a member who perceives a problem to address it in the newsletter and suggest it as a topic for discussion at the next monthly meeting. This gives everyone a chance to think about the problem and discuss it with his or her family or among friends before the meeting date. The member who originally brought the problem to the group's attention brings it up for meeting discussion. Sometimes a reminder for future behaviors is all that is required to resolve the problem, sometimes we need to change or add to our group policies or rules.

We've found it very important to cultivate a climate of respect in LVHE. Members need to be respected for the responsibilities they undertake for everyone's benefit. We frequently remind each other to RSVP spaces for an activity or event by an announced deadline, to get submissions in to the newsletter editor on time, to avoid (at all costs) last minute cancellations to events and to exercise similar common courtesies. This reminding seems to be a never-ending necessity; doing it makes a lot of difference in what kind of exchanges go on in the group. One year we faithfully reminded members every month how important it was for them to get to field trips on time. It took a while but the problem of late arrivals vanished the following year. It's also important to acknowledge people who are making contributions to the group. Writing appreciations in the newsletter, mentioning them at meetings and telling people in person are all good ways to keep people glad to be part of the group and willing to continue doing their best.

Respect for differences is particularly important to encourage. If this isn't evident in a support group, things can get messy and ugly really fast. Homeschoolers need to be aware of the many different ways intolerance has of creeping into groups and that it can come from any direction: Christian or non-Christian, liberal or conservative, unschoolers or school-at-home types.

As a counterbalance to our flexible and diffuse structure, we use our monthly newsletter and the monthly meeting to pull us together. These are at the heart of LVHE. They are meant to serve everyone, which can sometimes make them bones of contention. The newsletter represents the group, and members want to feel proud of it. That puts a lot of pressure on the editor. The job of editing the newsletter is important and valued, yet difficult, and fraught with conflict if the members don't like the product. Cultivating good editors to take over when veteran editors need to be relieved of the job is important. Encouraging lots of contributions to the newsletter is a good way to get people involved before they are ready to take on the job of editor. It also develops a broad base of talent and cultivates an appreciation for the difficulties of writing. And it makes a more interesting newsletter. Sharing the job with another member is a good policy. It avoids burnout, allows for help with proofreading, and provides compensating factors for weaknesses. An editor may be assisted by a willing member who can help by proofreading or typing the newsletter.

The monthly meeting has been an issue with which we've had to deal. The meeting time, place and format must not be subject to anyone's whim but needs to be thoughtfully discussed by the members before it gets changed. As for the format, we have a rule that everyone must have a chance to talk and be listened to at the monthly meeting. This is so we don't talk over each other or default the meeting to members who are domineering or have an agenda to promote. For the most part everyone is considerate, but the rule is for the exceptions. We rotate the role of facilitator at the meeting. The facilitator gets the meeting going, helps move things along when they bog down and makes sure everyone gets a turn to talk and gets listened to.

Field trip guidelines are important to have in place before scheduling the first trip and can keep potential problems from occurring. The push for guidelines arose out of my experience in another homeschool group which suffered some embarrassing fiascoes on field trips which were not well planned or controlled. I insisted our group have these, and everyone agreed. Our field trip organizers remind all the members to read them at the beginning of the year.

We did have one fiasco in our group, which I'd rather forget. Some property was damaged at an event in one of our member's homes. Those who attended the event recovered the good will of our hostess by taking up a collection to pay for the damages. Although we had strong suspicions, none of us knew exactly whose kids did the damage. We discussed the problem at a meeting and made it a policy to hold all participants accountable at homeschooling events for any property damage unless the culprit is known. This is to encourage adults who are present to take responsibility for watching over other children as well as their own and calling misbehavior to the attention of parents. If one person clearly is responsible for damaging property, that person or person's parents must pay to replace or fix it. It's not a perfect solution but better than letting the host bear the brunt of any damage.

Handling media contacts also bears forethought. While media coverage is important for homeschoolers, some homeschoolers have privacy concerns that need to be considered and honored, and the members need to discuss media contacts beforehand.

Another problem which sometimes gets mentioned is the "a few people do all the work" problem. I don't think this is a big issue for us. I'd say 40-60% of our members are heavy contributors. It would be too time consuming to apportion the work fairly to be worth the effort. The people who get the most out of this group are the people who do the work. Members do the work they want to do and their enthusiasm for their projects generates support for them. If they're not getting help or cooperation for their efforts, they'll most likely stop. Everyone in the group knows that, so they actively support things they value.

Conflict is part of group dynamics. The best policy is to rise above the petty and avoid personality conflicts. Also, don't try and micro-manage the structure of the group. Focus on the gifts each person brings. There are a few areas where you need to draw clear, firm lines. Draw them, make them stick, and watch your support group blossom.

Coastside HomeScholars
By Jackie Orsi

I have considered the matter of conflict resolution, and I frankly think it has its limits. There are some conflicts that are simply unresolvable, and trying to resolve them merely wears people out, or worse, causes lots of pain and sorrow. There are times when people are better off "taking their ball and going home."

My own group, Coastside HomeScholars, has survived for seven years now by keeping a collective sense of humor. However, a few incidents were not funny at all, and we had to take serious steps to deal with them by disassociating our group from the offending parties. Take, for example, the mother whose behavior on a camping trip turned so bizarre and appalling that we suspected drug use; she was dropped from the group by swift and unanimous agreement.

Another instance was not so clear cut, and indeed, points out how complicated human relations can be. A bouncy, friendly newcomer with an endless supply of ambitious ideas ended up nearly destroying the group. She committed us to complicated projects, then proceeded to disorganize us hugely. Members worked overtime to unscramble her messes and salvage her plans. She was virtually oblivious to the confusion, exhaustion, irritability, expense, and dissension that followed in her wake as she steamed on to the next disaster. She borrowed materials and returned them weathered and broken from having been carried in the back of her pickup truck for weeks. She was always "short on cash" and assumed other people would cover her tickets and other expenses until she could pay them back. Always smiling, she missed the fact that her children were as disorganized and as much in need of discipline as every other part of her life. All attempts to address our difficulties with her failed to produce changes. It became clear that she was hopelessly self-absorbed. At the end of two years, families were staying away in droves from any events her family signed up for. That cooked it. She was firmly asked to leave the group, and presented with a list of items she had borrowed and debts she owed. No one to this day has ever cast doubt on her good intentions, but we sure were glad to see her gone.

Coastside HomeScholars has never experienced a major rift, but I've observed other groups go through terribly divisive issues. Problems emerge when a group grows and cleaves between those who want an intense, proactive and structured group, and those who want a laid-back, informal group. When factions begin to vie for the heart and soul of a support group, I've seen it turn downright nasty. I have concluded that groups sometimes err in trying too long to keep together, when divergent needs would be better served, and much unpleasantness avoided, by going separate ways.

Inland Empire Area Homelearners
By Roberta Jackson

In order for our group to function and give support to homeschooling families effectively and efficiently, we decided that we needed to accomplish a few basic things. First, was to be well organized. Second, was to implement some policies. Third, we needed to be sure of what we wanted the group to be and also what we did not want it to be. Fourth, but most important, was to allow mothers the freedom to step forward to take on responsibility so that the other three things would materialize.

I learned from hearing about and visiting other support groups, that many develop personalities, which seem to reflect the founder's beliefs and philosophies. I strongly advise all families to visit a couple of groups before settling on just one. You want to be sure the personality of the group matches your own beliefs or philosophies.

One of the most difficult problems that can arise results from lack of personal responsibility. Mothers may become offended if they feel they are being told how to parent or how their child should behave. I understand their feeling. Unfortunately we have all witnessed parents who do not take enough responsibility to assure their child is not endangering, offending, or simply disrespecting another person or the person's personal property. A few who do not feel they need to abide by any rules can then create a negative situation that impacts the entire group. I have heard many times, "But who wants to play police and be the one to enforce the rules?" I wanted my children to be in a group where they could have enjoyable experiences, with reassurances of peace. Others in the group did too. I committed to be the person who would enforce policies.

One bit of advice I give to parents is that the group is not capable of being all things to all people. They are advised that the group should be looked upon the same as the public library. Although libraries carry many books and materials on everything you can think of, you only bring home what pertains to your personal interests and beliefs. I feel strongly that people should use our very diverse group in the same way they use their library; come for what they want or need and hopefully leave somewhat better off for having been part of the group.

Regardless of what rules or polices are put in place, I don't believe any group is immune to having conflicts. The few times we have had conflicts, we referred to our policies to resolve the problems. IEAH's "Policies and Procedures" are several pages long, so for brevity I've written an outline for setting up a policy:

1. Establish who is leader or founder (or create a panel) to determine who will make final decisions.
2. Explain the philosophy of the group and what purpose the group serves.
3. List each service the group offers, how to use the service and who helps assist with this service.
4. Explain up front what the group will not tolerate as unacceptable behavior and what the consequences are for not adhering to the group's policies.
5. Explain procedures for participating in field trips & other activities and what they need to do if they are unable to attend.
6. If a group e-mail list is established be sure the use of the list is clear.
7. Determine if you will allow members to advertise and solicit for their businesses and services in the newsletter and at meetings.

Special Events and Projects

Organizing a Cooperative Learning Group
By Ann Lewis, Lompoc Valley Home Educators

Over the years, I have become interested in group activities where there is a cooperative effort among the members to learn from each other. Therefore, when I started homeschooling, it seemed natural to start a small cooperative group so that my family could benefit from regular group activities. I felt this would give us the best of both worlds; time with other people, and private time together as a family.

I discussed the idea with members of our local support group, the Lompoc Valley Home Educators, to see if anyone was interested. One family joined right away, while another two joined a few months later. By the end of the first year, we had committed families interested in continuing as a cooperative group. This core of four families consisted of six girls and two boys, with ages ranging from four to twelve. I enjoyed having the different ages in our group and incorporating each family unit into our activities. The only change I would have made would have been to have a more equal balance between boys and girls.

In September, we would meet to discuss what we would like to explore and learn about for the upcoming year. After deciding on four to six subjects, we would then try to cover two or three of those subjects in a day. For example, since we met two days a week, for four or five hours at a time, we might schedule Art, Math and Music on one day, and Spanish, Drama and Science on the other. I found that it was important not to schedule too many activities in one day, as there would be too much pressure to get things done, and time for play became too limited. We enjoyed the luxury of being able to continue with an activity past its scheduled time, if stopping would interfere with the enjoyment and learning that was in progress. I would sometimes have tangrams, cuisinaire rods, geoboards, blocks or other activities out for people to do inbetween our regularly scheduled activities. I always had paper, pencils and markers available. Sitting around the table drawing and talking proved to be a popular activity, as was playing freeze tag or other games in our yard.

Sometimes we would just "socialize," especially if we hadn't met in a while. We did not meet in the summer and took breaks around holidays or other busy times of the year. If only one of the families couldn't meet as scheduled, the group would either take a break and wait until that family was available again, or the rest of the group would meet anyway to continue without interruption on the activities already planned. There was enormous flexibility with our scheduling, which helped each family follow it's own natural rhythm throughout the year. In this way we were able to use the schedule to our advantage, keeping to it when it truly met our needs.

We emphasized being considerate of others. Learning the subtleties of when to help someone and when not to became an important skill, since help is often not wanted even if it appears to be needed. It took great sensitivity on the part of everyone to recognize what approach would truly be the most helpful. It was important to learn that what was easy for one might be challenging for another, and to understand that this is perfectly normal and natural. Seeing how we all processed information differently was interesting, and helped everyone to respect the fact that we all had different strengths and weaknesses. This diversity proved to not only enhance our learning experiences, but add to the group's overall cohesiveness.

The first year that we met was spent experimenting and trying to develop and settle into a system that would work for all of us. In the group's second year, each child chose a subject to teach with their parent as backup. As teachers, the children learned that being flexible and responsive to their students' needs required the ability to compromise and negotiate, which was challenging to say the least. As is often the case, the teacher learned as much or more than the student. Some of the subjects explored were: Science Experiments, Spanish, Art Appreciation, Cooperative Math, Music/Note Reading, Drama, Clay/Arts and Crafts and Language Arts.

Each of the four parents taught the following year, with help from their children if desired. It was a pleasure to see each parent's unique talents shine through as they contributed their time and energy to the group. Everyone was encouraged to teach a subject that they were genuinely interested in and could really get excited about, since that enthusiasm would definitely be contagious to the rest of the group.

We put on three major events over the course of three years in addition to the regular classes that we held. The first event was a play and concert, the second was a geography fair, which the other LVHE members were invited to participate in with us, and the third and most elaborate was a performance called "A 'Round the World Extravaganza," in which we explored the dance, songs and folktales of nine different countries. The two performances required extra meetings, as well as a four- or five-day-a-week commitment for the entire month leading up to each performance. These events were definitely highlights for each one of us. The amount of work and preparation involved took all of the energy we could muster, and we rose to meet the challenge. Experiencing the thrill of performing as a group gave us an exhilarating feeling of togetherness. Needless to say, we have special memories from these events that will last a lifetime.

One of the satisfying things about this group was that we could develop and refine it in any way that we wished. We had total freedom to explore what worked for us and what didn't. There was a feeling of collaboration and camaraderie, of working towards a common goal to make it the best experience possible. This was the force that guided and unified us.

Celebration of Art
By Monica Cardiff, Lifelong Learners

Lifelong Learners' annual art show is a wonderful event. The children's art is displayed at a local library for one month. The art includes anything the students created during the preceding year: paintings, drawings, pottery, ceramics, sculpture, jewelry, macramé, photography, woodworking, papier mâché, and quilting.

The highlight of the month is the reception held one evening in the library's community room. The participants send invitations with the Lifelong Learner logo to family and friends.

Guests view the art work and talk with the artists. The students give original poetry readings and share their musical talent. Each participant is awarded a certificate and refreshments are enjoyed by all.

Drama Program
By Jackie Orsi, Coastside HomeScholars

From first casting to final performance, putting on a play is considerably more challenging than the old Mickey Rooney – Judy Garland "Hey, kids, let's do a show!" would have you think. It takes tons of creativity, saintly patience and endurance, incisive problem-solving skills, and nerves of steel from kids and parents alike.

We do drama in a big way. We've played to audiences of up to 125 people. Our rendering of A *Christmas Carol* featured 26 children on stage, and involved about 40 other children and adults as stage hands, lighting crew, costumers, ushers, and so forth. There are scenery painting workshops, elaborate sound effects, programs to design and print, and rehearsals upon rehearsals. They say an army marches on its stomach, and so does a drama troupe—they need a constant supply of snacks and junk food to keep them going in rehearsal. This past year we put on our first totally original play, *Who Killed Aunt Edna?* Previously, we took existing plays and rewrote them to accommodate our needs. We did a full-scale production of A *Christmas Carol* and a nutty spoof called *Red Ridinghood Goes 90s*. Our policy has been to find a part for every kid who wants to perform, so I have written in bit parts galore, and even our version of A

Christmas Carol included a scene in which eight children ages five to eight enacted Scrooge's childhood Christmas. *Red Riding Hood* had an abundant population of little forest creatures, each with one line to say.

Who Killed Aunt Edna? involved only kids age 11 and up, and they directed themselves for the most part. It was a demanding one-act comedy, and we accomplished the amazing feat of taking the whole show on the road. As usual, we performed once for parents, family and friends in a local community center. Then we took the sets, furniture, and lights by minivan-load to two other locations where we performed for other homeschoolers in our area.

At each performance, we include recitals by our many young musicians. This year we not only featured soloists, but also our very own orchestra comprised of three violins, one viola, one recorder, two keyboards, two guitars, and a percussionist playing classical pieces arranged by the student-conductor.

Drama is not for the faint of heart. When your backdrops made from refrigerator cartons are teetering, when a toddler in the audience wanders on stage in the middle of a scene, when a muffed line sends the whole cast into giggle fits, certain parents have been known to wonder why they let themselves in for such torture. Then when the play ends, and the audience is cheering, and the kids are beaming with justifiable pride, certain parents wipe a tear or two, and remember why.

Note: For a variety of support group forms, including field trip letters, policies, logs, planners, a medical authorization form and field trip ideas, see The California Homeschool Companion CD.

What Would I Do with a Computer?

"Thousands of software programs

have been designed to promote learning."

©Bill Taylor

Homeschooling and Computers

Many homeschoolers find that computers assist them in educating. They are so enthusiastic, that those homeschoolers who have no access to a computer sometimes worry about being left out of something very important. Is a computer necessary for educating? No, of course not! In fact, you'll find some experts who will tell you that there is way too much emphasis on computers and that too much of anything is not that good for children. But, there's also no doubt that computers are a great tool for homeschooling. Some families use computer programs for teaching certain skills, others for research, and still others find it's primarily used as a reference resource for the parents, who then share what they learn with their young children. No doubt about it, one of the greatest features of computers is that through the internet, homeschoolers no longer need to be isolated from each other. This free exchange of information has been very beneficial in spreading homeschooling information to parents all over the world.

Computers are indeed a great tool for homeschooling. Not essential, but a great tool, nonetheless. If you are looking for ways in which a computer might enhance learning, we can think of five:

Educational software

Thousands of software programs have been designed to promote learning. The good ones can make math drill fun, can help your child acquire pre-reading skills and new vocabulary, can be a rich source of science and history facts, can stimulate a child's thinking processes, and can even teach the child to play the piano!

Word processing and publishing

Kids enjoy writing stories, poems and essays on computers because it is so much easier than writing by longhand. Revisions and corrections are a snap, and the final printed product is neat and handsome. Spelling and grammar checkers can help build writing skills, so there's no fear that the child is "cheating." The reinforcement of observing that a word has been misspelled, and seeing the correct way is very helpful in the process of learning to spell. While special word processing and publishing software for children is available, most kids learn on adult programs with no problem. In fact, children learn so quickly, they sometimes end up assisting their parents!

Research

CD-ROMs contain vast amounts of information that can be searched in seconds. Multimedia capability combines written data, photography, art, audio and video. The same amount of information that would take hundreds of linear feet of bookshelves now sits in a small space in homes everywhere. A full encyclopedia is no longer a major family investment now that it can be purchased for less than $50 (we've even seen rebates that made them almost free!). Atlases, dictionaries, specialized references, complete literary collections and much more are available on CD-ROM.

Communication

Using online services, you can take classes online in what is known as Distance Learning. Homeschooling parents and children are also communicating via e-mail. It's a conduit to people of all kinds and all interests throughout the world, and increasingly, a way homeschoolers communicate with each other about matters related to homeschooling. There are thousands of free e-mail groups, including two for California homeschoolers that are sponsored by CHN. General homeschooling information and support is offered at the popular CaliforniaHS list and there is also a calendar list for California events. Information about subscribing is at CHN's website: *www.CaliforniaHomeschool.net/*. Other helpful sites are:

- Homefires~The Journal of Homeschooling Online *http://homefires.com/*

- Kaleidoscapes Refugees, a homeschooling discussion board *http://www.network54.com/Forum/180575*

- Vegsource "Homeschool Talk and Swap" There are many individual boards for all kinds of homeschool interests. *www.vegsource.com/homeschool/*

- Jon's Homeschool Resource Page *http://www.midnightbeach.com/hs*

- Learn in Freedom *http://learninfreedom.org/*

- Large list of e-mail groups
  www.geocities.com/Athens/8259/e-mail.html#OTHER

- A to Z Home's Cool *http://www.gomilpitas.com/homeschooling/index.htm*

Educational Sites

The Internet now makes it easy to find all sorts of information. Without leaving home, you can access awesome archives from all over the world, including The Smithsonian, The Louvre, the Library of Congress, plus arcane resources beyond imagining. Many homeschoolers have also found it to be an endless resource for educational ideas, with instruction offered for free in about every subject imaginable. Below is a sampling of just a few of the various educational sites. There are many websites with teaching plans and ideas, from math and science to foreign languages, and more:

General Resources
- Fun Brain (educational games online) *www.funbrain.com/*

- Quia (directory of thousands of online educational games)
  www.quia.com/

- Free Federal Resources for Educational Excellence
  www.ed.gov/free/

- ClickSchooling, a daily homeschool curriculum idea is e-mailed
  http://groups.yahoo.com/group/ClickSchooling

Math
- Natural Math *www.naturalmath.com/*

- Fun Fractions *http://math.rice.edu/~lanius/Patterns/*

- Math Stories *www.mathstories.com/*

- AAA Math *www.aaamath.com/index.html*

- Fractions
  http://pittsford.monroe.edu/jefferson/calfieri/fractions/FractionsMain.html

Science

- How Stuff Works *www.howstuffworks.com/satellite-radio.htm*

- Science Toys You Can Make With Kids
  http://scitoys.com/

- Science Experiments *www.brighterkids.com/experiment.html*

- Robert Krampf's Experiment of the Week. *http://www.krampf.com/*. Sign up for the free weekly e-mailed science experiement.

Language Arts

- Learn Spanish *www.studyspanish.com/*

- Spanish Language *http://spanish.about.com/homework/spanish/msub29.htm*

- 1,000 Good Books List
  www.classicalhomeschooling.org/celoop/1000.html

- Latin *http://eleaston.com/latin.html#wheelock*

- Resources for Classical Literature *http://www.dc.peachnet.edu/~shale/humanities/literature/world_literature/classical.html*

- Puzzlemaker *www.puzzlemaker.com/*

- Spelling
  www.katy.isd.tenet.edu/kisd/resources/spelling/spelling.html

- Worksheets for grammar, spelling and more *edhelper.com*

Music

- The Music Rack *www.sheetmusic1.com/music.rack.html*

- Free On-Line Piano Lessons *www.gopiano.com/*

History/Social Studies

- HyperHistory Online: 2,000 files covering 3,000 years of history
  www.hyperhistory.com/online_n2/History_n2/a.html

- Middle Ages: What was it really like?
  www.learner.org/exhibits/middleages/

- Geography
  http://geography.miningco.com/science/geography/msub17.htm

- Learn capitals and states with this fun game, one of many to be found
  http://www.scottforesman.com/resources/statescapitals/index.html

Computer Hardware

New homeschoolers often consider investing in a computer at the outset of their family's homeschooling adventure. We are frequently asked what sort of system we would recommend. It's an important question because you certainly want to invest in a system that will accommodate your needs now and for some time into the future. Like buying shoes for growing children, you want to allow a little toe room. It is also very true that children's software, with the typically heavy use of graphics, color, and sound, tends to require considerable RAM (random access memory) and hard drive space.

Each new generation of software demands more speed and more memory than the last. We find that manufacturers' recommended system requirements listed on software packages tend to represent the bare minimum you need to run the program; you may actually need much more system capability to run the program at an enjoyable speed and to avoid overwhelming your system. Given these factors, and with the explosive development of new technologies, the question, "how much system is enough" is therefore very hard to pin down; a reasonable answer today might be too conservative even six months from now. So, our best advice: get the most computer you can afford.

Getting Started with Computers

A book might help you get started, as might a class, or your local talk radio station may have a regular computer program (see *http://jefflevy.com/*). Others rely on friends, or jump in and start exploring the computer on their own. You might even find your computer savvy child will be your best teacher. We don't

315

know how, but some children almost seem to be born knowing about computers. If you want a book, you might be able to save money and find what you need at your local library. You aren't going to need training books for long.

Educational Software Buyer's Guide

With thousands of new programs coming out each year, and previously released titles still on the market, there are an overwhelming number of children's educational software programs to choose from at any given time. You may find that some are not worth the $30 to $80 they typically cost. Some are entertaining, but not educational at all, regardless of what the packaging claims. There are some companies that feel certain tactics are necessary in order to hold a child's attention, so amidst the quality programs, you'll also find some that rely on gimmicks such as shooting or some other violence, constant activity, or music that will soon leave you climbing the walls. How can you spend your software dollars wisely? There are no foolproof methods, but here are a few tips:

1. Look for certain features that characterize good programs:
    *   Allowance for individual pacing, such as freedom to set the answer response time.
    *   Multiple skill levels to allow growing room so a child can continue to use it as his skills expand.
    *   Customizing features, so that you can add your child's own spelling words, for example.
    *   Questions that require thinking, acting, and decision-making. Try to avoid programs in which the child is a passive receiver of the action on the screen.

    Turn to a catalog supplier that has a well-articulated selection criteria. Some of the choosiest ones reject 80% to 90% of the software they review. Some you might try are:

    *   Educational Resources 800/624-2926
    *   Mac Connection/PC Connection 800/800-2222

- AbleSoft 800/354-6150
- Homeschool catalogs. Some of the family-run homeschool catalogs sell only programs that they like, and they will often say why they like them. This is a review that can be very helpful, especially if over time, you learn that you share the views of the company.

2. Read magazines that review children's software.
   Be aware, however, that the magazines which accept advertising are not likely to "bite the hand that feeds them" by printing highly critical reviews. Some homeschooling magazines print reviews. Another source is to ask at your local support group or on an e-mail list such as CHN's CaliforniaHS list. Someone is bound to have experience, good or bad. Homeschoolers are known for being willing to generously share their experiences with others.

   - Magazines with no ads
     Children's Software: A Quarterly Newsletter for Parents 713/467-8686
     Children's Software Revue 800/993-9499

   - Magazines with ads (usually available at newsstands)
     Family PC 800/289-4849
     Mac Home Journal 800/800-6542
     Home PC 516/562-5309
     Computer Life 800/926-1578

3. Check out software review webpages
   PEP, Parents Educators Publishers *http://microweb.com/pepsite/*
   Children's Software Press *www.childsoftpress.com/*
   Learningware Reviews *www.learningwarereviews.com/*

4. Some stores offer demo areas, which is a great way to see what you are getting. Some magazines offer demo CDs, but they are a limited, "best-foot-forward" glimpse of the product, and not wholly reliable. Some libraries offer programs on loan.

5. Learn which software developers are consistently good, remembering that even the very best of them are capable of producing the occasional clinker.

6. If you locate a store with a liberal return policy, it can be worth making your purchases there.

7. Explore every other possible avenue for recommendations of good software and warnings about bad software. These might include friends, especially other homeschoolers, computer online forums and bulletin boards, and books of children's software reviews.

8. You might also investigate shareware (see *www.zdnet.com/downloads/*) where you download a program, and pay only if you decide to use it.

Even with the best of care, there will be some programs that you don't like as much as others do. It happens, and if it's really not something you want, sell it at the next homeschooler's sale in your community, or through one of the many online homeschool curriculum-selling sites, such as *www.vegsource.com/homeschool/*.

Parent's Concerns

Parents often worry about who might be conversing with their children in online chat rooms, or where their World Wide Web searches may take them. Unfortunately, creepy people and seamy webpages do exist. Having objectionable material pop up on your screen may not happen often, but it is always a possibility, and sometimes it happens inadvertently when the wrong URL is typed in. Some families use filters to attempt to block objectionable materials, and it's also very common for parents to establish certain ground rules for computer use, including using the computer in a busy room in the house, and only when the parents are home. Some parents feel that the internet is best used under some sort of supervised situation, but these are decisions that each family will have to reach for themselves. We would urge, for general safety, however, that your children be instructed not to release private information about themselves to people they meet on the internet. That would include their name, age, where they live, passwords, phone numbers, or any other personal information. While we don't want our children living in fear, it is important to know that there are some people on the internet who misrepresent who they are. Parents might also want to investigate:

- Online services—inquire about parental control features
- Software to filter the internet. These work with direct internet connections to block access to predetermined sites. Priced around $30-$50. For a comprehensive listing go to PEP, Parents Educators Publishers, *http://microweb.com/pepsite/*. Some search engines also offer this feature for free.
- Excellent child safety information: *www.safekids.com/*.

Distance Learning
By Karen Rafferty

In today's world the words "Distance Learning" are often equated with online learning, but Distance Learning began before computers were even invented. In the early 1890s the University of Queenland in Australia offered an external degree program. The real growth in Distance Learning began in the 1970s. Today the largest DL student body in the world is part of the University of South Africa. They have more than 200,000 people enrolled worldwide!

At its most basic level, Distance Learning takes place when a teacher and student are separated by physical distance. Bridging the instructional gap are audio tapes, instructional television, computers, phone, video, and print. Recent research indicates that DL is as effective as face-to-face instruction when the media used is appropriate to the instruction and there is timely student-teacher feedback.

What can Distance Learning do for a homeschooled teen? Enrichment experiences, high school courses and college degrees are available through Distance Learning. Where are DL resources found? Everywhere. Resource collections are available in books and on the web.

Mentoring

Mentoring provides the opportunity for contact with individuals actually involved in your area of interest. It is not always easy to find someone who lives close to you and has sufficient time and interest in mentoring. Enter telementoring, which allows your mentor to reside outside the geographical and temporal bounds of your community.

The Electronic Emissary (*http://emissary.ots.utexas.edu/emissary/index.html*) is one site dedicated to telementoring. In answer to the question of whether their services were open to homeschooling families or groups, Director Judi Harris wrote, "Of course! We have had several homeschooling families participate in the Emissary, as a matter of fact. Please note, though, that we do require that at least one parent or guardian actively involve themselves...." To assure a successful experience, the Emissary program will help bridge the communication gap between what you expect and what the mentor is willing or capable of providing.

Field Trips

Imagine escaping crocodiles, barely avoiding dangerous rapids, and meeting isolated tribes while kayaking down the Victoria Nile in Uganda to do scientific research. Perhaps you prefer the less dangerous, painstaking work at an archeological dig. Can't afford either one? Electronic field trips inexpensively enliven any course of study and give you access to real world field researchers. A fairly comprehensive list, organized by grade level, is available through the PBS Teacher Resource Service (*www.pbs.org/teachersource/*).

High School

Say, "high school," and panic sets in for many homeschoolers. Parents worry about whether they can remember enough high school biology let alone successfully reboot the brain cells that studied trigonometry. Teens worry about being prepared for independence and higher education. There are empowering resources available that address these concerns.

Cynthia Good's College and Career Planning Home Page has extensive resources that address both college and career concerns. The college section includes resources for financial aid, applications and SAT preparation. The career resources refer to aptitude tests, career pathways and career planning (http://www.bridge-rayn.org/CGood.html).

If you are certain that college is in your future, you might browse through the syllabus of College Prep-101 and work through the lessons of interest to you. Lessons cover admission standards, the application process, standardized tests, financial aid, choosing a major and much, much more (*http://collegeprep.okstate.edu/*).

Accredited high school diploma programs and individual coursework are also available through Distance Learning. Both traditional correspondence and online high schools are available. The resource section in Chapter 15 lists several of these schools (see pages 344-345).

College Without Walls

Howard Richman, director of Pennsylvania Homeschoolers for many years, coined the term "college without walls." It refers to doing coursework, even completing degree programs, without attending a college campus. Many respectable colleges offer correspondence study, credit for life and work experience, guided independent study done at home, and credit by examination. Depending on the admission requirements, many of these programs are available to teens.

A big benefit to Distance Learning college is reduced costs. In her article, "Save $40,000 on College," Joyce Swann writes, "We recently checked with four of the best universities which offer degrees through independent study and discovered that at each the cost of earning a degree at home is a fraction of that for attendance on campus." She then lists the University of Oklahoma at Norman (82% savings), Indiana State University (73% savings), Brigham Young University (76-79% savings) and California State University at Dominguez Hills (Masters in Liberal Arts, 40-52% savings). Note: as participation in Distance Learning programs increases, costs have also been increasing.

One of the drawbacks of Distance Learning degrees is public sentiment. Acceptance is growing, more rapidly in some fields than in others. It is worthwhile to interview workers and employers in your field of interest to see if DL coursework or a degree is readily accepted.

Consumer Savvy

The number of colleges and universities offering external degree programs is growing. In choosing Distance Learning courses or degree programs, be a wise consumer. Consider contacting the Department of Education in the state where the school is located. Talk to potential employers in the field and ask what they think. Contact the Better Business Bureau. If your career requires certification or licensure, talk to the licensing or certifying agencies about your choices. If you can, visit the physical campus. Check accreditation claims, but remember that accreditation is not necessarily a guarantee of quality. Be aware that many quality schools don't submit to the accreditation process because it is expensive, lengthy and complex. Most of all, listen to your own common sense. You are right to be concerned if the information packet you receive makes unbelievable promises or is poorly written or sloppily reproduced.

Distance Learning has many of the same benefits as homeschooling. A successful Distance Learning venture depends on self-motivation, confidence and discipline—all the qualities common to homeschoolers. Distance Learning can enrich a homegrown course of study, be a source for specialized coursework, provide a traditional high school diploma, or open the door to college. It is a way in which homeschoolers can retain control over their education.

From Uganda to Mars, Distance Learning Rules!
By Andrew Rafferty

By relating my personal experiences in Distance Learning, I hope to enlighten parents and teens on the pros and cons. Although I'm no expert, I have several Distance Learning experiences that I have found to be most useful.

My first experience was corresponding with scientists in the field while they traveled down the Victoria Nile in Uganda. This opportunity was through Adventures Online. The scientists e-mailed every night about their experiences. I could e-mail them with questions. When I suddenly stopped hearing from them, I wondered what was going on. They finally wrote to explain that they had been robbed and all their pictures, cameras, data and computers had been stolen.

I also participated in some Passport to Knowledge electronic field trips, one on the Kuiper Airborne Observatory and one on the Hubble telescope. Both of these were set up like Adventures Online with the ability to e-mail questions. They also had a teacher's guide and videos as supplemental materials.

During a project on Mars that involved lots of research, I sent questions to NASA scientists. Many professionals have web pages and are open to having you e-mail them about their area of expertise. This is not a formal setting, but you can learn a lot from informal correspondence.

Currently I'm taking a college-level, Visual Basic programming course. I will highlight my experiences from this current course because it is the freshest in my memory and my most formal experience with Distance Learning.

Communication has been one of the most persistent problems in the Visual Basic course I'm taking. The instructor I have likes to let the student discover what he did wrong, and, therefore, gives rather vague feedback. Although I'm all for discovering what I did wrong, at a certain point, I need my mistakes explained flat-out to me. I cannot ask my parents what is wrong, because neither one knows Visual Basic. The totally different communication style of my instructor has led to many complaints on my part and a reluctance to finish the course. Our communication was made harder by the fact that I couldn't talk to him face-to-face or have a real-time conversation. We finally ironed out our differences. Some of the parents reading this article might see my struggle to effectively communicate as a positive rather than a negative experience. All I can say is that it was very frustrating for me.

Delay in communication has been another problem area. There may be a significant time lag, sometimes over two weeks, between sending in my work and having it evaluated. Each programming lesson builds the foundation for future lessons. It is disconcerting to move ahead in lessons without the assurance that I've understood the previous principles. Sometimes I've had to backtrack.

On the brighter side, taking things at my own pace has been a godsend. Although I usually like to hurry through things and learn just enough to keep me going, I have been able, when I needed to, to slow down and take it step-by-step. Like in homeschooling, I can breeze through areas that come easily to me but take things slower in areas that are confusing and/or deal with precise work.

An additional benefit is that no one is looking over my shoulder. I can quit working on the assigned project, which is normally a business application, and apply what I've learned to projects of my own choice. This has led to several ongoing projects that I continue to add features to as my knowledge increases. I'm writing a password generator program and I'm developing a game.

Price can be a pro or con in Distance Learning. This is a big variable in Distance Learning opportunities. Many electronic field trips, such as Adventures Online and Passport to Knowledge, are free. The current course I'm taking cost several hundred dollars, but that included the software needed for the course.

In spite of some of the problems I've experienced, I am certain I'll be taking more Distance Learning courses in the future. Before taking another formal Distance Learning class, I would ask several questions. How quickly will I be evaluated? Is there a time limit for turning in my assignments? Can I negotiate what the assignments are? Can I arrange for a more informal approach where I send in my work for evaluation, but don't have to use the textbook assignments and tests? In other words, I might try for more of a mentoring experience my next time around.

Overall, Distance Learning is a great opportunity to pursue subjects that your parents can't teach. It is a good opportunity to get college credits while still in high school. It has some of the same benefits, like self-pacing, that we are familiar with in the homeschool setting. Try it! You may like it!

What Do I Need and Where Do I Find It?

"Just beginning?"

©Bill Taylor

Help is Available From Many Places

By Karen Taylor

If you are reading here, we can assume you have decided to homeschool, and are now wondering where to begin. This is the resource chapter, where you will get a start on locating some resources to help you. There are reading lists, curriculum resources, special resource lists for gifted and special education learners, lists of publications, information about academic testing, and information about state and national homeschooling organizations.

We recognize that the resources available to homeschoolers are extensive and ever changing, and so a more extensive list has been compiled at the CHN website, *www.CaliforniaHomeschool.net/*, where it will be updated regularly. For some people, too long a list is overwhelming, and what we offer here may meet your needs. But there will be others, new or experienced, who will want to know about every available resource they can find.

California Homeschool Network: Your First Resource!

How can CHN help you? At the beginning of this book, is a list of ways to reach CHN, from e-mail, to Local Contacts, the toll free number, the mailing address, and website. These are all ways to reach actual homeschoolers who are there to offer assistance. We are proud of our volunteer system, and hope you will take advantage of it, as thousands before you have.

Several outstanding, unique publications have been published to meet particular needs. They are available only through CHN (call, write, or visit the website):

The Guide Companion CD, version 2, edited by Karen Rafferty, one of CHN's original volunteers, and the one we go to when we have a question. She's a popular homeschooling speaker, as well as a long time homeschooler, and she knows what homeschoolers are looking for! This updated and improved CD-ROM contains many printable forms that homeschoolers have long wanted. Using your computer and this easy-to-use CD, you may print a copy of the required (but sometimes hard to find) health forms for your files, convenient teacher forms, your course of study, and attendance records, to aid in your record keeping. Report cards are not required, but some people like them, so a selection is offered, to suit the educational philosophy of individual families. There are recommended reading lists for high schoolers, and enough extras that this inexpensive CD is highly recommended because it's a great time saver!

Homeschooling Stands to Reason, a one hour video from a TV interview with Jackie Orsi, a nationally known homeschooling speaker/writer, as well as one of the founders of CHN. She thoroughly answers the many questions that the interviewer asks, and her discussion about the benefits of homeschooling is quite convincing. This video isn't flashy and fancy; it's the message that has been so reassuringly presented that makes this video popular. For those who would rather give skeptical family and friends a video to watch instead of a book, this is the one to get!

Homeschooling in California: Our Rights, Our Laws, and Our Children, written by Jackie Orsi, who is not an attorney, as you may have read in her amusing Chapter 3 interview. Instead, she's a homeschooling mom who saw the need for someone to research the law as it pertained to homeschooling. This 50 page publication is an in-depth look at our fundamental rights and how the State Department of Education has attempted to undermine them through misinterpretation and manipulation. For those seriously concerned with maintaining homeschooling liberty, it is edifying, revealing and empowering. There is nothing quite like this publication—buy one for your attorney too!

When Your Grandchildren Homeschool is a series of essays written by experienced homeschoolers, including some grandparents. This 50-page publication will do wonders to convince not only the grandparents, but also other concerned relatives— perhaps even your spouse—of the benefits of homeschooling. The introduction by Win and Bill Sweet (long time homeschoolers as well as homeschooling grandparents now, and authors of *Living Joyfully with Children*) is so inspiring. Reassure your loved ones with this publication written with them in mind!

Homeschooling the Child of a Divorce was written by Jackie Orsi, CHN's first legal chair. It is considered a work in progress, and feedback and information regarding your case will enable CHN to help others in the future. This publication is designed to help parents who must contend with a custody challenge due to their choice to homeschool. We don't claim to have all the answers here, but we offer this to help, because we care, and we recognize it is a very difficult time. If you need this publication, we will mail it free as soon as it is requested. A $3 donation after you receive it, while not required, would help defray the copy/shipping costs.

CHN Recommends . . . Reading!

Begin with a few basic homeschooling books, and then keep reading as many other books as you can find, or have time for. We have compiled a partial list of favorites here, and we enthusiastically declare we could have added many more.

How do you stop, when the subject is so interesting? Homeschooling has become such a popular subject that many of these books are being placed in libraries, which is very good news. Other books may be available on loan from your support group, and others you may decide to purchase (*see note below*). You will learn something from all of them, and as you do so, you will gradually become aware of how you want to approach homeschooling for your family, or perhaps become further inspired, or discover a new approach. You will find specialty books that deal with a particular age group, or with a style of homeschooling, or even the politics of it. You will find some books will tell you how the author views homeschooling, and others will offer practical hints of what works in some families.

Note: If you purchase any books from either Amazon.com or Laissez Faire, and enter their sites by clicking on their logo at CHN's website, a portion of the sale will go to homeschooling, at no additional cost to you. Book loving homeschoolers think that's a great deal!

Just beginning?

We'll start with a few general books that are often suggested for new homeschoolers. We have tried to keep this list short, and that is hard to do, since there are so many wonderful books to read, and new ones are being written every year!

Dobson, Linda, editor
The Homeschooling Book of Answers: The 88 Most Important Questions Answered by Homeschooling's Most Respected Voices
As the title says, the most respected homeschool activists and authors answer the most common, and some uncommon, questions about homeschooling.

Griffith, Mary
The Homeschooling Handbook
An overview of homeschooling and its different approaches, along with different main themes of homeschooling in the words of individual homeschoolers.

The Unschooling Handbook: How to Use the Whole World As Your Child's Classroom
For those who want an idea of what unschooling might be like for them, or for homeschoolers who want reassurance before trying a more unstructured approach.

Guterson, David
Family Matters: Why Homeschooling Makes Sense
A high school teacher making a compelling argument for the future of families learning together.

Holt, John
How Children Learn
Considered the "father" of the unschooling movement, Holt described in detail his first-hand observations of children, and how they approach learning.

Lahrson-Fisher, Ann
Fundamentals of Home-Schooling: Notes on Successful Family Living
A practical guide on how children learn, and how parents can help them.

Lande, Nancy
Homeschooling: A Patchwork of Days
A variety of homeschoolers speak for themselves. Every chapter features detailed descriptions of a different household on any given day.

Leistico, Agnes
I Learn Better by Teaching Myself and Still Teaching Ourselves
A mother's account of her children's experiences in self-directed learning and how she learned to trust this method of learning.

Moore, Raymond and Dorothy
The Successful Homeschool Family Handbook
A comprehensive book that is helpful for parents struggling with homeschooling. Emphasis is on parenting skills to produce a stress-free homeschool environment.

When You're Ready to Read More...

Note: A decision was made not to place these books into categories. We doubt any of us would agree on the same classification for some of these books anyway. You will find general books here, along with books for specific needs. It is hoped that in doing so, that a special book won't be overlooked by the reader. Please note that his list is not comprehensive, and many of these authors have written other outstanding books worth locating.

Albert, David
And the Skylark Sings with Me—Adventures in Homeschooling and Community-Based Education

Alvino, James, editor
Parents' Guide to Raising a Gifted Child

Anderson, Winifred
Negotiating the Special Education Maze: A Guide for Parents & Teachers

Andreola, Karen
A Charlotte Mason Companion: Personal Reflections on the Gentle Art of Learning
The Charlotte Mason method, presented in a way that many find easier to follow.

Armstrong, Thomas
Awakening Your Child's Natural Genius: Enhancing Curiosity, Creativity, and Learning Ability

Armstrong argues that every child has the bud of genius just waiting for an opportunity to bloom. Through practical suggestions and activities, he shows how parents can help their child realize his true gifts.

In Their Own Way: Discovering and Encouraging Your Child's Multiple Intelligences
Seven specific learning styles (eight in the latest edition) are identified. The potential within each child is affirmed, with suggestions to help develop their abilities.

The Myth of the A.D.D. Child: 50 Ways to Improve Your Child's Behavior and Attention Span without Drugs, Labels or Coercion

Bear, John and Mariah
Bears' Guide to Earning Degrees Nontraditionally

Blumenfeld, Samuel L.
Homeschooling: A Parents Guide to Teaching Children
He exposes some school-related follies (in some cases tragedies), and extols the virtues of the homeschooling family.

Is Public Education Necessary?

NEA: Trojan Horse in American Education

Cohen, Cafi
And What About College? How Homeschooling Leads To Admissions To The Best Colleges and Universities
Includes information about transcripts, record keeping, and how to apply to college. It is a popular resource for homeschooling a child who may want to go to college.

Colfax, David and Micki
Homeschooling for Excellence: How to Take Charge of Your Child's Education—and Why You Absolutely Must
A true homeschool success story, this is a personal account of one family's homeschooling experience in the 1970's.

Dennis, Jeanne Gowen
Homeschooling High School: Planning Ahead for College Admission

Dobson, Linda
Homeschoolers' Success Stories: 15 Adults and 12 Young People Share the Impact That Homeschooling Has Made on Their Lives
With homeschooled children reaching adulthood, the effectiveness of homeschooling can now be assessed.

Homeschooling The Early Years: Your Complete Guide to Successfully Homeschooling the 3- to 8-Year-Old Child

Duffy, Cathy
Christian Home Educators' Curriculum Manual. Elementary Grades and Junior/Senior High (two volumes)
Reviews of hundreds of books, games, videos, computer programs and parent helps, for all subjects. Information on teaching, learning styles and much more.

Government Nannies: The Cradle-to-Grave Agenda of Goals 2000 and Outcome-Based Education

Elkind, David
Miseducation: Preschoolers at Risk
Designed to help parents avoid the miseducation of young children. The risks of formal academic and physical instruction to pre-school children are explained.

All Grown Up and No Place to Go: Teenagers in Crisis

The Hurried Child: Growing Up Too Fast Too Soon

Flynn Keith, Diane
Carschooling: Over 350 Entertaining Games & Activities to Turn Travel Time into Learning Time

Gatto, John Taylor
The Underground History of American Education: A Schoolteacher's Intimate Investigation Into The Problem of Modern Schooling
This long awaited book is being hailed as one of the most important education books ever written. Many consider it to be a must-read for all parents and teachers.

Dumbing Us Down: The Hidden Curriculum of Compulsory Schooling

Goldberg, Bruce
Why Schools Fail

Greenberg, Daniel
Free at Last: The Sudbury Valley School

Hannaford, Carla
Smart Moves: Why Learning Is Not All in Your Head
A neuroscientist explains brain development, the effects of TV, causes of some learning disabilities, and why physical activity is so important.

Harris, Gregg
The Christian Home School

Healy, Jane
Endangered Minds: Why Children Don't Think—and What You Can Do About It
Discusses TV watching and video games, increased attention deficit, and how parents can make a difference in helping a child become a good learner.

Your Child's Growing Mind: A Guide to Learning and Brain Development from Birth to Adolescence

Hendrickson, Borg
Home School: Taking the First Step

How to Write a Low Cost / No Cost Curriculum for Your Home-School Child

Henry, Shari
   Homeschooling the Middle Years: Your Complete Guide to Successfully Homeschooling the 8- 12-Year Old Child

Hensley, Sharon
   Homeschooling Children With Special Needs: Turning Challenges into Opportunities

Hern, Matt, editor
   Deschooling Our Lives
   A collection of essays by notable authors on the subject of alternatives to schools.

Herzog, Joyce
   Learning in Spite of Labels
   A practical guidebook for homeschooling children with learning disabilities.

Hiona (a pen name)
   As Geese Fly South: a pioneer home school without the home
   The first of two stunning books written by a courageous mother who dared to homeschool against great odds in the early '60s, when it was considered very illegal to do so.
   Wild Rose Publishing PO Box 1837 Oroville, CA 95965.

Hirsch, E. D.
   What Your _Grader Needs to Know *(Core Knowledge Series)*
   The intent of this series is to provide the basis of language arts, fine arts, history, geography, mathematics, science, technology, and cultural literacy at each grade level. It is not a full curriculum, but an attempt to standardize a core of learning.

   Books to Build On: A Grade-by-Grade Resource Guide for Parents and Teachers
   A guidebook to materials and books categorized by subject through grade 6.

Holt, John
   How Children Fail
   The book that touched off the national education debate in the early 60s leading to alternative education reforms.

   Learning All the Time
   Holt observes the natural ability of all children to learn, showing that the model of formal training and institutions for learning is destined to failure.

   Teach Your Own
   Holt abandons his goal of public school reform and turns to homeschooling as the path for true education reform.

Hood, Mary
   The Relaxed Home School: A Family Production
   Hood presents simple methods to bringing a classical education to children, and compares her methods to the institutional school approach.

Kaseman, Larry and Susan
Taking Charge through Homeschooling: Personal and Political Empowerment

Kenyon, Mary Potter
Home Schooling from Scratch: Simple Living—Super Learning

Klicka, Christopher
The Right Choice: Home Schooling

Kline, Peter
The Everyday Genius: Restoring Children's Natural Joy of Learning—and Yours Too
A practical guide for producing confident, eager learners.

Kohl, Herbert
The Question Is College
College is not always the next step after high school. Alternatives are presented.

Kohn, Alfie
Punished by Rewards: The Trouble with Gold Stars, Incentive Plans, A's, Praise, and Other Bribes
Kohn examines the effect of rewards on behavior.

Kurchinka, Mary Sheedy
Raising Your Spirited Child: A Guide for Parents Whose Child Is More Intense, Sensitive, Perceptive, Persistent, and Energetic
Helpful to parents of children who might be labeled strong- willed or difficult.

Layne, Marty
Learning at Home: A Mother's Guide to Homeschooling

Leppert, Mary and Michael
Homeschooling Almanac: How to Start, What to Do, Who to Call, Resources, Products, Teaching Supplies, Support Groups, Conferences, and More!

Levison, Catherine
A Charlotte Mason Education: A Homeschooling How-To Manual
A simple, easy-to-understand introduction to the Charlotte Mason method of teaching.

Llewellyn, Grace
The Teenage Liberation Handbook
Teens and their parents appreciate this nontraditional view of educating oneself. There are sections on unschooling everything, how to get into colleges or find em ployment without the traditional education and transcript.

Markova, Dawna
How Your Child Is Smart: A Life-Changing Approach to Learning
Parents can take charge of their children's education by understanding their learning pattern.

Moore, Raymond and Dorothy
Better Late Than Early
According to the authors, "school" work should be delayed until age eight to allow for proper physical and psychological development.

School Can Wait
Describes the research that indicates that a young child's nervous system is not ready for formal education.

Morgan, Melissa L.
Homeschooling on a Shoestring: A Jam-Packed Guide

O'Leary, Jenifer
Write Your Own Curriculum: A Complete Guide

Pearce, Joseph Chilton
Magical Child

Peterson's Guide to Distance Learning Programs

Pride, Mary
Big Book of Homelearning (three volumes)

Reed, Donn
The Home School Source Book
Includes reviews on learning materials and books for all ages. Essays and articles supplement the trove of resources listed.

Richman, Sheldon
Separating School and State: How to Liberate America's Families
The shortcomings of public schooling are analyzed, and an alternative is presented.

Rothbard, Murray
Education: Free and Compulsory

Rupp, Rebecca
The Complete Home Learning Source Book: The Essential Resource Guide for Homeschoolers, Parents, and Educators Covering Every Subject from Arithmetic to Zoology
Truly a huge book—865 pages of very helpful resources.

Home Learning Year by Year: What Your Child Needs to Know from Preschool through High School

Schofield, Mary
The Highschool Handbook: For Junior High, Too

Sheffer, Susannah
Writing Because We Love to: Homeschoolers at Work

Silberman, Arlene
Growing Up Writing: Teaching Children to Write, Think, and Learn

Smith, Frank
Insult to Intelligence: The Bureaucrat Invasion of Our Classrooms
Today's teaching methods are contrary to how children actually learn.

Reading Without Nonsense

The Book of Learning and Forgetting

Sowell, Thomas
Late-Talking Children

Stehli, Annabel
Dancing in the Rain
Stories of exceptional progress by parents of children with special needs.

Stein, David B.
Ritalin Is Not the Answer: A Drug-Free, Practical Program for Children Diagnosed with ADD or ADHD

Sutton, Joe
Strategies for Struggling Learners: A Guide for the Teaching Parent

Sweet, Win and Bill
Living Joyfully with Children

Tobias, Cynthia
The Way They Learn: How to Discover and Teach to Your Child's Strengths

Every Child Can Succeed: Making the Most of Your Child's Learning Style

Walker, Sally
The Survival Guide for Parents of Gifted Kids: How to Understand, Live With, and Stick Up for Your Gifted Child

Wallace, Nancy
Child's Work: Taking Children's Choices Seriously
An intimate account of the daily lives of an unschooling family.

Waring, Bill and Diana
Things We Wish We'd Known
Advice from fifty veteran homeschooling families.

Waring, Diana, and Cathy Duffy
Beyond survival: A Guide to Abundant-Life Homeschooling

Webb, James T.
Guiding the Gifted Child: A Practical Source for Parents and Teachers

Willis, Mariaemma and Victoria Kindle Hodson
Discover your child's learning style

Wise, Jesse and Susan Wise Bauer
The Well-Trained Mind: A Guide to Classical Education at Home
A handbook on classical education, from kindergarten through high school.

Selected Resources

This section includes just a sampling of the many materials, curriculums, and catalog suppliers available to homeschoolers. A more complete listing may be found at the CHN webpage *www.CaliforniaHomeschool.net/*. Many of the listed programs and books may be purchased directly from the author or company, from a general homeschooling catalog, or from an internet bookseller such as *Amazon.com* (remembering, we hope, to access it through CHN's website so that homeschooling is benefited). While a large homeschooling education store will also carry most of these resources, that is usually not the case at local teacher stores, which typically cater more to public teacher needs. A teacher store is fun to browse in, but it is worth locating a homeschooling store, or shopping from a catalog to make certain you are not missing out on some exceptional products that teachers may not have heard about, or may not be allowed to use in their classrooms because it is not on their limited approved list, or because they simply don't have time to offer it.

English Language Arts

Composition

National Writing Institute
888/644-8686 for catalog, 888/688-5375 orders and customer service
www.writingstrands.com
This writing program was developed for use in a homeschool setting. It teaches students creative and expository writing plus research and report techniques.

Princeton Review
Writing Smart, Junior by C.L. Brantley and *Writing Smart* by Marcia Lerner
The Junior book is designed to stimulate your child's interest in writing with creative exercises. *Write Smart*, for the older set, is full of helpful tips and useful drills to improve both business and academic writing.

Grammar and Punctuation

Caught'Ya!: Grammar With a Giggle
By Jane Bell Kiester
It only takes 10 minutes a day to build grammar competency. Students correct grammar, punctuation and usage in an ongoing story that you construct. There are lots of examples so that you can create a story of interest to your particular student.

Daily Grams: Guided Review Aiding Mastery Skills
By Wanda C. Phillips
This is a series of books from second grade to 6th and above. Each page is a short review lesson of capitalization, punctuation, sentence combining and grammar. New information is introduced slowly, and designed to promote independent learning.

Princeton Review Series
Grammar Smart Junior: Good Grammar Made Easy/Grades 6-8 by Liz Buffa
and *Grammar Smart: A Guide to Perfect Usage* by Nell Goddin, Erik Palma (Editor)
Well known for its irreverent humor which is guaranteed to capture the imagination of secondary-grade students. These are good for grammar usage remediation.

Literature

Chinaberry
800/776-2242 *www.chinaberry.com*
This is a great guide to good literature for your children.

Jim Weiss Storytelling Tapes
800/477-6234 *www.greathall.com*
Storytelling is a wonderful introduction to good literature, and Jim Weiss is a great storyteller, and recipient of many awards. Highly recommended!

Newbery Medal Award Winning Books
This annual award recognizes authors who contribute to American literature for children. A complete list of the winners is available in local libraries, or you can find it on the internet at: *www.ala.org/alsc/nmedal.html/*.

Reading Lists for College Bound Students
By Doug Estell, et al.
Contains reading lists from 100+ colleges and universities and an annotated list of the 100 books most often recommended by leading schools. It provides guidance for setting up your reading program.

Reading

At Last: A Reading Method for Every Child
By Mary Pecci
A simplified step-by-step guide for teachers and parents/ Grade K- Adult. Comes highly recommended for all children and especially useful for learning disabilities.

Flyleaf Publishing
800/449-7006 *www.flyleafpublishing.com*
The Books to Remember series—phonetic stories for beginning readers.

Sing, Spell, Read and Write
800/321-3106
This phonic-based program utilizes songs, games, storybook readers, and consumable texts. Assessments are built in. Spelling and writing are also taught.

Spelling and Vocabulary

Help You Spell and Enjoy Reading
800/464-2066
Designed to provide a foundation in reading and spelling skills. Particularly helpful if you have students needing remedial assistance because of learning disabilities.

Making Words: Multilevel, Hands-On Developmentally Appropriate Spelling and Phonics Activities
By Patricia M. Cunningham, Dorothy P. Hall
This is a how-to book based on phonics. It really does have a hands-on approach with hundreds of lessons which you can adapt to your student's particular need.

Vocabulary from Classical Roots
By Norma Fifer and Nancy Flowers
800/225-5750 *www.epsbooks.com*
This series of books teaches a root and then the words derived from it are studied.

Fine Arts

Art

Gordon School of Art
800/210-1220 *www.newmasters.com*
A home study course with instruction manual, student art book, videotaped demonstrations of all worksheet exercises and projects, and monitoring by teachers.

Drama

Pioneer Drama Service, Inc.
800/333-7262 *www.pioneerdrama.com*
Excellent catalog of plays and musicals and all theatrical resources.

Music

Classical Kids Series
800/757-8372 *www.childrensgroup.com*
Eight cassettes/CDs combine the music of a classical composer with a story.

Music Masters Series
www.voxcd.com/ (available in many homeschool catalogs)
The lives and music of the great composers are presented on 18 very enjoyable cassettes/CDs. A narrator discusses the composer's life while representative music is played in the background. This is an excellent introduction to music appreciation.

Foreign Language

Artes Latinae
Bolchazy-Carducci
847/526-4334, 800/392-6453 to order demo *www.bolchazy.com*
A programmed, self-teaching Latin course which is popular with homeschoolers. They have a variety of books in Latin including some Dr. Seuss books.

Cambridge Latin Course
Cambridge University Press *http://uk.cambridge.org*
This textbook/workbook approach includes a stimulating story line, grammatical development and cultural information.

The Learnables
800/237-1830 *www.learnables.com*
Students look at pictures and follow along while listening to a tape. Then they begin thinking the words. It has been described as a method similar to how babies learn to speak. First they listen, and then they understand, and finally they speak.

Power-Glide Foreign Language Courses
800/596-0910 *www.power-glide.com*
The series was developed for homeschoolers and is designed to move you beyond vocabulary memorization and verb conjugation to actual communication.

Math

Key Curriculum Press
800/995-MATH *www.keypress.com*
Lower grades use hands-on Miquon Math materials. Upper grades have an inexpensive, well-developed workbook program that is incrementally designed.

Mathematics: A Human Endeavor: A Book for Those Who Think They Don't Like the Subject
By Harold R. Jacobs
Technically a textbook, this book is an excellent read. The author uses a wide range of real-life examples and humor to introduce the reader to mathematical sciences.

Math-U-See
800/454-6284 *www.mathusee.com*
This manipulative-based program includes video instruction. It teaches not only the how-to but the why of math. The manipulatives with minor add-ons are used through high school math, which makes the program cost effective in the long run.

Saxon Publishing, Inc.
800/284-7019 customer service; homeschool help 580/338-4477
www.saxonpub.com
The lessons build incrementally and the instructions are easy to understand. This is a traditional approach to math, with lots of drill.

Science

Backyard Scientist
By Jane Hoffman
714/551-2892 *www.backyardscientist.com*
Easy to perform experiments using fairly common household items.

Janice VanCleave's 202 Oozing, Bubbling, Dripping and Bouncing Experiments
By Janice VanCleave
This former science teacher has written more than 26 educational activity books. The books give good instructions for experiments, with easy-to-find materials.

Tobin's Lab
800/522-4776 *www.tobinlab.com*
Tobin's Lab catalog is comprehensive and has high quality products from dissecting equipment and specimens microscopes. They are very helpful on the telephone.

Wild Goose
888/621-1040 *www.wildgoosescience.com*
Great science kits designed for K-8 that launch burning projectiles, use matches, and require safety goggles and protective gloves. Safe and sane instructions.

Social Sciences

Bluestocking Press
800/959-8586 *www.bluestockingpress.com*
History, government, and geography books, documents, music, toys, audiotapes and many unusual products. Well respected resource for these materials.

Greenleaf Press
800/311-1508 *www.greenleafpress.com*
The book descriptions make this a must-have catalog.

History of US
By Joy Hakim
A culturally well-balanced look at American history which includes non-judgmental explanations of why people did what they did. It provides information on what was happening in other parts of the world. This is a very popular series.

Across the Curriculum

Catalogs

Critical Thinking Books & Software
800/458-4849 *www.criticalthinking.com*
This catalog has critical thinking and problem-solving products.

Excellence in Education (EIE)
626/821-0025 *www.excellenceineducation.com*
Shop online and or at the bookstore in Monrovia, CA. They offer educational games to enhance any curriculum, and are creators of the Fun Game Curriculum.

Rainbow Resource Center
888/841-3456 *www.rainbowresource.com*
They offer educational materials at discount prices. Their catalog is huge!

Timberdoodle Company
360/426-0672 *www.timberdoodle.com*
Everything has been tested and approved by this homeschooling family. It's a great catalog to start your homeschooling adventure or to find nice educational gifts.

Games

Aristoplay, Ltd.
800/634-7738 to order *www.aristoplay.com*
Quality educational games that are favorites of homeschoolers.

LEGO Shop-at-home
800/453-4652 *http://shop.lego.com/*
Locate small parts, plus sets not always available in stores.

MindWare
800/999-0398 *www.MindWareonline.com*
A Parents' Choice approved catalog with "brainy toys for kids of all ages".

Turn off the TV
800/949-8688 *www.turnoffthetv.com*
Specializing in games that promote interaction and togetherness.

Young Explorers
888/928-3285 *www.youngexplorers.com*
Excellent selection of educational toys and books.

Children's Magazines

Boomerang
800/333-7858 *www.boomkids.com*
A monthly, 70-minute audiocassette tape, for ages 6-12. Parents' Choice Award.

Cobblestone Publishing, Inc.
800/821-0115 *http://cobblestonepub.com*
Cobblestone publishes a variety of children's magazines and resource materials covering history, world cultures, science and the language arts.

Kids Discover
800/284-8276
One subject is covered in each issue: Elephants, The 5 Senses, Space, Weather, Amazon, etc. Back issues of this magazine are available and worth acquiring.

National Wildlife Foundation
800/588-1650 *www.nwf.org/kids*
"Ranger Rick" is for ages 6-12 and "Your Big Backyard" for ages 2-5. Spectacular photography and fun activities heighten their understanding of wildlife.

Pre-Packaged Curriculum

Calvert School
888/487-4652 *http://home.calvertschool.org/hs/homeschool_title*
This is a structured non-sectarian correspondence program with teacher assistance. Grades K-8, established in 1897 and has an excellent academic reputation.

KONOS, Inc
972/924-2712 *www.konos.com*
Biblically based unit studies curriculum written by two educator/homeschool moms.

Oak Meadow
802/387-2021 *www.oakmeadow.com*
A Waldorf inspired homeschool curiculum. Traditional subjects are studied, but painting, drawing, music, writing poetry, building things, and learning through experience are included in the curriculum.

Sonlight Curriculum
303/730-6292 *www.sonlight.com*
This literature-based program offers the flexibility of purchasing a few books or the complete curriculum. While based on Biblical principles, Sonlight provides a non-propagandistic education with an international flavor, and is popular with secular homeschoolers too. You can teach several grade levels because it is literature based.

Distance Learning

American School of Correspondence
708/418-2800 *www.americanschoolofcorr.com*

Cambridge Academy
800/252-3777 *www.cambridgeacademy.com*

Center for Media and Independent Learning
A division of the University of California extension program
510/642-4124 *www-cmil.unex.berkeley.edu*
Provides a core curriculum of high school courses meeting UC's "a-f" requirements.

Clonlara School Home Based Education Program
734/769-4511 *www.clonlara.org*
Grades K-12. A contact teacher is assigned to each family, and students graduate with a private school diploma.

Indiana University Homeschool Courses for High School Students
800/334-1011 *http://scs.indiana.edu/hs/hs_courses.html*
Dual-credit courses allow teens to earn transferable university credits while meeting high school requirements. Budget friendly. AA and BA degrees available too.

Laurel Springs School
800/377-5890 *www.laurelsprings.com*
K-12 online curriculum, textbooks, customized curriculum, transcript, diploma.

Keystone National High School
800/255-4937 *www.keystonehighschool.com*

University of Missouri Center for Distance and Independent Study
800/609-3727 *http://cdis.missouri.edu*
Elementary-level through university-level courses. Mail-in, e-mail and online courses offered. Open enrollment with 12 months to complete each course.

Private Independent Study Programs (ISP)

- Almaden Valley Christian School (Special needs)
  6291 Vegas Drive San Jose, CA 95120 408/997-0290
  www.almadenvalleychristianschool.com

- Bay Shore School
  PO Box 13038, Long Beach, CA 90803
  562/434-3940 *http://www.bayshoreeducational.com/*

- Bear Hollow School
  650/856-6463 *www.bearhollowschool.org*

- Bethal Baptist Christian ISP (Special needs)
  901 South Euclid Street, Santa Ana, CA 714/527-5807

- Branford Grove School
  PO Box 341172, Arleta, CA 91334
  818/890-0350 *www.branfordgrove.com/home.html*

- Cedar Life Academy
  5528 Cedar St., Glen Avon, CA 92509
  909/681-4449 *bkymaxwell@hotmail.com*

- EIE Academy
  527 Franklin Place, Monrovia, CA 91016
  626/357-4443 *www.excellenceineducation.com*

- Family Learning Center
  3590 Peralta Blvd., Fremont, CA 94536   510-793-0540

- HCL-Boston
  PO Box 2920, Big Bear City, CA 92314
  909/585-7188 *www.bostonschool.org*

- Kolbe Academy Home School (Orthodox Catholic, classical education)
  2501 Oak Street, Napa, CA 94559 707/256-4306 *www.kolbe.org*

Academic Testing

Academic testing is not required of private schools in California and is strictly optional for homeschoolers. However, some families choose to administer these tests for their own evaluation purposes, keeping the results in their children's permanent records. There are several kinds of standardized tests available, each described briefly below with examples:

- **Achievement Tests.** These measure student's knowledge of concepts and subject matter in the grade level being tested. The Iowa Test of Basic Skills (ITBS) and the Stanford Achievement Test (SAT) are K-12th grade, nationally normed, covering all academic areas. Student's test results are compared with the national average. The Comprehensive Test of Basic Skills (CTBS) is administered in public schools throughout California for students in K-8. CTBS tests all academic areas; student's scores are compared against the state norm.

- **Learning Abilities Tests.** These tests assess student's aptitude in reasoning and problem solving using verbal, numerical, and nonverbal skills. The Iowa Cognitive Abilities test for grades 3-12 can be taken separately from or in combination with the Iowa Test of Basic Skills. The Otis-Lennon School Ability Test for grades 2-12 must be administered in combination with the Stanford Achievement Test.

- **Diagnostic Tests.** These tests are designed to provide information about student strengths and needs in particular subject areas. There are three separate Metropolitan Diagnostic Tests focusing on reading, mathematics, and language. The Gates-MacGinitie Reading Inventory tests only reading skills, vocabulary development, and comprehension.

Test Distributors

Some distributors are now selling to parents, while others continue to require that parents meet qualifications in order to administer certain tests.

- **Hewitt Homeschooling Resources** 800/ 348-1750
  www.hewitthomeschooling.com/. Testing for homeschoolers.
- **Thurber's Educational Assessments** 919/967-5282 *http://thurbers.net*
  Supplies the California Achievement Tests to homeschoolers.
- **Family Learning Organization** (509) 467-2552 *www.familylearning.org*
- **Bob Jones University Press** 800/845-5731 *www.bjup.com/services/testing*
- **Bayside School Services** 800/723-3057 *www.baysideschoolservices.com*
- **The Sycamore Tree** 800/779-6750 *www.sycamoretree.com*

College Testing

ACT Assessment Tests
319/337-1270 *www.act.org*

SAT I, II
609/771-7600 *www.collegeboard.com*

PSAT / NMSQT
609/771-7070 *www.collegeboard.com*

Advanced Placement Tests
888/CALL-4-AP *www.collegeboard.com*

Special Resources

(For books, see the recommended reading list at the beginning of this chapter.)

Accelerated Learners

- **California Association for the Gifted** *www.cagifted.org/* 310/215-1898
- **Mensa, Gifted Children's Program** 703/527-4293
- **National Association for Gifted Children** 202/785-4268 *www.NAGC.org*
- **Center for Talented Youth** (CTY) The Johns Hopkins University 410/516-0337 *www.jhu.edu/~gifted*

Special Education

- **SERI—Special Ed Resources on the Internet** *http://seriweb.com*
- **Homeschooling Kids With Disabilitties** *http://members.tripod.com/~Maaja/index.html*
- **Special Education** *http://specialed.about.com/education/specialed*
- **Shirley's Wellness Café.** Holistic health for children with special needs. *www.shirleys-wellness-cafe.com*
- **The Institutes for Achievement of Human Potential.** Introduces parents to the field of child brain development. *www.iahp.org/* 215/233-2050
- **California Department of Education, Director of Special Education** 515 L St, Suite 270, Sacramento, CA 95814. 916/445-4602. *http://www.cde.ca.gov/spbranch/sed/*. Can request state regulations booklet governing special education.
- **California State Offices, Early Intervention.** 800/515-2229
- **Council for Exceptional Children (CEC)** 800/CEC-SPED *www.cec.sped.org*
- **Moore Foundation.** Helps each child reach his potential. *www.moorefoundation.com/* 360/835-5392 Box 1, Camas, WA 98607
- **NATHHAN: Nationally Challenged Homeschoolers Associated Network.** Provides lists of homeschool friendly professionals and companies. Newsletter and support. *www.nathhan.com/* 208/267-6246

- **National Academy for Child Development.** Individualized home programs. PO Box 380, Huntsville, UT 84317, 801/621-8606, *www.nacd.org/index.html*
- **National Information Center for Children and Youth With Disabilities (NICHCY).** 800/695-0285 *www.nichcy.org*
- **Parent to Parent Project Beach Center.** 913/864-7600. Veteran parents of children with disabilities offer emotional and informational support.
- **Parent Training and Information Programs (PTIs).** 916/ 327-3700 *http://www.cde.ca.gov/spbranch/sed/caprntorg.htm*
- **Protection and Advocacy, Inc. (PAI)** 800/952-5746 *www.pai-ca.org/*

Homeschooling Publications

California Homeschool News (CHNews)
　800/327-5339. Bimonthly, included with membership in CHN.
California HomeSchooler
　888/472-4440. Bimonthly, included with membership in HSC.
The Drinking Gourd: Multicultural Home Education Magazine
　PO Box 2557 Redmond, WA 98073 425/ 836-0336
F.U.N. Family Unschoolers Network
　888/386-7020 *www.unschooling.org*
HELM - Home Education Learning Magazine
　941/359-3628 *www.helmonline.com*
Home Education Magazine
　800/236-3278 *www.home-ed-magazine.com*
Home Educator's Family Times
　888/300-8434 *www.homeeducator.com/FamilyTimes*
Homeschooling Parent (a free homeschooling newspaper)
　936-756-2226 *www.homeschoolingparent.com*
Homeschooling Today
　970/493-2716 *www.homeschooltoday.com/home.htm*
Life Learning
　800/215-9574 *www.lifelearningmagazine.com/*
The LINK (a free homeschooling newspaper)
　888/470-4513 *www.homeschoolnewslink.com*
Moore Report International
　360/835-6322 *www.moorefoundation.com*
The Old Schoolhouse
　530/823-0447 *http://theoldhomeschoolhouse.com/*
Practical Homeschooling
　800/346-6322 *www.home-school.com*

Homeschooling Organizations

California

California Homeschool Network (CHN)
PO Box 55485, Hayward, CA 94545
800/327-5339 *www.CaliforniaHomeschool.net*

Christian Home Educators Association of California (CHEA)
PO Box 2009, Norwalk, CA 90651
800/564-2432 *www.cheaofca.org*

HomeSchool Association of California (HSC)
PO Box 868, Davis, CA 95617
888/472-4440 *www.hsc.org*

National

Adventist Home Educator
PO Box 836, Camino, CA 95709
530/647-2110 *www.tagnet.org/ahe*

Alliance for Parental Involvement in Education (ALLPIE)
PO Box 59, East Chatham, NY 12060-0059
518/392-6900 *http://croton.com/allpie*

Alternative Education Resource Organization (AERO)
417 Roslyn Rd., Roslyn Heights, NY 11577
800/769-4171 *www.educationrevolution.org*

Catholic Homeschool Network of America
PO Box 6343, River Forest, IL 60305-6343
www.geocities.com/Heartland/8579/chsna.html

Jewish Home Educators Network
2122 Houser, Holly, MI 48442
www.snj.com/jhen/index.htm

Latter-day Saint Home Educators Association
2770 South 1000 West, Perry, UT 84302
801/723-5355 *www.ldshea.org/*

Muslim Homeschool Network and Resource
PO Box 803, Attleboro, MA 02703
508/226-1638 *www.muslimhomeschool.com*

National Association of Catholic Home Educators
   PO Box 787, Montrose, AL 36559
   www.nache.org

National Home Education Network (NHEN)
   PO Box 7844, Long Beach 90807
   www.nhen.org

National Home Education Research Institute
   PO Box 13939, Salem, Oregon 97309
   503/364-1490 *www.nheri.org*

Native American Homeschool Association
   PO Box 979, Fries, Virginia 24330
   www.expage.com/page/nahomeschool

Separation of School and State Alliance
   4578 N. First #310, Fresno, CA 93726
    559/292-1776 Information request line: 888/338-1776
   www.sepschool.org

We have made every attempt to ensure that the resource information in this chapter is accurate. If you discover an error, or if you know of a resource you think we should include in future editions of The California Homeschool Guide or on CHN's website, please let us know by contacting CHN.

California Homeschool Network
www.CaliforniaHomeschool.net
800/327-5339
CHNmail@CaliforniaHomeschool.net
PO Box 55485, Hayward, CA 94545

Appendix

© Bill Tayolr

Selected California Education Codes

The following are the California Education Codes most frequently referred to by homeschoolers. This is important information that each homeschooler should be familiar with. The complete California Education Code may be accessed from the CHN website: *www.CaliforniaHomeschool.net/*.

§33190, 48222 and 48415—*The codes pertinent to your right to file the PSA*

§33190. Every person, firm, association, partnership, or corporation offering or conducting private school instruction on the elementary or high school level shall between the first and 15th day of October of each year, commencing on October 1, 1967, file with the Superintendent of Public Instruction an affidavit or statement, under penalty of perjury, by the owner or other head setting forth the following information for the current year:

(a) All names, whether real or fictitious, of the person, firm, association, partnership, or corporation under which it has done and is doing business.

(b) The address, including city and street, of every place of doing business of the person, firm, association, partnership, or corporation within the State of California.

(c) The address, including city and street, of the location of the records of the person, firm, association, partnership, or corporation, and the name and address, including city and street, of the custodian of such records.

(d) The names and addresses, including city and street, of the directors, if any, and principal officers of the person, firm, association, partnership, or corporation.

(e) The school enrollment, by grades, number of teachers, coeducational or enrollment limited to boys or girls and boarding facilities.

(f) That the following records are maintained at the address stated, and are true and accurate:
  (1) The records required to be kept by Section 48222.
  (2) The courses of study offered by the institution.
  (3) The names and addresses, including city and street, of its faculty,
    together with a record of the educational qualifications of each.

(g) Criminal record summary information has been obtained pursuant to Section 44237.

Whenever two or more private schools are under the effective control or supervision of a single administrative unit, such administrative unit may comply with the provisions of this section on behalf of each of the schools under its control or supervision by submitting one report.

Filing pursuant to this section shall not be interpreted to mean, and it shall be unlawful for any school to expressly or impliedly represent by any means whatsoever, that the State of California, the Superintendent of Public Instruction, the State Board of Education, the State Department of Education, or any division or bureau of the department, or any accrediting agency has made any evaluation, recognition, approval, or endorsement of the school or course unless this is an actual fact.

The Superintendent of Public Instruction shall prepare and publish a list of private elementary and high schools to include the name and address of the school and the name of the school owner or administrator.

§48222. Children who are being instructed in a private full-time day school by persons capable of teaching shall be exempted. Such school shall, except under the circumstances described in Section 30, be taught in the English language and shall offer instruction in the several branches of study required to be taught in the public schools of the state. The attendance of the pupils shall be kept by private school authorities in a register, and the record of attendance shall indicate clearly every absence of the pupil from school for a half day or more during each day that school is maintained during the year.

Exemptions under this section shall be valid only after verification by the attendance supervisor of the district, or other person designated by the board of education, that the private school has complied with the provisions of Section 33190 requiring the annual filing by the owner or other head of a private school of an affidavit or statement of prescribed information with the Superintendent of Public Instruction. The verification required by this section shall not be construed as an evaluation, recognition, approval, or endorsement of any private school or course.

§48415. In the case of attendance upon private school, exemption from the requirements of attendance upon compulsory continuation education shall be valid only after verification by the attendance supervisor of the district, or other person designated by the board of education, that the private school has complied with the provisions of Section 33190 requiring the annual filing by the owner or other head of a private school of an affidavit or statement of prescribed information with the Superintendent of Public Instruction. The verification required by this section shall not be construed as an evaluation, recognition, approval, or endorsement of any private school or course.

§48224 Credentialed Tutor Exemption

Children not attending a private, full-time, day school and who are being instructed in study and recitation for at least three hours a day for 175 days each calendar year by a private tutor or other person in the several branches of study required to be taught in the public schools of this state and in the English language shall be exempted. The tutor or other person shall hold a valid state credential for the grade taught. The instruction shall be offered between the hours of 8 o'clock a.m. and 4 o'clock p.m.

§44237 Parental Exemption From Fingerprinting

a) Every person...offering or conducting private school instruction on the elementary or high school level shall require...background clearance criteria that meets or exceeds the requirements of this section, to submit two sets of fingerprints...(4) This section does not apply to a secondary school pupil working at the school he or she attends or a parent or legal guardian working exclusively with his or her children.

§49069 Parental Right To View Records

Parents of currently enrolled or former pupils have an absolute right to access to any and all pupil records related to their children which are maintained by school districts or private schools. The editing or withholding of any such records, except as provided for in this chapter, is prohibited....

§51210 and 51220—*California Private School Requirements*

§51210 Course of Study, Grades 1-6

The adopted course of study for grades 1 to 6, inclusive, shall include instruction, beginning in grade 1 and continuing through grade 6, in the following areas of study:

(a) English, including knowledge of, and appreciation for literature and the language, as well as the skills of speaking, reading, listening, spelling, handwriting, and composition.

(b) Mathematics, including concepts, operational skills, and problem solving.

(c) Social sciences, drawing upon the disciplines of anthropology, economics, geography, history, political science, psychology, and sociology, designed to fit the maturity of the pupils. Instruction shall provide a foundation for understanding the history, resources, development, and government of California and the United States of America; the development of the American economic system including the role of the entrepreneur and labor; the relations of persons to their human and natural environment; eastern and western cultures and civilizations; contemporary issues; and the wise use of natural resources.

(d) Science, including the biological and physical aspects, with emphasis on the processes of experimental inquiry and on the place of humans in ecological systems.

(e) Visual and performing arts, including instruction in the subjects of art and music, aimed at the development of aesthetic appreciation and the skills of creative expression.

(f) Health, including instruction in the principles and practices of individual, family, and community health.

(g) Physical education, with emphasis upon the physical activities for the pupils that may be conducive to health and vigor of body and mind, for a total period of time of not less than 200 minutes each 10 schooldays, exclusive of recesses and the lunch period.

(h) Other studies that may be prescribed by the governing board.

§51220 Course of Study, Grades 7 to 12

The adopted course of study for grades 7 to 12, inclusive, shall offer courses in the following areas of study:

(a) English, including knowledge of and appreciation for literature, language, and composition, and the skills of reading, listening, and speaking.

(b) Social sciences, drawing upon the disciplines of anthropology, economics, geography, history, political science, psychology, and sociology, designed to fit the maturity of the pupils. Instruction shall provide a foundation for understanding the history, resources, development, and government of California and the United States of America; instruction in our American legal system, the operation of the juvenile and adult criminal justice systems, and the rights and duties of citizens under the criminal and civil law and the State and Federal Constitutions; the development of the American economic system, including the role of the entrepreneur and labor; the relations of persons to their human and natural environment; eastern and western cultures and civilizations; human rights issues, with particular attention to the study of the inhumanity of genocide, slavery, and the Holocaust, and contemporary issues.

(c) Foreign language or languages, beginning not later than grade 7, designed to develop a facility for understanding, speaking, reading, and writing the particular language.

(d) Physical education, with emphasis given to physical activities that are conducive to health and to vigor of body and mind.

(e) Science, including the physical and biological aspects, with emphasis on basic concepts, theories, and processes of scientific investigation and on the place of humans in ecological systems, and with appropriate applications of the interrelation and interdependence of the sciences.

(f) Mathematics, including instruction designed to develop mathematical understandings, operational skills, and insight into problem-solving procedures.

(g) Visual and performing arts, including art, music, or drama, with emphasis upon development of aesthetic appreciation and the skills of creative expression.

(h) Applied arts, including instruction in the areas of consumer and homemaking education, industrial arts, general business education, or general agriculture.

(i) Career technical education designed and conducted for the purpose of preparing youth for gainful employment in the occupations and in the numbers that are appropriate to the personnel needs of the state and the community served and relevant to the career desires and needs of the pupils.

(j) Automobile driver education, designed to develop a knowledge of the provisions of the Vehicle Code and other laws of this state relating to the operation of motor vehicles, a proper acceptance of personal responsibility in traffic, a true appreciation of the causes, seriousness and consequences of traffic accidents, and to develop the knowledge and attitudes necessary for the safe operation of motor vehicles. A course in automobile driver education shall include education in the safe operation of motorcycles.

(k) Other studies as may be prescribed by the governing board.

PRIVATE SCHOOL AFFIDAVIT

Fall 2002

R-4 (Rev. 08/02)

Return the original between October 1 and 15, 2002 to:

California Department of Education
Policy & Program Coordination – Affidavit
1430 N Street, Suite 4309
Sacramento, CA 95814

CHN Sample R-4 Affidavit

DEPARTMENT USE ONLY
Identification Number ___ DO ___ SD

Do not write here

*THIS AFFIDAVIT IS A REQUIRED REGISTRATION DOCUMENT ONLY
AND IS NOT A LICENSE OR AN APPROVAL TO OPERATE A PRIVATE SCHOOL.*

Who should file an affidavit

The Private School Affidavit is for:

* Persons, firms, associations, partnerships, or corporations offering or conducting full-time day school at the elementary or high school level
* For students between the ages of 6 and 18 years.

Home schooling is generally understood as a situation where a noncredentialed parent teaches his or her own children, exclusively at home, whether using a correspondence course or other types of courses. Defined in that way, home schooling is not authorized in California. Filing an affidavit does not, by itself, change the home instruction into a private school.

Filing does not grant state approval, recognition, or endorsement

Filing of this affidavit shall not be interpreted to mean, and it shall be unlawful for any school to expressly or impliedly represent by any means whatsoever, that the State of California, the Superintendent of Public Instruction, the State Board of Education, the State Department of Education, or any division or bureau of the Department, or any accrediting agency has made any evaluation, recognition, approval, or endorsement of the school or course unless this is an actual fact (see Education Code section 33190). Filing an affidavit does not mean that any accrediting agency has made any evaluation, recognition, approval, or endorsement of the school or course.

I. School Information   *Required fields*

Is this a new school (if you have been operating only as a pre-school, consider yourself a new school)   X Yes ___ No   County * Pleasant

Name of School * Sunny Hills Academy   Telephone Number * (408 456-7890

Street Address * 808 Monterey Ave

City * Pleasantville   Zip Code * 95123

Mailing Address (if different)

Mailing City   Mailing Zip Code

Former Name of School (leave blank unless you are changing your school name)

Site Administrator * Paul M. Jones   Title * Principal

Other Administrator (if any)   Title

Type of School *
(Do not include preschool)
X Coeducational
___ Boys Only
___ Girl Only

School Accommodations (Select one) *
___ Residential Boarding Only
X Day Only
___ Both

High School Diploma Offered *   X Yes ___ No

Public School District in which the school is located * Pleasant Unified

Grades Offered * 1-12

NDSL Certification—Full-time teachers in private nonprofit schools having concentrations of students from low-income families may have National Direct Student Loans (NDSL) canceled. (Title 20, United States Code, § 1087ee; Title 34, Code of Federal Regulations, §674.53.) If you believe your school can qualify in either or both categories, check "Yes"; otherwise, check "No." **   ___ Yes   X No

II. Statistical Information

Range of students' ages (Do not include preschool) * 8-14

Enrollment on available date October 1-15, 2002
(Do not include preschool enrollment)

	Number of Pupils *	Number of School Staff * (Count each staff only once) (Do not include preschool staff.)	
Kindergarten		Full-time Teachers	1
Grade 1		Part-time Teachers	1
Grade 2		Number of Administrators	
Grade 3	1	Other Staff (instructional aides, therapists, secretaries, etc.)	
Grade 4			
Grade 5			
Grade 6			
Grade 7	1		
Grade 8			
Grade 9	1		
Grade 10			
Grade 11			
Grade 12			
Ungraded Elementary			
Ungraded Secondary			
Total Enrollment	**3**		
Number of Twelfth Grade Graduates in 2000-2002 School Year *	0		

See pages 51-52

School has been granted: *
___ Tax-exempt, NONPROFIT status under section 501(c)(3) of the 1954 U.S. Internal Revenue Code
___ Tax-exempt, NONPROFIT status under section 23701d of the California Revenue and Tax Code
___ Property tax exemption under section 214 of the California Revenue and Tax Code
X No tax exemption

CHN Sample

PRIVATE SCHOOL AFFIDAVIT
Fall 2002
R-4 (Rev. 08/02)

DEPARTMENT USE ONLY
Identification Number   DO   SO
Leave blank

Classification of School *(Select one)* *   Note: check religious or secular

____ Church-affiliated • Denomination (Use codes below to complete denomination.) ____
____ Religious school, not church affiliated
____ Secular

III. Directors, if any, and Principal Officers

Name * Paul M. Jones   Position Principal
Street Address * 808 Monterey Ave.
City * Pleasantville, CA   Zip * 95123

Name Patty Jones   Position Teacher
Street Address 808 Monterey Ave.
City Pleasantville, CA   Zip 95123

IV. School Records — The attendance records required by Education Code section 48222 and the records of courses of study, names, addresses, and educational qualifications of the faculty, as required by subdivisions (f)(2) and (3) of Education Code section 33190, are maintained by the person and at the place listed here and are true and accurate.

Name of Custodian of Records *
    same as above

Address of Location of Records *
                                 City *   Zip *

When school ceases operation, every effort should be made to give a copy of pupil's permanent records to his or her parents. If records cannot be given to the parents, it is recommended that the school's custodian of records retain the records permanently so that former pupils may obtain copies when needed for future education, employment or other purposes.

This school offers programs for children with the following disabilities *(if any)*:

____ Autism	____ Deafness	____ Deaf/Blind
____ Emotional Disturbance	____ Hearing Impairment	____ Mental Retardation
____ Other Health Impaired	____ Orthopedic Impairment	____ Specific Learning Disability
____ Speech or Language	____ Traumatic Brain Injury	____ Visual Impairment

Do not check here

V. Certification — I hereby certify under penalty of perjury that:

(a) Each applicant for employment by this private school in a position requiring contact with minor pupils, who does not possess a valid California state teaching credential, or who is not currently licensed by another state agency that requires a criminal record summary, has obtained from the Department of Justice a criminal record summary which has been forwarded to the administrator(s) of this private school;

(b) No person has been employed in such a position prior to the receipt of the report from the Department of Justice;

(c) No person has been employed in such a position who has been convicted of a violent or serious felony as defined in subdivision (g), except as provided in subdivision (b), (i) or (j), of Education Code section 44327; or who would be prohibited from employment by a public school district pursuant to any provision of the Education Code because of his or her conviction for any crime;

(d) That this private school is not owned or operated by a person who would be prohibited from employment by a private school pursuant to Education Code section 44237(e)(1) and;

(e) To the best of my knowledge and belief, the information contained in this Private School Affidavit is true, accurate, and complete.

Signature of Owner or Chief Administrative Officer *   *Paul M. Jones*   Date * 10-1-02

Name of Person Preparing Form * Paul M. Jones

Title * Principal   Telephone Number * 408-456-7890

Private school authorities are responsible for initiating contact with the appropriate local authorities (city and/or county) regarding compliance with ordinances governing health, safety, and fire standards, business licensing, and zoning requirements applicable to private schools.

REQUESTING SCHOOL RECORDS
SAMPLE LETTER

Better Idea Academy
123 Homesbest Drive
Future's Bright, CA 99999
September 3, 2001

Our Public Elementary School
101 ABC Way
Anytown, CA 00000

Re: REQUEST FOR STUDENT RECORDS

The following children will be enrolled in Better Idea Academy, effective
September 3, 2001:

Sara Smith (2nd Grade) (Date of Birth)
Paul Smith (6th Grade) (Date of Birth)

Please forward their records and cumulative files to Better Idea Academy as
soon as possible.

Sincerely,

Patty Smith

Patty Smith
Better Idea Academy

Index

A

B

C

Private independent study program
55
Private school affidavit, see R-4
Private School ISP, see ISP
Prom 31, 80
PSAT 234, 347
Public school, hidden cost of 267
Public school ISP, see ISP

Q

Qualifications to teach 50, 99, 327
requirement 54
worries 90, 98, 102

R

R-4 (Private School Affidavit)
approval 48
deadline for filing 47, 62
evaluation 48
processing fee 49, 50, 64
requirements 50
state address 50
where to get 50
Record keeping 53, 241, 327
Research 12
academic achievement 13
National Home Education Research
Institute (NEHRI) 14
psychological 72
studies of genius 10

thinking processes of
homeschooled students 130
Resources 337
art 339
catalogs 342
children's magazines 343
composition 337
drama 340
foreign language 340
games 342
grammar and punctuation 338
literature 338
math 341
music 340
pre-packaged curriculum 343
reading 339
science 341
spelling and vocabulary 339
social sciences 342
Rutherford Institute 60

S

SAT 233, 237, 347
Schedules 116
School at home 139, 172, 204
School officials
contact by letter 53
contact by phone 53
dealing with 52, 65
evaluation 48
misinformation 45
School records
access to 53

ISBN 155212712-5

9 781552 127124

Made in the USA
Lexington, KY
23 September 2012